RUGBY'S
GREATEST
Characters

D1135763

RUGBY'S
GREATEST
Characters

Colourful tales of fantastic fullbacks, inspirational leaders and jokers in the pack

JOHN GRIFFITHS

BOOKS

First published in Great Britain in 2009 by
JR Books, 10 Greenland Street, London NW1 0ND
www.jrbooks.com

Copyright © 2009 John Griffiths

John Griffiths has asserted his moral right to be identified as the Author of this
Work in accordance with the Copyright Designs and Patents Act 1988.

All rights reserved. No part of this book may be reproduced or utilised in any form
or any means, electronic or mechanical, including photocopying, recording or
by any information storage and retrieval system, without permission in writing
from JR Books.

A catalogue record for this book is available from the British Library.

ISBN 978-1-906779-15-3

1 3 5 7 9 10 8 6 4 2

Printed and bound in the UK by Thomson Litho Ltd

CONTENTS

INTRODUCTION

For its first 125 years as an international sport dating from 1871, rugby union was an amateur game that proudly upheld the ethos handed down by its founding fathers in the Victorian Age. Gradually the sport became one of the world's most popular outdoor team games, yet even when it launched its own World Cup in 1987 it remained strictly amateur. Players came from all walks of life to participate in a game they loved and from which they never expected to reap material reward. It meant that teams comprised players whose livings were made working with their hands, or their wits or their brains, or sometimes all three. Yet the camaraderie engendered by the sport set it apart from others where players at the top level were professionals, men brought together by a common desire to be paid for parading their sporting skills at the highest level.

It was arguably the great freemasonry of rugby union that gave the game its character and greatest characters. This book sets out the backgrounds and stories surrounding some of the larger-than-life personalities who have graced the game, characters who have stood out not necessarily for their deeds as players but for their heart, their courage or their ability to make those around them enjoy the game for what it was always intended to be: one for gentlemen from all classes of life, but especially for those who enjoyed their rugby even more when there was a laugh attached to it.

Different people would choose different characters among their leading five dozen or so, but few could argue that this collection lacks variety. Wavell Wakefield and Alex Obolensky, a baron and a prince, were outstanding personalities in English rugby between the wars whose names are still celebrated today at Twickenham Stadium. And from the other end of the spectrum came the groundsman's son, Billy Bancroft, rugby's first fabulous fullback, whose dedication to practice and supreme self-confidence were essential components in early Welsh successes on the rugby grounds of the late 19th century. Then there were the jokers in the pack. Men like Peter Robbins, whose love of practical tricks terrorised victims and endeared him to a generation of English forwards in the 1950s and 1960s; Clem Thomas, the wholesale butcher from Wales who was accused by opponents of practising his profession on the field; and Gareth Chilcott, who was later engaged to tread the boards in Christmas pantomime owing to his reputation as one of rugby's funniest men.

Inspirational leaders are also represented. Dave Gallaher is still remembered and revered in New Zealand for the pioneering course he and his original All Blacks steered through Britain, Ireland and France in 1905. And in Wales Clive Rowlands, the captain and coach of several Welsh Triple Crown sides, is renowned for appealing to the emotions of his troops with outpourings of rhetoric that would have stirred David Lloyd George.

Although those included in this selection were not chosen for the excellence of their rugby – readers will search in vain for the Jonny Wilkinsons, Daniel Carters or Will Carlings – several were undoubtedly outstanding rugby players and pure box-office. David Campese, the brilliant wizard of Oz, would be a contender for any All-time World XV to meet Mars, yet it was his teasing of English rugby and his general outspokenness about teams that were reluctant to entertain that sharply defined his character, prompting even his own team coach to declare that Campo had a wire loose somewhere between his brain and his mouth. Jonah Lomu would no doubt partner Campo as the other wing in an all-star XV. He really was larger than life. Did any man do more to advertise rugby's wonderful capacity to entertain than Jonah when he first hit the headlines at the 1995 World Cup? Probably not.

There have been plenty of cheeky chappies who have graced the game, too. Back at the dawn of the 20th century, when Welsh rugby was sweeping all before them, a brilliant little schoolmaster from Cardiff named Percy Bush was the outside-half who made even the All Blacks fear to tread when they came to Wales in 1905. He somehow managed to trade his rugby fame off against his teaching duties, missing 50 per cent of term-time for one reason or another while turning out regularly for Cardiff and helping Wales. He was as much a will-o'-the-wisp to the Cardiff Schools Management Committee as he was to opponents on the rugby field.

Fast forward 60 years and another young Welsh fly-half made his debut as a student teacher. Barry John's initial meeting with Gareth Edwards, who was to be his halfback partner in many famous wins, showed the laconic side to the great man. Edwards, bubbly and keen in contrast to the confident and laid-back John, wanted to get the calls right and pestered Barry into an out-of-hours practice before a big trial match. Having got up early, Barry soon tired of his partner's constant questioning. 'Look Gareth, you just throw 'em and I'll catch 'em,' he said, and with that he walked out on the practice . . . and so began one of the most famous partnerships in rugby history.

And who but the cheeky Austin Healey of more recent vintage would get up to intercept the morning post and conceal a flatmate's Lions' tour invitation, as he did to poor unsuspecting Will Greenwood on the morning of the announcement of the 1997 Lions' squad to tour South Africa? As Greenwood said, 'With friends like Austin, who needs enemies?' Who says that the modern game doesn't throw up characters?

For the material included in this book, thanks go to the rugby union writers and journalists who down the years have carefully recorded the comings and goings, the antics and tricks of the sport's characters. The game has always been lucky enough to enjoy a media that has overwhelmingly had the love of rugby at its heart. Even in today's hard-nosed era of investigative journalism the critics continue to promote the game by emphasising the positives and refer to the negative aspects only when the very wellbeing of rugby, its players or followers is threatened.

Special thanks are due to old friends Tim Auty, Tony Lewis, Geoff Miller, Willow Murray and Dave Richards, of Rugby Relics in Neath, for their practical support unearthing cuttings and references regarding some of the older characters covered. Compiling this book has been a labour of love and final mentions should go to Jeremy

Robson, for his encouragement for the project and enthusiasm in commissioning this selection, and to Lesley Wilson at JR Books for her calmness managing the project.

John Griffiths

IN A CLASS OF THEIR OWN

WILFRED WOOLLER
A Man for all Seasons

The giant of Welsh rugby in the 1930s was the tall, long-striding three-quarter, Wilf Wooller. He was born at Rhos-on-Sea in north Wales on 20 November 1912 and educated at Rydal School, where he originally played in the back row. But he made such an impact on the Welsh selectors while playing as a schoolboy centre for Sale that they drafted him into the final international trial side in January 1933.

On his first appearance in senior rugby in south Wales he starred for the Possibles in a side that included Vivian Jenkins, Harry Bowcott and Maurice Turnbull. The junior side surprised everyone, winning 15–6 at Swansea, but the selectors, unsure of their best combination, insisted on Jenkins and Wooller turning out again. They played for Glamorgan against Monmouthshire on the Thursday of the following week, before the selectors finally announced the side. 'Wooller', it was reported in *The Times*, 'was the first to distinguish himself, his long, raking stride carrying him from his own 25 almost as far as his opponents'. It was an impressive run . . . and ended in a great try'. He scored two tries, Glamorgan won 23–8 and later the same evening Wooller, along with Jenkins, Bowcott and Turnbull, was in the Welsh side to play England at Twickenham. He learnt of his selection while motoring home with his father after the match. They stopped at a garage to fill up with petrol and were told the latest news by the pump attendant.

Much was expected of the young 20-year-old who, in order to qualify for a place at Christ's College, Cambridge, had returned to school to study Latin. The press had already likened him to another great Welsh centre of an earlier age, Gwyn Nicholls, and on the morning of the Twickenham game, Owen L. Owen in *The Times* continued to wax lyrical: 'So far, [Wooller] has exceeded all expectations. His passing is beautifully timed and balanced, even when he runs up to the man and takes the bump.' The 6ft 2in Wooller proved the press and selectors' faith in him well-founded, playing a strong defensive role in the team that, at the 10th attempt, finally managed its first win at Twickenham. He had alongside him in the centre that day his Sale partner Claud Davey, whose tackling was the perfect foil to Wooller's abrasive running and siege-gun kicking. He was ever-present in the Welsh side that year, though the promise of Twickenham quickly evaporated into defeats for Wales at Swansea (against Scotland) and in Belfast.

And that was the end of Wooller's Welsh rugby for nearly two years. Going up to Cambridge in October 1933 he duly won the first of his three rugby Blues, playing at the shoulder of another great Welsh player, Cliff Jones. Curiously he was omitted from the Welsh trials that autumn and missed all of Wales's three internationals in 1934. Then a brilliant performance for the Cambridge side that routed Oxford 29–4 in December 1934, when Wooller dropped a goal from just inside his own half, brought him sharply back into the focus of the Welsh selectors. 'That dropped goal pitched in the upper deck of Twickenham's North Stand,' he once reckoned. When Idwal Rees withdrew from the Probables in the final trial the same month, Wooller was reinstated and returned to the international side in January 1935. He was the mainstay of the side thereafter and missed only one match (through injury) up to the outbreak of the war.

It was during his Cambridge and Cardiff days that the best was seen of him, playing alongside the will-o'-the-wisp fly-half, Cliff Jones. Wooller could win matches with wonderfully creative play, often scoring near-impossible tries or kicking towering goals. Yet he could also save apparently certain tries by delivering a shattering crash tackle. Even so, it was his sheer determination and never-say-

die attitude that helped Wales to their most famous victory of his
era, against New Zealand in 1935. With Wales trailing 12–10 and
a man short, Wooller's opportunism led to the thrilling late winning try. He made the carefully judged kick ahead that deceived
the All Blacks and allowed Geoffrey Rees-Jones in for the decisive
score. The move was practically a carbon-copy of one involving
the same players earlier in the match which had led to Wales's
second try.

The *Daily Telegraph*'s Howard Marshall, the leading critic of the
day, described Wooller's rugby talents as 'like the sacrificial car of
Juggernaut, leaving a trail of prostrate figures in his wake'. Wooller
captained Wales in 1939, but it was in the Middlesex Sevens of that
year that he achieved what he considered the highlight of his club
rugby career: leading Cardiff, as the guest side, to victory. 'Six of us
had never played sevens before,' he said many years later. He was
still in his prime when the outbreak of war effectively brought his
international rugby career to an end. He was commissioned into
the Royal Artillery serving with the 77th Heavy Anti-Aircraft
Regiment, but still managed to figure prominently in many of the
popular wartime charity internationals staged in 1939–40.

All that was missing from his otherwise impeccable rugby CV
was a place on a Lions' tour. He would have been a sight to behold
against the Springboks on the firm pitches of the veldt. But in
1938, when he was invited to make the visit to South Africa with
Sammy Walker's tourists, business commitments with a Cardiff
company prevented him from accepting.

After coming down from Cambridge in 1935 he had entered the
coal trade that flourished in Cardiff docks working for the business
tycoon Sir Herbert Merrett. Wooller could not afford to take
unpaid leave for the duration of a major tour. Still, if one door
closed another opened, for in mid-June of that summer he made his
Glamorgan cricket debut taking 5–90 at Cardiff Arms Park on the
opening day of the championship match against Yorkshire. He
played as part of his annual paid leave. Later his cricketing commitments would prevent him from covering a Lions' tour as a critic. It
was one of the few regrets he had in a career that otherwise brought
him complete fulfilment. His last international rugby appearance

was at the Parc-des-Princes in February 1940, when a British Army side, playing exhilarating rugby, demolished France 36–3. Wooller scored a hat-trick of tries.

In 1942, he was captured by the Japanese at Java and imprisoned at Changi jail for the rest of the war. In *The Skipper*, Dr Andrew Hignell's biography of Wooller, the former POW told of the physical and mental toughness he needed to survive that horrendous ordeal. 'If I was to get anywhere, I'd have to achieve it myself by sheer drive and force.' These were qualities that the remarkable prisoner showed he had by the bucketload. He successfully bartered for a strip of land in which he was able to grow bananas. 'The skins were an important source of fibre,' he said. He survived, but returned to Cardiff a shadow of the physical giant who had put the wind up the All Blacks, and after one postwar appearance for Cardiff never played rugby again.

During the war Wooller had married Lady Gillian Windsor-Clive, but the marriage was dissolved shortly after his return to Britain, and in 1948 he married Enid James. This was the start of a long and happy family life that accelerated his physical recovery. He had resumed the county cricket career that had flourished before the war, when he had also won two cricket Blues at Cambridge, and quickly established himself as an all-rounder with leadership potential at Glamorgan. He succeeded Johnnie Clay as the county's captain in 1947 and led the Welsh county to its inaugural County Championship title in 1948. He finally stood down as captain in 1960 and played his last match two years later, but remained a strong influence on Glamorgan cricket, serving as secretary until 1977. Later he was their president. A true-blue amateur, he brought a thoroughly professional approach to his cricket and was highly respected as an England selector between 1955 and 1961 during Peter May's successful captaincy.

Cricket is a game that reveals much about character, and many of the incidents that Wooller was involved in illuminated his determination to win and his larger-than-life presence. Whether true or apocryphal, the stories about his antics on the cricket field convey his hatred of losing and the barracking he could give batsmen. Peter May allegedly once took umbrage when Wooller ran him out backing up before the bowler had released the ball during a county championship match with Surrey.

May enquired politely: 'Isn't it customary to give the batsman a warning?' 'Not in Swansea,' replied Wooller. Tom Graveney was another fine England batsman who was once sent packing by a typical Woollerism after knocking Glamorgan around. 'That was the worst double-hundred I've ever seen Tom,' he declared in his stentorian voice as Graveney, no doubt feeling quite pleased with himself, headed back to the pavilion.

Another dispute at Swansea, when Wooller was secretary, has been well documented. He became so annoyed by Brian Close's captaincy during a Somerset match at St Helen's in 1972 that he announced over the tannoy: 'In view of Somerset's negative approach, we are happy to refund the admission money of any spectator who wishes to call at the county office.' He ruled Glamorgan with an iron fist; there were never any velvet gloves around when Wooller was present. Some players, even on his own side, were intimidated by his overbearing manner; others – usually opponents – resented it. But his heart was always in the right place and he put Glamorgan cricket on the national map. Vivian Jenkins, his old rugby and cricket friend, recalled that Wilf was always the first to buy the opposition a pint afterwards, no matter how heated the cut and thrust of the game had been. Superficially he could appear brash and arrogant; inside he was shy and modest. It was a view corroborated by J.B.G. Thomas, who referred to him as 'The Godfather of Glamorgan Cricket'. Thomas worked closely with Wooller as a journalistic colleague in the rugby season and reported Glamorgan cricket in the summers. Thomas described him as enigmatic. 'To those who know him well [he] is, deep down, a shy and kindly man, far more retiring in manner than his public image would suggest.'

A compelling figure, Wooller was an outspoken broadcaster as well as a trenchant critic for the now defunct *News Chronicle* after the war. Years later, on *Welsh Sports Parade*, a Monday evening sports magazine put out by BBC Wales television, he once very publicly took to task a well-known Wales wing three-quarter who had missed a try-scoring pass in a losing international. Arguments and disagreements were frequent, though there was never any lasting malice. His observations on sport, perceptive and provocative but always honest, continued to entertain readers, listeners and viewers in Wales. He spoke with enthusiasm and a depth of knowledge. One of his most memorable outside broadcasts came from St Helen's on a lazy Swansea afternoon in the late summer of 1968 when cricket history was made by Gary Sobers. Playing for Nottinghamshire, the former West Indies' captain knocked six sixes off a Malcolm Nash over while Wooller was at the microphone.

Wooller campaigned vigorously in support of sporting relations with South Africa at the time of the anti-apartheid demonstrations against the rugby and cricket tours in 1970. He argued that politics should not relate to sport. He was blithely scornful of the views of sports ministers – Conservative and Labour – and told the Archbishop of Wales that supporting demonstrators was disgraceful. He sent the cleric off with a flea in his ear: 'It's time the Church confined itself to the spiritual matters I find sadly lacking in these permissive times.' Wooller never backed down and never bowed to political correctness. Even as a pensioner on the Cardiff crown-green bowls circuit his combative spirit, by all accounts, was still to the fore. He relished challenges. How he would have loved 21st-century Britain! Once, though, he was completely disarmed by bureaucracy gone mad.

In 1961, when the *Sunday Telegraph* launched as a national broadsheet competitor to the *Observer* and *Sunday Times*, Wooller was installed to comment on rugby and cricket. He became the backbone of the newspaper's sports pages. In late October 1973 their correspondent was due to do a weekend report of the Cardiff v. Cambridge University rugby match – his two former clubs as it happened. He was denied entry to the Arms Park. An officious steward who knew Wooller well demanded to see his press pass. He didn't have it. His report the next day was hilarious.

'I must admit that as I know most stewards and committee men on most of the grounds in Wales I thought this joker was joking, but as I moved to enter, [the steward] forcibly stopped me assisted by another gateman. So, not having a pass, I quitted the premises, a sadder and perhaps wiser man.

'The irony of the situation later struck me. I joined Cardiff as a player in 1936. Then as a serving soldier after the committee had closed down the club accounts, I captained and rallied the team and before the end of the [1939–40] season we had handed many thousands of pounds to war charities before the timid committee came back to take over. After the war I served the club as a committee man. In short, a serving, fully paid up member for 38 years, a paid up member of the NUJ, but still rudely stopped watching Cardiff play Cambridge, for whom I played in 1933–34–35: the two clubs in my life, in fact.

'Prominent old Cardiff players have often growled about the bureaucratic set-up in the club, several stay clear because the better they were as a player the less they felt welcome; but personally this is the first time I have seen it in action. The next time I approach the holy of holies I shall take my prayer mat, kill a fatted calf, crawl in on my knees and ask to be pardoned. I am sure that splendid rugby committee will consider my case favourably if I bow low enough.'

It was pure Wooller.

His favourite rugby match was the 1967 Wales–England encounter when Keith Jarrett, a teenager playing out of position at fullback, scored 19 points to deny England the Triple Crown. Wales won by the then staggering scoreline of 34–21. In Wooller's five appearances for Wales against England in the 1930s the two sides accumulated only 26 points. 'This spectacle, to one who had fought England over dour 80-minute periods, was something one could not quite believe,' he told readers. 'The pace was as hot as the [spring] weather and it never let up for an instant of the 80-odd packed minutes of movement. Spectators at this memorable contest will no doubt forget the score, if not the broad outlines of the game, but I doubt very much whether any single individual present will ever forget Jarrett's superb try in all its glorious technicolour. And the strangest thing of all is that happened in a game between England and Wales.'

Welsh sport's man for all seasons – he had even played centre forward for Cardiff City in 1939 and was a squash international – died in his sleep in March 1997, aged 84. Among the many tributes paid, Sir Tasker Watkins VC, president of the Welsh Rugby

Union, said Wooller was 'one of the greatest sportsmen Wales has ever produced, indeed there is any amount of evidence to suggest that he was the greatest of them all'.

PETER ROBBINS
Life at One Hundred Miles an Hour

Writing in the *Daily Telegraph*, its rugby correspondent John Mason perfectly summed up the life and times of England flanker Peter Robbins: '[He] had many strings to a finely tuned bow – humorist, linguist, businessman, journalist and staunch friend. He was a magnificent back-row forward who roamed the field bent on creation more than destruction. Support was his constant theme linked with a considerable physical presence. On and off the field [he] lived his life to the full.'

Knocking over fly-halves with hard, fair tackles was second nature to Robbins, the genuine open-side who featured prominently in the England sides that won Five Nations honours in the late 1950s and early 1960s. He was perpetual motion personified on the field and always scrupulously fair as a player. He covered the ground with lightning pace to set up second phase possession – he was always first to the breakdown – and tackled like a thunderbolt in defence. Robbins, it was said, always got his man.

Peter Robbins was born on 21 September 1933 in Coventry and it was at Bishop Vesey Grammar School in Sutton Coldfield that the rugby fire that burned brightly throughout his life was kindled. From there he went up to Oxford to study modern languages and after two eye-catching performances in the Varsity Match he was drafted into Eric Evans's England side to meet Wales in 1956. Robbins was one of 10 new brooms in that XV and many survived to take part in the clean sweep a year later when England secured their first Grand Slam for 29 years. Robbins had already made a name for himself as a tactician at Oxford and the England captain, Eric Evans, paid warm tribute to Peter's constructive support: 'If I was a good captain, it was because I had Peter Robbins beside me: he was a great asset,' he said. Evans led England to another championship title in 1958 and after his retirement many critics canvassed Robbins's talents as successor. In Evans's last year as England's skipper P.G.D., as Robbins was known to his friends, had transformed a physically small Oxford side into one of the fittest teams ever fielded by the university and his agile tactical brain enabled the Dark Blues to achieve a famous 3–0 victory over Cambridge. He would later skipper Moseley, Coventry and a successful Warwickshire county side. Yet the England selectors dropped a bombshell by omitting him in 1959 from a team that went on to score just three penalty goals in the entire Five Nations campaign. Robbins, it was argued, did not push in the scrums and palpably inferior flankers were promoted ahead of him. He was recalled for the Triple Crown season in 1960, when England shared the Five Nations title with France, but he lost his place after successive defeats by South Africa and Wales in 1961, giving way to a young Budge Rogers. Peter's 19th and last cap was against Scotland in 1962, but his Test career record spoke volumes: 11 wins, four draws and only four defeats as well as those three Five Nations titles.

Apart from the sheer class he showed on the field he was the life and soul of the party off it, a born practical joker. Neddy Ashcroft, an England back-row contemporary, cherished memories of P.G.D.'s water-pistol shoot-outs on visits to the Chiswick Empire on the eves of Twickenham internationals. One year Lonnie Donegan was on stage and found himself at the sharp end of a Robbins onslaught from the front row. When the England team returned a month later before another Twickenham engagement Donegan was well-prepared, retaliating with a soda siphon. At the *Folies Bergères* nightclub the same season, while celebrating after an England match in Paris, Robbins and his sharpshooters wreaked havoc with a salvo of ice-cold water on the dancers' naked flesh.

Then there was the classic passport trick that Robbins played on an Oxford colleague while the university side was on its way by road to play Cardiff in November 1957. Near the Welsh border Robbins asked the big South African lock, Dennis Bouwer, if he had remembered to bring his passport. He hadn't, so at Robbins's insistence Bouwer was concealed in the luggage hold of the coach until they were into deepest Wales and clear of the 'border control point'. The unsuspecting South African, an occasional member of the side who had been drafted in for the Cardiff match while England's John Currie was rested, had the misfortune to fracture his collarbone after only 20 minutes of the match. Fearing that he would be taken for an illegal immigrant if admitted to a local hospital, he insisted on making the journey back to Oxford in pain before seeking treatment.

Dudley Wood, erstwhile secretary of the Rugby Football Union, an Oxford flanker and modern linguist a couple of years ahead of Robbins, remembered playing against Robbins in a Waterloo–Moseley club match in the 1950s. Robbins told him at the first line-out: 'I've got your French notes.' At the next line-out he said: 'I also had your French tutor,' and at the third: 'And that's why I got such a bloody awful degree,' leaving Wood totally bemused.

Even so, the degree was good enough to launch him on a successful 10-year career as a schoolmaster at King Edward's, Birmingham, where one of the first XV captains in his early years was outside-half and future birdwatcher, Bill Oddie. Robbins impressed on his pupils that sport was a recreation and that life should be fun. Teaching gave him the spare time to keep up his rugby contacts and during vacations he managed combined Oxford/Cambridge tours overseas. He never stayed still for long. One trip to South Africa illustrated his gift of the gab. There had been a riotous assembly among the tourists in Durban with matters escalating completely out of hand after a match against the Central Universities. The worst incident involved a bedstead plummeting several storeys from a hotel window into the street. Robbins smoothed matters over masterfully afterwards and by all accounts almost had the hotel manager thanking him for preventing a more serious incident occurring. Robbins had blagged his way out of potentially a very serious situation by telling the manager – who was unaware that Robbins himself had been proactive in the caper – that

Oxbridge students weren't used to drinking such strong, fine South African wines.

He left teaching for business and developed a sideline in the rugby media, covering the big matches for the *Financial Times* and later the *Observer*. As a critic he was as sharp as he had been a player, and the feature of his writing was the ability to fill his columns with insight, never relying on players' post-match quotes to bulk out his copy. Wearing a black beret and with his trusty pipe never far out of his reach, he continued to roam the rugby world with light-hearted menace, attracting a large circle of friends – journalists, former players and business acquaintances – to share in his revels. He was renowned for his love of food and drink and an evening out in his company was an education. The late John Reason of the *Telegraph* once told the story of a Robbins meal during the Hong Kong Sevens where P.G.D. cleared not only his own plate but also finished off the leftovers from nine fellow diners. As the party settled up to leave Robbins asked the waiter: 'Right, where's the nearest McDonald's?'

Alas, he missed out on the highest honour in rugby through injury. Although considered not good enough to play for England in 1959, the Four Home Unions selectors regarded Robbins as an automatic choice for the British/Irish Lions' tour to Australia and New Zealand that summer. But playing for the Barbarians against Newport on their Easter tour he broke his leg and had to withdraw from the party. In later years the myth arose that he had actually injured himself jumping into an empty swimming pool at the club's Penarth hotel, trying to sober up after a bit of a thrash celebrating the night before. Definitely wrong – he did that on the 1957 Baa-Baas' tour of south Wales, damaging his shoulder so severely that he had to withdraw from the Barbarians' tour of Canada. There was also some damage to the swimming pool.

Peter Robbins died aged 53 on 25 March 1983, bringing sorrow to those whose lives had been touched by his boundless energy. His son said that his father had lived life at one hundred miles an hour, a phrase used by the journalist Michael Blair as the heading for an engaging biography of Robbins. 'They understated the speed,' said Tony O'Reilly when he heard of the title.

TREMAYNE RODD

Fighting Individualist

There was only one Tremayne Rodd. He was a scrum-half who qualified to play for Scotland through a grandmother and brought a fighting spirit to a national side that had suffered a long and bleak run of defeats. Scotland had endured 17 losses on the trot in the early to mid-1950s and had managed only a couple of odd victories when Rodd was selected to partner his Royal Navy colleague Gordon Waddell in the Scottish side in January 1958. The pair were an odd couple – Rodd had a weak service and a strong individual streak to his game while Waddell, too, revelled as a soloist. But for sheer grit and determination their combination proved to be just what Scotland needed.

In their early games together they masterminded Scottish wins against France and Australia. 'Courageous', 'heroic' and 'resourceful' were words used to describe Rodd's play. He was particularly dangerous breaking solo from the base of the scrum and it was such a move that led to a try by his wing Grant Weatherstone in the Dublin match against Ireland in 1958. Later the same season he effectively closed down the English attacks with a brilliant defensive display, frequently smothering his famous opponent Dickie Jeeps like a blanket on a fire. Rodd's strength that day played a big part in Scotland holding England to a draw and at the end of the season the Scots could reflect on a relatively successful campaign. Overseas duties as a naval officer ruled him out of international rugby for the 1959 Five Nations and probably robbed him of the opportunity to tour Australia and New Zealand with that year's British and Irish Lions.

He returned with renewed enthusiasm for the 1960 campaign and was prominent in an outstanding open game at Murrayfield in January, which gave international rugby a wonderful shot in the arm. The French were playing exhilarating rugby at the time and Scotland joined them in a fast-flowing game that yielded five tries. Despite getting an unpleasant elbow in the face from a French forward just after half-time, Rodd's tricky runs were instrumental in Scotland's second-half rally.

Thereafter, Rodd was in and out of the Scottish team, the strong vein of individualism that ran through his game not always winning favour with the Scottish selectors. Throughout his career he played in England, mainly with London Scottish for whom he was an outstanding member of their invincible sevens outfit that ruled the Middlesex Sevens in the early 1960s. But when he was recalled to Scotland duties he never let his side down. His penchant for a break made him a more-than-useful outside-half, and he was versatile enough to fill that position with some success for Hampshire in the English County Championship competition, helping them to reach the final in 1962 when they were narrowly beaten 11–6 at Twickenham by a powerful Warwickshire side.

Arguably his finest hour came in early 1964 when, playing with all his customary resource, he battled through a hard match against France at Murrayfield where Scotland were 10–0 winners. His tactical nous – in particular knowing when to keep the game tight against a marauding French back row – was a major factor in the victory and when, a fortnight later, he gave a repeat performance as Scotland held New Zealand to a point-less draw, countless laurels were heaped upon him. The Scottish pack was pulverised by the All Blacks and Rodd had to deal with a steady stream of untidy possession. But he always revelled in adversity and it was his resourcefulness dealing with scrappy heels and resilience in the face of the New Zealand back row that more than anything kept Scotland's line intact. Scotland, in fact, has never had a better result against New Zealand in over a hundred years of matches. Scotland went on to share the International Championship title with Wales in 1964, their best achievement in the competition since 1938. He played the last of his 14 games for Scotland in 1965 and went on to show the same qualities of character in his public and private life off the field.

He had joined the merchant bank Morgan Grenfell, where his

uncle Lord Rennell was then a director, after leaving the navy but decided to throw in his City job in order to follow the 1966 Lions' rugby tour of Australia and New Zealand as a freelance journalist. His articles for the *Scotsman* and *Observer* were to lead to his being professionalised by the Scottish Rugby Union, for in those days writing about rugby for gain led to an automatic ban from playing. Rodd, ever the fighter, appealed to the Rugby Football Union, which overturned the ban and he continued playing among his friends at London Scottish until the International Board finally upheld the Scottish Union's view and ruled in March 1970 that he was a professional.

During the 1966 Lions' tour, their manager Des O'Brien was relaxing at the team's plush hotel on a rest day between matches. He saw Rodd enter the reception area and immediately rose to tell the freelance that there were no press events planned for the day. Rodd brushed off the hapless manager with a smile, telling him that he was staying there and had a suite on the second floor.

He was well-liked as a young naval officer, popular with his rugby cronies and well-connected. He belonged to gentlemen's clubs in Belgravia and Knightsbridge, where those who shared his passion for backgammon and cards included his cousin the painter Dominic Elwes, John Aspinall and Lord Lucan. In November 1975 Rodd, who was once described in a pen-picture before an international match as having 'plenty of punch in his play', was involved in a much-publicised fracas after a Mayfair memorial service for Elwes, who had committed suicide. John Aspinall gave an address which offended Rodd, who took immediate action, punching Aspinall on the chin saying: 'That's what I think of your bloody speech.' Rodd afterwards told the press: 'I'm glad I did it. If I hadn't thrown that punch I would have regretted it for the rest of my life.'

Tremayne Rodd was born on 28 June 1935 and educated at Downside and the Royal Naval College at Dartmouth. It was at Dartmouth that his rugby blossomed – and his punching, for he was a Home Fleet Boxing champion during his service days. His mentor there was the former Irish scrum-half Mark Sugden, who was quick to spot Rodd's potential. '[He] had the eye and ability to profit from the smallest loophole in the defence,' Sugden wrote in the college magazine, 'and his constant and clever breaking from the scrum had a most upsetting effect upon the opposition.' It was said that Rodd showed greater respect for Sudgen than he did for an admiral during his naval days.

After his brief flirtation with journalism he set up his own company, Marks of Distinction, which produced medals and trophies and later branched out running corporate and sporting promotions. Typically, he brought plenty of style to all his enterprises. In 1978 he succeeded his uncle as Lord Rennell and was prominent in House of Lords activities. In his late 50s he proudly promoted and played for 'The Rugby XV of the Houses of Parliament of Westminster of Her Majesty's Government' – whatever happened to that IB ban? Overturned by Parliament, perhaps, though in truth, despite his high connections, he always seemed to have a healthy disregard for authority. He worked his old journalistic connections to publicise the matches and one invitation, for the morning of the England–New Zealand Twickenham match in November 1993, was typical of his enthusiasm. The Commons & Lords XV was due to play The David Kirk New Zealand Select XV at Richmond with Lord Rennell himself at scrum-half against the former New Zealand World Cup winning captain. 'Hope I may see you there,' he wrote to his contacts. 'K.O. 11.00am. Don't be late – I might not last!'

Lord Rennell died of cancer on 9 December 2006. He certainly attracted his critics but for his cheerful and positive character it was impossible to dislike him.

JACK KYLE
The Greatest

In the early 2000s the Irish media conducted a poll to discover the leading players in Irish rugby history. The man who came out as the greatest of them all was Dr Jack Kyle, the outside-half who played 46 times for his country and appeared in six Lions' Tests between 1947 and 1958. As a player of consummate skill he could float like a butterfly in his running and sting like a bee with tackles and kicks – long before another in a different sport invented the phrase. Jack Kyle was rugby's chivalrous icon.

He was born on 10 January 1926 in Belfast and educated at the Belfast Royal Academy where, after a brief flirtation as a forward and fullback, he was transferred to outside-half for his last two years at school. He went up to Queen's University in Belfast to study medicine in 1944, and it was there that the player whose elusive runs did wonders for Irish esteem in the immediate postwar seasons first emerged. Few sights on the rugby field excite the spectator more than an outside-half tearing defences to shreds with will-o'-the-wisp breaks, but Kyle was far more than just a mazy runner. His contributions to Ireland's purple patch between 1948 and 1951 were beyond measure. The way he managed to take a game by the scruff of the neck and instinctively knew the tactics most likely to benefit his side were phenomenal talents.

Ireland had an intelligent pack, and Kyle would be the first to acknowledge the splendid service he received from his skilful scrum-halves – Ernie Strathdee, Hugh de Lacy and later John O'Meara. But his spontaneous skills in the pivotal role were the keys that unlocked Ireland's potential for honours. In appearance he was short and slender with a shock of dark hair. On the rugby field he possessed the instinctive judgement to know what to do without having to think about it. The best place to position yourself, the Irish players said when Kyle was playing, was two metres away from him. He could land a tactical kick on a sixpence, he could sniff out an opening where ordinary bloodhounds would be senseless, and his uncanny positional sense enabled him to pop up at unexpected moments in defence to make try-saving tackles.

He had a reputation for being completely unflappable – off the pitch as well as on. He would, apparently, nod off on the bus to big matches when others were uptight. And he could become absorbed in a book or poem and nearly miss a team talk or training session. He was the living embodiment it seemed of Kipling's inspirational 'If'. Even when controlling tactics in the hurly-burly of an international, as at Twickenham at the start of the second half in 1948, Kyle was the model of stability. The score at half-time was 5-all, but England were expected to fare better with the wind at their backs after the break. But they had not reckoned with the genius of Kyle. The Irish pivot was the mainspring behind the first of two tries in the opening five minutes of the half when he accelerated through on the blind-side of a loose scrum on the English 25 to score in the right corner without an English hand being laid on him.

Although there was no Grand Slam for Ireland in 1951, the Irish were outright champions. In the opinion of many leading critics, that side was the best of the postwar Irish XVs – better even than the Grand Slam achievers of 1948. It was Kyle who took them to the brink of a Grand Slam that season. With wins over France, England and Scotland under their belt, Ireland found themselves 0–3 down to Wales at Cardiff in March. A flash of Kyle genius gave the old Arms Park crowd a try to live in the memory. From a line-out in the Welsh 25 he looped around his inside centre to receive a return pass. Next he overlapped his outside centre and, tucking the ball under his right arm, accelerated through a gap to take him head on to the Welsh fullback. A sidestep off his right foot left the Welsh defender sprawling and Kyle's try squared the match. Near the end he stopped the Welsh sprinter Ken Jones in his tracks, the tackle saving a certain winning score.

Ironically, before that match Ireland's Karl Mullen had given his customary captain's speech, ending with his usual invitation for any questions from his team. 'I have a question,' said centre Noel Henderson, one of the quieter members of the side. 'I want to know if our out-half will be taking his man for a change?' Henderson was Kyle's brother-in-law and the banter was at the expense of the outside-half's tackling skills – not usually the strongest part of his game.

The same afternoon, while the two sides were walking from the changing rooms to the pitch, another aspect of Jack's character was revealed. Modest and unassuming, he was respected as one of the kindest men to play international rugby. His opposite number, making his debut for Wales that day, was the great Cliff Morgan, who went on to win 29 caps in the position. As the sides filed on to the field, Morgan felt a kindly hand on his shoulder. It was

Kyle. 'Have a great game, Cliffie. Good luck,' he said. Morgan rated Kyle the greatest fly-half of his time.

The same kind thoughtfulness of character was shown to young team-mates and unknown youngsters. He enjoyed such a long career in the Irish side that many who later played with him had hero-worshipped him as boys. When John O'Meara was selected to partner him for the first time in 1951 his biggest dilemma was should he address his outside-half as Mr Kyle or Dr Kyle. The kindly doctor, of course, put his young colleague at ease immediately and one of the most productive Irish halfback partnerships was born. Kyle was also invariably the last to leave the pitch after a match, signing autograph books for all and sundry. Moreover, postal requests from enthusiasts on the British mainland were answered with a personally addressed studio portrait of the great man neatly signed 'With best wishes'.

He went on thrilling rugby crowds with his wonderful feats until 1958, when his international career finished on a then world record of 46 caps for his country. He also played six Tests on the 1950 Lions' tour. Old-timers still rate him the best outside-half ever to have visited New Zealand. In 1953, after he very nearly engineered another famous win over England in Dublin (the match finished drawn), R.C. Robertson-Glasgow of the *Observer* put him 'on the shortest list of the great' in the outside-half position. 'In defence, some may have been more obviously and noisily robust,' he wrote. 'In attack, a few, a very few, may have been more incalculably elusive and more swiftly penetrative. But who ever exceeded Kyle in the two arts taken together?'

The modest Ulster doctor carried on playing rugby for fun for several more seasons, serving his club, North of Ireland, as a full-back on their third XV. There, in front of the proverbial old man walking the dog, he seemed to derive as much pleasure from the game as when he had played for Ireland in front of thousands. Later he practised his medical skills in Indonesia and spent 30 years in Zambia before retiring home to Northern Ireland, where he still enjoys watching rugby and reminiscing with modesty about his wonderful playing days.

AMÉDÉE DOMENECH
The Duke

It's rare for one man to exercise such influence that he transforms his club into a household name. Yet that was the achievement of Amédée Domenech, the larger-than-life French prop of the 1950s and 1960s whose club Brive became a force in European rugby. The club even named its home ground after him.

On the pitch he was likened in appearance and personality to a Roman gladiator. Immensely strong with dark aquiline features, he had a fierce stubbornness to his character. Early in his career he disliked being told what to do and often ended up in hot water for his truculence. At Twickenham in 1955 his captain, Jean Prat, was barking out orders left, right and centre when Domenech, tired of being told to do this or do that, unexpectedly found himself in possession and tossed the ball to his skipper saying: 'Here – see what you can do with it.' Prat dropped a goal.

Then in 1961, when French rugby was riding the crest of a wave, the national side had big international matches on successive Saturdays in February and the players were told to rest between games. Domenech didn't. After playing a stormer for the Tricolores in a famous scoreless draw against the Springboks he decided to ignore the French Federation's directive and on his way home from Paris on the Sunday after the Test stopped off in Orléans to play for his beloved Brive. He scored two tries as a makeshift wing, was promptly fined by the FFR and paid up with a grin. Six days later he was in top form for France against England at Twickenham, even briefly deputising as a wing for injured team-mate Jean Dupuy and frightening the living daylights out of John Young, his English opponent.

Off the field he enjoyed a colourful life as a bar/restaurant owner, local politician and film/television star, careers which all added to the Brive and Domenech legends. He once saved a local from drowning when the river Corrèze overflowed and he was offered a life-saving certificate. 'It was only three feet deep,' said Amédée modestly. 'Mind,' he added, 'the fellow drank a bottle of my cognac. I'll take the certificate.' On another occasion the river flooded and washed away part of his bar, including a mural bearing the inscription: 'Love and Rugby while away the hours', a slogan that gave an accurate insight into the happy-go-lucky nature of the popular restaurateur. Years later, when Brive had become a force in the Heineken Cup competition, an English team turned up for a match at his club's ground and complained about the state of the pitch. Domenech, by then a respected local councillor, gave them short shrift. 'What have you come here for? To play rugby or to graze?'

He was universally known as 'The Duke', partly on account of his uncommon given name (Amédée was the handle of a line of the Dukes of Savoy) and partly as a reflection of his full-blooded, noble bearing. Another version has it that Domenech once called André Boniface, a famous French three-quarter, the 'king' of players to which Boniface replied: 'Well, if I am the king, then you are the duke.'

Amédée Domenech was born in Narbonne on 3 May 1933 and played as a back-row forward in his youth, displaying the running and handling skills that would have impressed a basketball coach. He joined the Vichy club while he was stationed there during his national service and was called into the French Test side as a 20-year-old in 1954. As a loose-head prop he was to become the cornerstone of the French teams that created history by winning for the first time shares of the Five Nations in both 1954 and 1955 (France shared the title with Wales and England n 1954, and with Wales in 1955). On completion of his military service he settled in Brive where he quickly made his mark by helping the club to reach the top flight of the French Championship. Before he arrived there, the town in the southwest of France was virtually unknown to rugby followers and barely mentioned in the French press. By the time he retired, Brive was a rugby force to be reckoned with and has remained so to this day. Domenech had put the town on the map.

Immensely strong for his age and with energy to burn in the loose, he looked set for a long tenure in the national side and was ever-present in the Five Nations teams of 1956 and 1957, before his world started to fall apart a year later. France's intoxicating era of champagne rugby under Lucien Mias was uncorked in 1958, but it opened with 'The Duke' out of favour. He was deemed unsuitable for the forward collectivism propounded by Mias. It was never disputed that Domenech had the potential to fit into the Mias scheme, but he was judged to be incurably individualistic. Some critics labelled him a butterfly because he fluttered on the verge of the pack instead of adding to its cohesion. 'Do I look like a butterfly,' he retorted, but by his own admission he was deeply disappointed by his omission and after absorbing Mias's ideas he became committed to the captain's tenets. He finally returned to the French side in 1960 and when his recall was announced he appeared on French television with Roger Lerou, the chairman of selectors. Friends expected 'The Duke' to make the odd crack or two for the cameras, but he was practically mute throughout the interview. Monsieur Lerou congratulated him afterwards. 'But I was almost dumb,' said Domenech. 'Exactly,' replied Lerou. 'You were excellent.'

There was to be a new role for Domenech. The Mias era had given rise to a tactical development known as the ploy, a forward move that involved the entire pack working in harmony to launch attacks. 'The Duke' was deputed to peel off from the front and take tap-downs off the back of line-outs before heading upfield at the head of a wedge-shaped attack. He became a pivotal figure in France's Five Nations sides that won titles in 1960, 1961 and 1962, raising the peel to an art form and playing the best rugby of his life. He won his 52nd and final cap in 1963, having featured in five winning Five Nations seasons.

Amédée Domenech, who went on to become as big a character on Brive's political stage as well as in French film and television circles, died on 21 September 2003 having lived his three-score years and ten to the full. Rugby in France and life in Brive has never been quite the same without him.

JEFF BUTTERFIELD
Ahead of his Time

Jeff Butterfield was one of rugby's most creative exponents in the dreary years of the mid-1950s. His stylish running and polished handling illuminated many Test and club matches at a time when tactically the game was passing through a sterile period. Off the field his professional approach to a strictly amateur sport placed him ahead of his time in terms of physical fitness and tactical appreciation. In short, it is no exaggeration to conclude that he would have been equally at home at Test level as a player and coach/manager in the modern professional game.

Jeff Butterfield was a Yorkshireman. He was born in Heckmondwike on 9 August 1929 and educated at Cleckheaton Grammar School before attending Loughborough College, where he qualified as a PE teacher. Fitness was the keynote of his playing career and the high standards he set himself as a college student never waned throughout his days in first-class rugby. He worked hard to improve his stamina, strength and speed. Representative honours came early in his career. He played for Yorkshire and the Army during his national service, and when he took up a teaching post at Wellingborough Grammar School he joined Northampton, the leading club in England during the 1950s. There he blossomed into an all-round centre whose hallmarks were bravery and perfect judgement, in sharp contrast to the bluster and bludgeon that were the principal midfield weapons of the generation that preceded him.

Skilful handling was the most striking feature of his centre three-quarter play. He had the intuition of the natural ball-player, could give a carefully placed pass in one smooth movement and had the ability to exploit an opening in a split second. Colleagues purred at the thought of playing outside him. When Jeff sensed that the back division was being forced across the field he had no trouble straightening the line; if the moment cried out for a swift pass to the wing then he would deliver his colleague a perfectly weighted try-scoring pass. Don White, his contemporary at Northampton and later an England coach, said Butterfield 'was a superb passer of the ball and a joy to play with'. His qualities did not go unnoticed in the rugby league territory of his native county and many lucrative offers to turn professional were turned down.

Jeff's skills carried him into the England team against France in 1953 and, through his consistency and fitness, there he stayed for 28 consecutive international matches. He showed his capacity as a finisher, scoring tries in each of his first two matches for England and helping them to the Five Nations title. In 1954, his burgeoning centre partnership with Phil Davies was a significant factor in England's Triple Crown season under Bob Stirling, and he and Davies were the first-choice pair for the 1955 Lions, who became the first of the 20th century to share the spoils of a series in South Africa.

That visit found him at the peak of his powers. He relished running on the firm pitches and South African critics showered praise on his deft attacking touches. He scored tries in each of the first two Tests of the visit and his unexpected left-footed drop-goal – the only one he scored in his first-class career – opened the scoring at Pretoria in the Lions' third Test win. Kicking, in fact, was seen as the only weakness of his game, but his goal helped place the Lions one up in the series with only one to play – a position that no British/Irish touring side in South Africa had found itself in since the 1890s. Moreover, his organisational skills and knowledge of fitness made him the ideal player to oversee the coaching that took place on tour. The 1955 Lions were regarded as the best-ever side up to that point to have visited South Africa and the tourists' manager, Jack Siggins, singled Butterfield out for special mention at the end of the visit. It was the first time that tactical appreciation and a balanced fitness regimen had been considered important in the preparation of a Lions' team. Butterfield's contributions, on the field of play and practice grounds, were instrumental to the Lions' success.

Back home, his midfield vision as a creator of tries and a

destroyer of opposition attacks was the key element of England's Five Nations dominance in 1957 and 1958, when the side were unbeaten in nine Tests. England carried off the Grand Slam in 1957 and beat the Fourth Wallabies with a famous last-minute flourish at Twickenham in 1958, when Butterfield played for an hour of a brutal match at fly-half despite being laid out three times by heavy tackles. It was said that only his winning mentality and strong determination held together a gallant 14-man effort that day after Phil Horrocks-Taylor had had to retire with a leg injury after barely 25 minutes. Butterfield captained England in 1959, becoming his country's then most-capped back, and toured Australia and New Zealand with Ronnie Dawson's Lions that summer. It was to be his international swansong, for a recurring thigh injury sidelined him for much of the visit. Later he was troubled by an arthritic hip and forced to retire prematurely in 1962, aged 33, after 223 appearances for Northampton.

But his long association with the game was still only in its infancy. His dedication and attention to detail as a player made him the RFU's ideal choice as a member of the coaching panel convened to produce the first short manual on this aspect of the game. It was published in the mid-1960s with Jeff's pamphlet on back play becoming compulsory reading for all aspiring to play and coach at the highest level. He propounded the theories of straight-running, swift and accurate passing, and attack as a valuable form of defence – quite simply the classic approach that had characterised his own playing style. His thoughts were to influence the thinking that led to the 1971 and 1974 Lions' triumphs when, for the first time in the modern era, British/Irish sides won series against the southern hemisphere superpowers New Zealand and South Africa.

After his playing days were over he left teaching and flirted briefly with the paint industry and the property business. In the 1970s he helped launch the Rugby Club of London, where his urbanity, business skills and high standing in the rugby world helped turn the Hallam Street club into London's most popular watering hole for rugby-lovers. For 25 years he managed the club with his wife Barbara, who looked after the catering side of the business. They built the enterprise into a going concern and

'Buttercup's' – the nickname had been coined by Cliff Morgan on the 1955 Lions' tour – became a popular venue for Lions' reunions, rugby book launches and eve-of-international press receptions and was a Mecca for those of a rugby persuasion visiting the capital, either from the four corners of the British Isles or from overseas. He sold his interest in the club in the late 1990s at about the same time as undergoing major heart bypass surgery. When he died, aged 74, on 30 April 2004 many of his colleagues and friends in the game found his passing hard to believe, for in his 60s the man who had been 20 years ahead of his time as a player had always appeared as fit and sharp as one 20 years younger.

GORDON BROWN
Broon from Troon

Few players in any sport have managed to put their home town on the map to the same extent that Gordon Brown did in his rugby career as a Scotland and Lions' lock in the 1970s. With his cherubic appearance he was known as the baby-faced assassin when he first entered the Scottish team in 1969, but by the end of the 1970s he had stamped his irrepressible personality on the game to such a worldwide extent that the little Ayrshire coastal town of Troon, famous for its Open Championship golf links, became inextricably bound with his name. Troon had its fair share of Browns, but the one and only 'Broon frae Troon' was the larger-than-life Gordon of that ilk.

The man who was to grow up to be even bigger than his myth was born there on 1 November 1947, the youngest of three sons of Jock Brown, the Scotland and Clyde Cup-winning footballer of the 1930s. Father had also been a noted golfer while the boys' mother was a noted basketball and hockey player, so it was no surprise that all three Browns were primarily skilful, ball-playing sportsmen whose size dictated that they become rugby line-out forwards. Gordon followed his elder brother Peter, also a lock, into the Scotland team and made his debut in the match against the 1969–70 Springboks, partnering Peter Stagg. When Peter Brown was selected a couple of months later to make his return to the Scottish pack for the Five Nations match in Cardiff, he immediately called Gordon to tell him the good news. The brothers were always close but enjoyed the rough banter that goes with sibling rivalry. 'Who's out?' asked Gordon. 'You are,' said Peter. But the match against Wales was to give the brothers a unique place in international rugby's records, for Peter was injured early in the second half and replaced by Gordon – the first time that a brother had subbed for a sibling at Test match level.

By the end of the season the two brothers were first choices in the Scottish pack, Gordon staying as the hard-core partner to the giant Stagg with Peter Brown accommodated at Number Eight in the back row. The next season, when Peter took over as captain of the Scottish side, the pre-match banter between the brothers became a looked-forward-to diversion for the other members of the Scottish teams. Indeed, when Scotland achieved their first Twickenham victory for 33 years in 1971, it was one of Gordon's observations that broke some of the last-minute pre-match dressing room tensions. Peter was delivering an impassioned captain's speech imploring his XV to remember Stirling Bridge and Bannockburn and got so carried away that he added, 'and lads, don't forget Culloden!'. The baffled silence that followed was gently broken when Gordon piped up, 'Peter, I don't think we did very well at Culloden.' Peter responded with conviction: 'Gordon, I said "*remember* Culloden," and that's what I meant: after Culloden they didn't have to get changed and have dinner with the bastards!' The Browns were outstanding in Scotland's 16–15 victory that day, Gordon being the first to congratulate Peter after he had converted Chris Rea's late try to secure the winning points.

The match itself was witness to some off-the-ball argy-bargy among the forwards, particularly in the line-out where the French referee adopted a laissez-faire approach. It was more mischief than malice but led to an amusing exchange between Broonie and an opponent at the after-match banquet. The two sides were due to meet again in Edinburgh a week later in a special match outside the Five Nations arranged to celebrate the centenary of the fixture. The conversation went something along the lines of:

Opponent: 'That was a bit untidy at times, wasn't it?'

Brown: 'If that's what you think, just wait till Murrayfield next week.'

Opponent, with a slight air of superiority: 'We simply don't play the game that way.'

Brown: 'Well, you've got seven days to learn.'

Scotland won, achieving a run of three successive victories over England for the first time since 1927, and Gordon had played in all three games.

The summer of 1971 saw the Lions make their historic winning Test tour to New Zealand, where Gordon Brown came of age as a serious contender for rugby's hall of fame and coach Carwyn James hailed him the best all-round lock of his time. Brown was a good jumper at the line-out, capable of plucking the ball out of the air with the same two-handed certainty that his goal-keeping father had used to cut out crosses. In the tight he was a useful blocker and his immense strength in the scrums gave tremendous impetus to the Lions' pack. He replaced Delme Thomas to win his first Lions cap in the Third Test, at Wellington, when the series was delicately balanced at a win apiece.

Excited about his selection, Brown asked his line-out partner, Willie John McBride, what to expect from their famous New Zealand opponent, Colin Meads. 'He'll probably give you a punch in the eye at the first line-out,' Willie John explained, 'and he'll give you a hit on the nose at the second,' he continued, before asking Brown: 'What do you intend to give him in retaliation?' Gordon replied: 'All the line-out ball he wants!' He didn't, of course, but he did play a significant part in curbing the All Black forwards and winning good ball for Barry John and Gareth Edwards to give the Lions an unassailable early lead that put the tourists 2–1 up with one to play. In the final Test he played a brave part in the Lions' first-half rearguard action when the All Blacks threw the kitchen sink at the tourists as they strove to square the series in Auckland.

Brown survived an early punch and ended the drawn game with more than a dozen stitches in a badly gashed knee.

Knee, ligament and tendon injuries bedevilled his Scotland career in the seasons that followed, but his knowledge, confidence and experience were to prove invaluable to the Lions again when they made their invincible tour of South Africa in 1974. It was this second tour of his three Lions visits that brought him to the top of the tree. He played a dozen games, including the first three winning Tests, in the course of which he became an unlikely yet prolific try-scorer by crossing eight times. Difficult to stop when running like a Sherman tank at full tilt, two of his tries were crucial scores in the Tests.

Always an uncompromising player on the field, he enjoyed the company of friend and foe off it. Indeed, there was even an occasion *on* the field when he managed to lighten the intensity of battle in a rare break in play. During the savage do-or-die struggle at Port Elizabeth in the Third Test, the hardest of rugby men found themselves reduced to tears of laughter at the sight of Gordon Brown, bent over on all fours carefully combing the ground to help his opponent, Johan de Bruyn, find his glass eye. It had been sent flying during one of the several punch-ups that marked the early exchanges of the game. In later years Brown could not restrain his joy in telling of standing next to De Bruyn at a subsequent line-out and seeing the false eye with grass and mud hanging from it after it had been replaced in its vacant socket.

The last of 30 caps for Scotland was against Ireland in 1976. Later the same year he was seen retaliating viciously to a provocative stamping offence playing for Glasgow in an Inter-District match. Quicker intervention by the referee would have averted Gordon's reaction, but for this sole blemish on his sporting career he was suspended by the SRU for three months and missed the entire 1977 Five Nations. Even so, his playing credentials were never doubted by the Lions' selectors and he went to New Zealand for that summer's tour. A superb tourist, he was the Lions' honorary choirmaster, making 'Flower of Scotland' a number one hit with his team-mates, and worked tirelessly to raise morale on a disappointing tour. He played one of his best matches in the second Test when the Lions squared the series in Christchurch and kept his place as the nucleus of a Test pack that, in the end, narrowly failed to draw the series with the All Blacks.

He played in September of that year in the Queen's Silver Jubilee match when the returning Lions beat the Barbarians at Twickenham, but at 29 his Test career was over. Recurring injury ruled him out of Scotland contention and, even though as late as 1980 there were positive signs that he might recover in time to make the Lions' tour to South Africa, in the end a troublesome shoulder forced him into early retirement. His best rugby was undoubtedly seen in the red jersey of the Lions. By his own admission he was a reluctant trainer, but the strict regimen of a Lions' tour raised his fitness levels. Still, his record for Scotland was an impressive 14 wins in 30 matches, and to put that statistic into perspective it's worth mentioning that Scotland won only two of the 19 Tests they played after his departure from the squad in 1976.

The love of rugby never left him. He had been a successful building society manager in his professional career but gave it up to become one of the most popular and most sought-after after-dinner speakers on the rugby circuit. He wasn't a side-splitting jokester but had audiences eating out of his hand with hilarious tales from his own playing days. It was the way he told them. Chris Rea, a Scotland contemporary, said his humour wasn't so much infectious as 'rampantly contagious'. Often, it was said, fact and fiction were united, but the stories always complemented his warm personality and added greatly to the kilted Broon from Troon legend. Demand was great – he once managed six Murrayfield lunchtime speaking appointments before an international – but he also raised thousands for charitable causes. Even when he wasn't performing live, life with Broonie was a laugh a minute. Another friend who had accompanied him on a shuttle flight from Glasgow down to London for a Burns Supper tells the story that the stewardess interrupted their banter. 'We're concerned that your hilarity will cause residents living under the flight path to complain about the noise,' she jokingly told them.

Even after the onset of the early cancer that led to his premature death he continued to tell his stories for a living. As part of his medication he had to drink huge volumes of liquid. 'I used to play rugby for my country,' he said, 'Now I can definitely pee for it.' Three weeks before his death, a special tribute dinner was held in his honour at London's Grosvenor Hotel. More than 1,400 were in attendance as Broonie, greatly diminished physically by his awful illness nevertheless showed that his spirit remained indomitable, laughing uncontrollably as his favourite stories were retold in front of an appreciative audience. Then he was genuinely overcome near the end of the evening to be given a special present by his old Springbok sparring mate Johan de Bruyn. They hadn't met for 27 years but De Bruyn had travelled over to give Brown that old glass eye, suitably mounted on a miniature wooden rugby ball. 'Now I can keep my eye on you for ever,' De Bruyn said.

Three weeks later, on 19 March 2001, Gordon Brown died, aged 53, and another capacity crowd of family and rugby friends turned up at the Old Parish Church in Troon to pay their final respects. Gordon had even sat down with his old friend, the Reverend Howard Haslett, to plan his funeral service. Predictably the occasion was one of joy – Broonie wouldn't have had it any other way – with the Rev. Haslett protesting to the congregation that Gordon had issued such a volley of instructions concerning the funeral arrangements that he had even wondered to the genial giant why Brown himself shouldn't conduct the service. The warm, genuine ovation for Broonie that Rev. Haslett encouraged from mourners spoke volumes for the strength of friendship they felt for the man who typified the good fellowship that rugby engenders.

FULLBACKS ARE
DIFFERENT

BILLY BANCROFT
Supreme Confidence

Welshman Billy Bancroft was the most confident rugby player of the late Victorian era. As a youth he had practised the game's fine arts to such a degree that on the field of play he backed his speed and skill against anyone. Whether he was facing the biggest, hardest forwards of the day or the fastest three-quarters, Bancroft always had a trick up his sleeve to outwit his opponents. Invariably, too, it was a trick that infuriated opponents.

As a fullback he was expected to be the master of the arts of kicking, catching and tackling, and these were the regular skills he mastered as a boy practising on the famous St Helen's turf in Swansea where his grandfather was the groundsman. Many fullbacks, though, are frustrated three-quarters and Bancroft was no exception, for contemporary commentators vouched for the fact that he did more running than any other fullback of his generation.

He was not an attacking, running fullback in the modern sense. Instead he perfected a ruse that was designed to tire out opposing three-quarters. Catching the ball from an opponent's long kick ahead, Bancroft would hesitate as if thinking about an orthodox return kick to the touchline. Then he would set off running at speed slightly sideways and towards a touchline. This move was designed to make opposition forwards chase him in the hope of catching him. But they very rarely did. Having dared forwards to try and close him down, Bancroft would then accelerate and, while running at full pelt, he would kick spectacularly to the touchline, often gaining his side 40 to 50 yards. It was a novel attacking tactic that demoralised opponents, who were forced to traipse back half a pitch length for the line-out to restart the game.

It was a tactic that particularly annoyed Irish forwards who, in the 1890s, were not renowned for their staying powers. Ireland arrived in search of the Triple Crown at Cardiff Arms Park in 1899 when the famous Ryan brothers from Tipperary decided to sort Bancroft out before he could get up to his usual antics. The game attracted great interest and more than 30,000 spectators turned out to see the match of the season. The huge crowd overran the enclosures and encroached the touchlines, giving the Ryan brothers their opportunity to deal with the cheeky Bancroft.

With the game nearly 20 minutes old, the Ryans closed in on Bancroft like a pair of street fighters as the Welsh fullback was about to perform his party piece. Bancroft cleared to touch with a long, raking kick but the Ryans caught him late and tossed him into touch. Bancroft landed awkwardly among the encroaching spectators, cracked a couple of ribs and took no part in the remainder of the game. Ireland managed a try and finished 3–0 winners, but it was the only time in a long career that anyone got the better of the Welsh fullback on the rugby field.

Another of his tricks involved letting the ball drop in front of him, giving opponents hope that they could bear down on him and smother him, ball and all. But the daring Bancroft perfected the soccer art of reaching forward to the ball with his foot, meeting it as it hit the ground and returning it high over the advancing forwards' heads. A Scottish enthusiast, watching the wily Welshman perform this trick at Raeburn Place in the 1893 international against Scotland, was heard to comment: 'That's not [rugby] football.' To which a Welsh follower familiar with his compatriot's unorthodoxy replied: 'No, that's Banky.'

Bancroft wasn't afraid to back himself against authority. At Cardiff in 1893 Wales were losing 11–9 to England as the game entered its final phases. Wales were awarded a penalty and their skipper Arthur Gould asked Bancroft to take a place-kick. The pitch was slippery after snow and ice and Bancroft defied his captain, saying that he wanted to try a drop-kick instead. A blazing row ensued and Gould threw the ball to the ground in frustration, whereupon Bancroft picked it up and nonchalantly drop-kicked it over the crossbar to give Wales a famous 12–11 victory and set them on course for a first Triple Crown.

His dedication to practice would perhaps be described by today's cricket writers as 'Boycottian'. In his own heyday, the Welsh press called his fabulous fullback play quite simply, 'Bancroftian'. He spent hours at St Helen's perfecting his kicking: punting, drop-kicking and place-kicking. He would begin his goal-kicking sessions by uprooting the corner flags and then aim to curl the ball through the uprights. Then he would move infield along the arc of a circle to pot goals from every possible angle before finishing up with his party trick of placing a goal from virtually beneath the crossbar. As his fame with Swansea and Wales grew, so the band of hero-worshippers increased. At the height of his fame his famous practice sessions attracted large numbers of interested observers. Certainly he never lacked for ballboys willing to collect his various kicks. A contemporary player was the Welsh-born English scrum-half Dai Gent, who later became the rugby correspondent of the *Sunday Times*. Gent described Bancroft as 'short, dapper, very quick off the mark, a superb judge of pace, flight and the kicking of a rugby ball, and under all circumstances the coolest person on the field'.

Bancroft knew he was good. In his 80s he was asked by a rugby journalist what he thought of the 1953–54 All Blacks' fullback, Bob Scott, who was making a name for himself as an accurate all-round kicker during the tour of Britain, Ireland and France. Back came the terse reply: 'Ask him if he can kick goals from the halfway line, *with either foot.*' It was clearly a trick that Bancroft had perfected 60 or so years earlier.

Billy Bancroft – he was known to his family and playing colleagues by his initials 'W.J.' – was born on 2 March 1871 in Swansea and played his first senior match for the town as an 18-year-old against Newport in October 1889. The same season he was called into the Wales team to meet Scotland at Cardiff when the Newport fullback, Tommy England, had to call off through injury. He went on to play 33 consecutive matches in an international career that extended to 1901 at a time when there were no matches against overseas nations. During that time he was entrusted with every place-kick and penalty that Wales were awarded. His penalty against England in 1893 was the first ever kicked in an international match. When he stood down in 1901, he was international rugby's record cap-holder (33) and record points scorer (60) at a time when scoring values were frequently altered. He also captained Wales in his last 11 matches between 1898 and 1901, leading them to seven victories, including their second Triple Crown in 1900. He was the first Welshman to play in two Triple Crown sides and probably the first man to accumulate over a thousand points in first-class rugby. A *Western Mail* tribute to 'W.J.' on his 80th birthday estimated that his haul came to the grand total of 1,108.

The late A.A. Thomson, a prolific and elegant writer on both rugby and cricket, paid arguably the finest tribute to Billy Bancroft in *Rugger My Pleasure*, published in 1955. As a youth, Thomson had seen Billy's younger brother, Jack, play fullback for Wales at Twickenham in 1912 and told the story of how he had marvelled to his Welsh friends that he had seen the great Bancroft. 'That you have not,' his friends informed him. 'Of course I have,' replied Thomson, 'and he was wonderful.' The Welshmen replied: 'Maybe the man you saw was wonderful, but he was not the great Bancroft. He was merely the great Bancroft's little brother,' and they went on to describe the legendary feats of the great 'W.J.'. Thomson concluded: 'My own feeling was that if Billy was all that better than Jack, he must have had wings as well.'

Billy was a little man, about 5ft 5½in tall and always immaculately turned out – on and off the field. For Welsh team photographers of the 1890s he presents a relaxed and confident pose, neatly attired with barely a hair or whisker out of place. Even in 1954, when Newport's Ken Jones equalled Dickie Owen's Welsh appearance record against Scotland at Swansea, Bancroft turned out in a carefully pressed suit while on stewarding duty to formally congratulate the Welsh winger on his great achievement.

When he retired from playing in 1903 his opinions were frequently sought by journalists. Bancroft could be outspoken and his quotes invariably provided good copy for the popular press. In

1908, when Wales beat a fledgling French side at Cardiff by 36–4 in the first ever match between the countries, Billy boldly predicted to reporters that France would never win in the Arms Park as long as he lived. He was almost right. France's first victory there came 50 years later in March 1958. Poor old Billy was finally proved to be wrong at 87 years of age, and he died a year later, the day after celebrating his 88th birthday.

ERNIE CRAWFORD
The Ventriloquist

Irish rugby has produced more than its fair share of players with an impish streak. Down the years colourful characters like Phil O'Callaghan, Tony O'Reilly and Mick Quinn stood out for the fun and laughter they brought to the Irish dressing-room. Then there were the non-stop talkers like Noel 'Noisy' Murphy and Ken Kennedy, players with more rabbit than Watership Down. But long before them, the father of Irish rugby wit and master of the art of chat, not to mention a little ventriloquism, was a Belfast accountant called Ernie Crawford, whose escapades during a long career as Ireland's fullback and captain singled him out as one of rugby's greatest characters in the 1920s.

Ernie Crawford was born in Belfast on 17 November 1891 and first played rugby at the city's Methodist College, where he was acknowledged as a fine all-round games-player. Indeed, in 1913–14 he regularly turned out for the top Ulster soccer side, Cliftonville, on weekends when his Saturday morning accountancy studies prevented him from travelling to away rugby matches with Malone, whom he had joined soon after leaving school. When the Great War began in 1914, he was among the first to volunteer, joining the Inniskilling Dragoons and later serving with the London Irish Rifle Brigade.

After the armistice, he took up an important post in local government in the Dublin area and quickly became a mainstay of the Lansdowne club whose ranks had been tragically depleted as a result of the war. In his late 20s, he was one of the senior players in a club that relied heavily on recent school-leavers and Dublin students for its playing force. Matters were pretty disorganised in that first full rugby season after the Great War and Ernie began his Lansdowne days as a centre before transferring to his favoured fullback position in mid-season. He somehow managed to play for *both* Ulster and Leinster in the Irish Inter-Pro Championship that season, quite an achievement while the Irish Troubles were at their most intense.

After appearing in Ulster's 8–6 win in the season's opener against Munster, he was dropped for the match a week later played in Belfast against Leinster. Ernie knew he had to keep his name at the front of the Irish selectors' mind so managed to talk the Leinster officials into picking him to face his native province, for whom Joe Stewart from Queen's University, Belfast, was at fullback. Stewart and Crawford were the main contenders for the position in the Irish XV. Ulster won 14–5 against a side that was without some of its star players but, according to legend, Stewart said afterwards that Ulster were without their star player too. 'Ernie Crawford couldn't get his place on the Ulster side because I've got it!' Crawford had the last laugh, however. He eventually beat Stewart to the Irish jersey by making his Test debut in February 1920, aged 28, in the Lansdowne Road clash with England. It was an inauspicious start to his international career, Ireland losing all four matches to finish whitewashed in the Five Nations for the first time. But Crawford more or less dominated the fullback position in the Irish side for the next seven years and went on to make 30 Test appearances, a record for an Irish fullback that stood until the 1960s.

Ernie became so popular with the youngsters in the Lansdowne side – he used to constantly shout abuse at them from the back in his distinct Ulster brogue – that within two years of joining the club he was appointed captain, leading them to Leinster Senior Cup honours in his first season at the helm. It was said that the louder he shouted at his young charges the better they played because, in order to block out Ernie's stream of insults, they focused sharply on their game. He must have done an awful lot of shouting that season. He became famous for his non-stop chat, sometimes using it as a form of gamesmanship which, allied to his uncanny knack of throwing his voice without moving his lips, often worked to his team's advantage. Once, playing against the French, he was faced by an attack down the wing that seemed certain to produce a score. His opponents had an overlap and Crawford was faced with the dilemma of which player to tackle. In his best French he called 'pass it'. The trick worked, the Frenchman transferred the ball to the wing he thought had called for it and Ernie coolly shepherded the attacker into touch. Quite how French spoken with a thick Ulster intonation could mislead a native speaker remains a mystery. Crawford must have been the only rugby player to use ventriloquism to give him an edge on the field.

One of his adventures in gamesmanship led to a change in the laws. In 1927, Lansdowne were playing Cardiff in Dublin when, with the scores square at 6-all, they were awarded a penalty on the visitors' 25. The Cardiff boys retreated, expecting a kick at goal, whereupon Ernie stepped forward, sized up the situation and told the team's kicker to pick the ball up and go for a try. The trick worked, Cardiff actually copied it the week later and the International Board eventually changed the law, ruling that penalty kicks should travel a minimum of 10 yards before the kicker's side could again touch the ball.

As a person he was the complete opposite of his on-field character. The English forward, Wavell Wakefield, described him as 'a cheery companion off the field' but as a sinister presence on it, 'a kind of brooding intelligence, directing the play, crouching and waiting like a spider for the unfortunate player who tried to pass him'. Crawford was reliable under the high ball, a safe if unspectacular touch-finder and one of the deadliest tacklers seen between the wars. His personality made him an ideal captain and he led Ireland 15 times. Their national side had suffered tough times reorganising after the Great War, but under Crawford's steadying influence performances rapidly improved. His first season in charge was 1924, when England made their one and only Test appearance in Belfast. It was supposed to be Ulster rugby's red-letter day, marking the opening of their new Ravenhill ground with Ernie, one of the city's best-loved sons, leading his country. Alas, he was plagued by lumbago, played the worst game of his life and Ireland were beaten by Wakefield's Grand Slam side. He was subsequently dropped in favour of his old rival, Joe Stewart, for the next match. But they couldn't hold a good man down. Ernie returned at the end of the season and in 1926 and 1927, as an old fox of 35, led Ireland to shares (with Scotland in both years) of the International Championship title. Only a last-minute miss from a drop at goal by Tom Hewitt against Wales in Swansea denied his side the Grand Slam in 1926.

After retiring from the game he became an upstanding member of the Irish Rugby Union. He was an Irish selector for many years, choosing the side that carried off the Grand Slam in 1948, and served as president of the IRU in 1958. He was also a staunch supporter of the Barbarians and it was during one of their tours of south Wales that he was credited with the invention of the word 'alickadoo', a noun describing any rugby club administrator or hanger-on who is no longer a player – later christened by Will Carling in less decorous language as an 'old fart'.

Ernie Crawford, part-time ventriloquist and the player who pushed gamesmanship to its limit, died in Belfast on 12 January 1959. The *Playfair Rugby Annual*, the game's bible, paid generous tribute to him. 'He developed into one of those almost legendary figures about whom people delight to tell stories. He certainly was remarkable for his cool head and grim wit, neither of which failed him, even in defeat.'

BOB HILLER
The Boss

The French daily sporting newspaper, *L'Equipe*, perfectly captured Bob Hiller's value to English rugby in a headline that read 'Hiller 14, France 14' after France had drawn at Twickenham in 1971. It reflected the feelings many countries had when facing England between 1968 and 1972 that Bob Hiller, the fullback, called the tune to such an extent that he was almost a one-man team. So often he pulled matches out of the fire for them or was their only source of points.

He was the scourge of the Irish in particular, his goal-kicking regularly depriving them of victory. At Twickenham in 1970 he landed two late, towering drop-goals from almost identical positions. The goals were scored barely three minutes apart, prompting one horrified Irish supporter to ask if he was watching a TV action replay. And when Hiller went on tour to South Africa with the 1968 Lions, his prodigious goal-kicking feats combined with his commanding form led spectators to nickname him 'The Boss'.

It was an appropriate title for one who appeared to be such a perfectionist in his approach, a player who oozed confidence on the field. With his immaculate appearance and long, dark sideburns he resembled a haughty taskmaster from a Dickensian novel, but the pre-conceived impressions were far from accurate. Yes, he certainly maintained high standards in his play, but he was a popular person-ality among players and his strong leadership skills, repartee and sense of fun made him a well-respected captain in the teams he led.

During the Lions' tour of 1971 when John Dawes, the tour captain, was due to be rested for the match against Manawatu/Horowhenua, Ireland legend Willie John McBride was honoured with the captaincy. Owing to a late injury to a three-quarter, Dawes finished off having to play. Afterwards, he boasted to his compatriot Barry John of his great rugby achievement: 'I've played under the captaincy of Willie John McBride,' in an attempt to get one up on the Welsh fly-half. But Barry, as always, had the last say and dismissively replied: 'But you haven't played under the captaincy of Bob Hiller.' John, who had been in the side led by the Englishman against Wairarapa-Bush the previous month, clearly considered this to carry greater status.

Robert Hiller was born in Woking on 14 October 1942, educated in south London and joined Harlequins in 1962 after making a name for himself with the Surrey Schools side. He was to become a mainstay of the Surrey senior county XV, and after taking his civil engineering degree at Birmingham University won Blues for both rugby and cricket while studying for a postgraduate teaching diploma at Oxford. *Wisden*, the cricketer's bible, listed him (incorrectly) as 'R.B. Hiller' – the 'B.' was for Bob presumably and, after all, any self-respecting sportsman should have at least two initials – and it was as R.B. Hiller that he often appeared in match programmes and press lists. He was touted as the answer to England's perennial fullback and place-kicking problem as early as the mid-1960s, but it was not until January 1968 that he was finally awarded his first cap, for the Twickenham match against Wales. Bob was accustomed to enjoying a couple of pints at his local on a Friday night. Seeing no reason to change his routine just because he had been selected to play for England, he and a like-minded team-mate set out for a quiet eve-of-debut nightcap. Imagine their surprise when, having got their drinks in, they adjourned to a quiet table only to find the England selectors sitting adjacent to them. In fairness to the selectors, they were unperturbed and even bought Bob and his colleague a round before closing time – those were the days!

After a successful first season in the Five Nations he went to South Africa with the 1968 Lions and was hugely influenced and impressed by the overseas approach to team preparation and coaching. That tour and the previous 1966 Lions' trip to New Zealand brought home to the British/Irish players the huge advances in team organisation that had taken place in the southern hemisphere. The Home Unions had clearly been left behind. Bob scored 104 points in South Africa before returning to captain 'Quins in 1968–69, immediately putting into practice some of the 'professional' methods seen on tour. He insisted that potential first-team players trained regularly if they were to compete for selection and he had the force of personality to carry out his convictions. He'd been shouting at forwards for years he said, coaching them was little different. His pathfinding work with Harlequins resulted in his elevation to the England captaincy the following season, the selectors taking the unprecedented step of nominating him two months in advance of the Twickenham match with South Africa and naming Don White as coach to the side. The upshot was England's first-ever victory over the Springboks.

Hiller's place-kicking routine was a source of controversy in the late 1960s. He took his duties seriously. His kicking boot was carefully filed off to increase purchase on the ball. Moreover, his on-field preparation involved the meticulous creation of a massive crater and tee before he made his straight run-up and kicked with his right toecap. In Wales they said that the reason the Wales–England Cardiff fixture was moved from January to mid-April in the late 1960s was to ensure that the harder ground in spring hindered Hiller's dig-for-victory antics. Even poor old Robin Prescott, the RFU Secretary at the time, used to despair at the damage Hiller did to the Twickenham turf. Prescott once took him to the top of the old West Stand after an international to show big Bob the pockmarks left by his place-kicking routines. Even so, the proof of the pudding is in the eating, and in his 19 Tests for England between 1968 and 1972 Bob Hiller scored a then-record 138 points. In 1971, he accounted for 49 of the 55 points England registered in the five matches he played, his haul including tries in three successive Twickenham internationals – the first ever scored by an England fullback at HQ. When he was dropped, for the Paris Tests in 1970 and again in 1972, the England selectors immediately regretted the folly of their ways, the side suffering 35–13 and 37–12 hidings in the French capital.

The barracking he received from restless crowds for his endless kicking routine was sometimes supplemented by edgy comments made by referees anxious to ensure that time was not wasted. These invariably triggered the famed laconic Hiller humour. The edge of his tongue was as sharp as the aim of his boot. One referee, urging him to get a move on barely seconds after awarding a penalty in an international match, became engaged in an exchange which prompted the official to ask the English kicker, 'Which of us is refereeing this match?' Hiller's quick reply was, 'Neither of us, sir.' During his career the laws of the game relating to place-kicking were changed so that any time taken beyond 40 seconds should be added on at the end of the half. Once, in New Zealand on the 1971 Lions' tour, a spectator at Gisborne shouted in louder and louder tones, 'Do you want a shovel?' as Hiller began excavations for a shot at goal. At the third time of asking, Hiller's stentorian voice boomed around the ground: 'Just pass your mouth over, it's big enough.' Laughter all round . . . as he kicked the goal.

That kick took him past a century of points on a Lions' visit for the second time and the tour manager, Dr Doug Smith, spoke for all that evening when he singled Hiller out to say: 'I would like to pay tribute to one of the greatest tourists I have ever met.' Bob had been understudy at fullback to the tour captain, Tom Kiernan, in South Africa in 1968 and had to play second fiddle to J.P.R. Williams in New Zealand. As a result he never appeared in a Test for the British/Irish Lions. That would have been a bitter disappointment to lesser players, but Boss Hiller was always cool and pragmatic. He was unfazed about his playing fate and set about ensuring the success of the dirt-trackers – the mid-week tour side – which was so important to the overall morale of teams in the days of the four-month-long tour. Hiller's unselfish and competitive instincts were beacons for all.

When he was dropped from the England side in 1972 he announced his retirement from Test rugby but continued to play for Surrey and Harlequins well into his 30s. He remained a loyal servant to the Twickenham-based club long after his playing days ended, serving as selector and vice-president – the perfect embodiment of the 'Quins' famed *esprit de corps*.

VIVIAN JENKINS
A Life in Rugby

Vivian Gordon James Jenkins was the son of a headteacher and used to say that the heroes of his youth were the 'wizards' of Aberavon RFC. He was born in Port Talbot on 2 November 1911 and as a boy used to crawl through the club's perimeter fence to catch a glimpse of the town side in action. That was the beginning of a lifelong love affair with rugby. Cricket was another passion, but hours devoted to rugby during schooldays at Llandovery College enabled him to develop into a powerful centre, the position where he later won three Oxford Blues between 1930 and 1932 and was never on the losing side.

His fondest memory of Oxford, however, was of the cricket field. In 1933, in his final year studying classics as an exhibitioner at Jesus College, he was called up at the eleventh hour to keep wicket in the Varsity Match and his defensive batting on the final day of a rain-affected match earned Oxford a draw. He also played occasionally for Glamorgan between 1931 and 1937.

It was at the whim of the Welsh rugby selectors that the tall, leggy Jenkins was transformed into a fullback. W.J. (Willie) Llewellyn, the Bridgend club secretary and a committee member of the Welsh Rugby Union, asked Jenkins to fill the fullback role for Bridgend during the Christmas vacation in 1932 so that the Big Five could watch the club's three-quarters, all contenders for caps, perform in the Boxing Day game against Newport at Rodney Parade. The displaced centre, however, proved the standout player that day. In his new role he was chosen for the Possibles XV that defeated the Probables in the final Welsh trial and then was selected to face England in January 1933.

For the first time in 10 attempts Wales triumphed at Twickenham and, despite playing with a high temperature, the new fullback fielded immaculately and sent long torpedo punts spiralling into touch. Additionally, he and Willie Llewellyn, who was also a well-known international referee and the Welsh touch-judge at Twickenham that day, featured in an incident that was to lead to a change in the laws.

England had opened the scoring when Don Burland broke through in the first half to send Walter Elliot in for a try. Soon after the interval, however, Wales took the lead when wing three-quarter Ronnie Boon dropped a goal from a loose maul 20 yards from the English posts. That pushed Wales 4–3 ahead with all to play for. Then Ronnie Boon put Wales further in front with a try. Welsh centre Claude Davey drew the English fullback perfectly to release Boon on a run that took the wing arcing outside the defence for a try near the posts. Jenkins lined up the simple kick and sent the ball, so the Welsh supporters and Welsh touch-judge thought, straight between the posts. Even the scoreboard operator believed that the kick was good, for he marked up a Welsh lead of 9–3 with time running out. Converted tries were worth only five points at this time, so most of the crowd and players felt that Wales were virtually safe with England having to score twice to win.

Not so. Only at the end of the match was it made clear by the referee that Jenkins's conversion kick from close range had failed. What was true was that Willie Llewellyn had signalled the goal. Knowing Jenkins's abilities as a goal-kicker, Llewellyn presumably could not believe that the young place-kicker would miss a goal from such a good position. The score had come 10 minutes from full time and the misunderstanding could have had a profound influence on the outcome of the match. The fact was that England only needed another breakaway try and conversion to win. Whether or not the English players were aware of the position is not recorded, though it was reported that the Welsh forwards so dominated the closing stages of the match that it was as much as England could do to prevent Wales from increasing their lead.

Until 1933 all restarts had been taken as place-kicks. To prevent future confusion, the International Board altered the kick-off law a year later to read: 'the kick-off is a place-kick after a goal has been kicked, or a drop-kick after an unconverted try.' That way players and spectators would know whether or not a conversion had been successful.

Jenkins went on to become the leading fullback of the day, noted not just for his kicking and defensive qualities but also for his flair for attack, the legacy of his earlier days as a centre. Against Ireland in 1934 he created quite a stir by scoring a try, a feat never previously performed by a Welsh fullback. 'It was not the done thing,' he once recalled.

For his heroic rugby deeds in 1935–36 he became a household name. His two conversions and a heroic try-saving race against All Black winger George Hart helped Wales to a 13–12 victory against New Zealand – 'by that lovely point,' Arthur Rees, the Welsh pack-leader and his lifelong friend since schooldays, used to say. Jenkins always maintained that it was the most nerve-wracking match he ever took part in.

'In most big games,' he later wrote, 'the needle a player feels before the kick-off usually evaporates once the game has started. After five or 10 minutes, action has provided its own sedative. The cut and thrust continues but the opening fever dies down. Not so in that Wales v. New Zealand match. I have it on the authority of the Welsh fullback that day that the needle continued right up to the end.' The 'Welsh fullback that day' was a meticulous man, both as a player and later as a journalist. A fortnight after Wales defeated the All Blacks, England also did so, by 13–0, a veritable thrashing in those far-off days. England's hero was a certain Prince Alex Obolensky on the right wing and the scorer of two spectacular first-half tries.

The next international match on the calendar was the Wales–England game at Swansea a fortnight later to launch the International Championship season. Jenkins, hearing of Obolensky's remarkable speed and unorthodoxy, thought he should do some preparation before facing the Russian. He took himself off to a London cinema and sat through 80-odd minutes of some dreadful B-film – twice – in order to catch a couple of 40-second newsreel glimpses of Obolensky in action. The preparation paid off. Wales held England to a 0–0 draw. Later the same season, Jenkins kicked the penalty that gave Wales the International Championship title in a tight decider with Ireland.

He toured South Africa as vice-captain of the 1938 Lions. A persistent hamstring injury curtailed his appearances on tour, but he kicked three penalties – including one monster effort from his own half – in the opening Test at Ellis Park in Johannesburg. For many years the eight-panelled South-African-made ball from that Test match had pride of place among the hats and brollies in the porch of his Hertfordshire home, a talking point for new visitors or old playing colleagues.

He retired from international rugby after the England match in January 1939, aged only 27, to build a career in sports journalism. He joined the *News of the World* to cover rugby, cricket, motor-racing and tennis but his career was promptly interrupted by the outbreak of the war. He had joined the Territorial Army in August 1939, served in the anti-aircraft command and was promoted to the rank of captain. He returned to Fleet Street after the war and twice covered MCC cricket tours of Australia and New Zealand: with Walter Hammond's side (against Bradman) in 1946–47 and Freddie Brown's in 1950–51.

For the next 25 years until his retirement in 1976 he reported every important rugby match and major tour. He transferred to the *Sunday Times* in 1955, transforming rugby coverage in the newspaper, and later the same year he and Bryn Thomas of the Cardiff *Western Mail* became the first British journalists to cover a Lions' tour when they travelled to South Africa. When the tourists, spearheaded by Cliff Morgan, unexpectedly beat the Springboks 23–22 in the opening Test of that visit, rugby became big news back in Britain and Ireland. As journalists, they proved to be trailblazers because in 1962, when the Lions next visited South Africa, every Fleet Street newspaper sent its rugby correspondent to provide coverage.

The 1955 tour was followed by the publication of his book *Lions Rampant*. It was a rugby classic, as was his follow-up to the 1959 Lions' tour, *Lions Down Under*. Yet despite numerous subsequent invitations, that was to be his last foray as a book author. In addition to his writing, he helped launch *Rugby World* magazine and in 1960 was a moving force behind the formation of the Rugby Union Writers' Club.

As a campaigning journalist he argued for changes to the game's laws. On tour with the 1959 Lions he had seen the New Zealand fullback, Don Clarke, kick six penalties at Carisbrook to pip the Lions' four tries by 18–17 at a time when tries were valued at three points. He proposed raising the points value of the try to encourage teams to adopt positive attacking tactics. Later he became a vigorous campaigner for the Australian dispensation law that restricted direct kicking to touch and was the first to lobby for the introduction of the differential penalty. Eventually all three entered the law book.

Typically he remained prominent in rugby after his retirement from the *Sunday Times* in November 1976. For its first 10 years he edited the *Rothmans Rugby Union Yearbook*, building the annual into rugby's bible. It was 'putting something back into the game' he used to say. Mind, those poor contributors and correspondents who witnessed first hand his characteristic attention to detail wished that he'd have practised putting that something back in to the game just a little later in the day. They were often phoned at ungodly hours as he queried a fact or figure.

Another of his rugby interests was the Crawshay's Welsh RFC, the 'Welsh Barbarians' he called them. He was an active member of the club that encouraged young Welsh players, and during his stint as *Rothmans* editor Jenkins always ensured that the club's fixtures featured prominently in the calendar of the year's forthcoming big matches. A highlight of his rugby year during retirement was touring with the club. A story he told against himself involved a long coach journey with the club in the south of France. A young player struck up a conversation with the former Lions' vice-captain and Wales fullback: 'Did you ever play the game yourself, Mr Jenkins?'

He must have set the world record for attending rugby dinners and parties – the only one he reckoned he missed was the traditional Twickenham post-match banquet after his first cap in 1933, when he had to retire to his bed with a 100-plus temperature and feeling like the symptoms listed on a medicine bottle. Even as a senior citizen his stamina barely waned. His 80th birthday coincided with the England–Australia Rugby World Cup Final at Twickenham in 1991, while his annual Christmas newsletter for 2001 revealed that his 90th birthday had been a marathon of celebration – numerous special occasions, including one bash thrown by the Welsh Rugby Union in Cardiff where Sir Tasker Watkins VC gave him a generous tribute.

Vivian Jenkins died in January 2004 after four-score years and twelve packed with rugby, cricket, friends and family. The memorial service celebrating his life, held near his Hertfordshire home, attracted a galaxy of Barbarians, Wales and Lions' stars, including Cliff Morgan, who paid a warm and fitting tribute to a Welsh rugby man who has been greatly missed.

TOM KIERNAN
Irish Hero

There was no particular reason to suspect that the neat, fair-haired Tom Kiernan would become Ireland's No. 1 fullback. At his school, Presentation Brothers College in Cork, he had shone as a scrum-half and his early senior honours were won as a centre, a position in which he had few technical weaknesses. Indeed, he was once selected for Ireland in the centre. But arguably the crucial game of his career took place in January 1960.

As a commerce student at University College Cork, in the city where he was born on 7 January 1939, he won a place as fullback on the Irish Universities' side against their English counterparts, the UAU. Only a couple of days short of his 21st birthday, he played such a magnificent game in a 19–5 victory at Donnybrook that his credentials for the Ireland side could not be ignored. His tackling, covering and calculated kicking were manna from heaven to the Irish selectors, who were desperately seeking a fullback with a big-match temperament. Tom got the nod and made the first of his 54 appearances for Ireland in an inexperienced side that was unlucky to lose, 5–8, at Twickenham against an England side that went on to win the Triple Crown and championship. A young Frank Keating saw that international match and Kiernan clearly made a big impression on the *Guardian*'s future sportswriter. 'Tom Kiernan had a wonderful game. He had the kick of a Kinsale mule, the whooshing deadly tackle of a midsummer Sligo scythe, and still a gentle open face as serene and warm as a turf fire in a cosy cottage,' Keating told his readers more than 20 years later.

Assurance and application were the distinguishing features of his international performances in the 1960s and he was at the peak of his form when he took part in the famous 18–5 obliteration of England at Twickenham in 1964. He had all the traits of the gifted fullback that day and added three invaluable conversions. A flair for attack and his keen sense of anticipation made up for a slight lack of pace.

Later, as captain of Ireland in a then record 24 Tests, his team warmed to his charming, modest nature. Tom's outgoing personality made him the ideal leader on the field, despite the difficulties inherent in leading from the fullback position. The madcap reputation that attends many Irish rugby characters never applied to him; his approach to captaincy, like his way of life, was measured – more velvet glove than iron fist – but effective. Before matches he could raise team morale with a passionate appeal to national pride and found time for moments of individual encouragement of team-mates. Playing the English often brought out the best in him and the friendly rivalry he had with his opposite number Bob Hiller – as both fullback and captain – was an interesting 'play within the play' in the fixtures of the late 1960s and early 1970s.

Hero status was assured when his Irish side beat France and England in the opening two away games of the unfinished 1972 Five Nations, and his stock ran high again in January 1973 when Ireland held the Sixth All Blacks to a 10-all draw in Dublin – their best result against New Zealand to date. He was an excellent ambassador for Irish rugby and he commanded respect as an international player with a wealth of experience.

He twice toured South Africa as a Lion. The selectors first showed their confidence in him in 1962, but he was dogged by injuries and appeared in less than half the tour matches. By 1968, however, he had established himself as such a respected leader at international level that he was invited to captain the tourists. His experience of South African conditions was invaluable. He judged his place-kicking to perfection and finished the tour with a haul of 84 points from 13 games. He even deputised on one occasion at scrum-half – his old school position. But it was in the Test series that he made his mark on the record books. At Pretoria in the first international he established a new mark for most points by a Lion in a Test, kicking 17. And his haul for the series (35 of the 38 points the Lions scored) represented the biggest return ever gained by a tourist. Ireland's hero returned a Lions' hero.

Tom remained the unwavering guardian of Ireland's defence until 1973, 13 years after his first appearance. He passed 150 points for his country, including a try in the corner at Murrayfield in his final international, but his links with Irish rugby lasted long after his playing retirement. The pinnacle of a distinguished coaching career came when he helped guide Munster to their famous 12–0 win against the All Blacks in 1978. It was allegedly one of the few occasions when the unflappable former fullback got carried away. After the match a journalist asked him if the win had been a fluke. 'If you play the All Blacks two or three times you can expect to lose nine times out of ten,' he is reputed to have answered. Everyone knew what he meant, though it was not the kind of remark expected of a respected chartered accountant. That was also the occasion that Irish rugby fanatic, Richard Harris, while filming on a set near Johannesburg, wired Kiernan's men that all South Africa had been captivated by Munster's win. He went on to say that he had spoken to his pal Richard Burton, who passed on congratulations, but with a touch of jealousy.

Tom Kiernan was again elevated to hero status in his own land in 1982 when, now in his second season as coach of the Irish national side, he masterminded a famous Twickenham win on the way to his country's first Triple Crown for 33 years. His nephew Michael was a key player that year and became the backbone of the Irish back divisions of the 1980s, while Tom went on to fill Irish rugby's top job – president of the IRU – in 1988–89.

ON A WING AND
A PRAYER

JONAH LOMU
Man Mountain

It is hard to imagine a player who made more of an impact on the Rugby World Cup than Jonah Lomu. The 'Player of the Tournament' honour at both the 1995 and 1999 finals that defined the beginning of rugby's professional era went to the man mountain from New Zealand. Everything about him was big – even down to the headphones blasting out his favourite music.

He was the monster in rugby kit. Relatively unknown in 1995, he became a household name after scoring seven tries – four against England in the semis – to create a new record for the finals. At 6ft 4in and weighing 19st, he remains the biggest three-quarter who has played Test rugby. Lomu loomed over opponents at that tournament like a dark cloud over a summer's morning. In New Zealand's first pool game, against Ireland, he trampled through them several times, scoring two tries with several would-be tacklers bouncing off him, and bulldozing a path to the Irish line for Josh Kronfeld to score near the end. After that match Colin Meads, part of the New Zealand management team, was asked if he had ever seen anything like Lomu before. 'Yes,' replied the former lock who was known as 'Pinetree', 'but never playing on the left wing.'

He continued to fill the hearts of opponents with terror – ask Tony Underwood and several others from the England side who were steamrollered 45–29 by Lomu and the All Blacks in the semi-finals. It was Will Carling, the losers' captain, who spoke for everyone at that event when he said after the game: 'He's awesome, a freak and the sooner he goes away the better. I never want to see that man again. The difference between the sides was on the left wing.' Jason Leonard, veteran England prop, was more direct, saying: 'There's no doubt about it, he's a big b******.' Lomu on the charge against Mike Catt, Will Carling and Tony Underwood in that 1995 semi-final was like watching a real-life Gulliver leading the Lilliputians against their neighbours.

Jonah Lomu was born in Auckland on 12 May 1975 and was educated at Wesley College. Originally a back-row forward as a schoolboy, he was converted to a winger before becoming the youngest New Zealand Test player of all time when he made his international debut against France in 1994. As a schoolboy he had built up his powers by running while attached to a cricket-pitch roller. He had clocked 10.8 seconds for the 100 metres and the sight of him on the run, ball waving in one hand as he bounced would-be tacklers off his ample body, provided the abiding memory of the 1995 World Cup, when New Zealand coasted to the final, only to be defeated in extra time by the host nation, South Africa. Speed alone is not a passport to success in rugby, neither is bulk. But when the two are combined, as they were most effectively in Lomu's case, the resulting momentum generated is phenomenal. The impulse that he gave to the New Zealand team was his most telling contribution on the field. It was not only his try-scoring runs that took their toll on opponents. His drives invariably took out so many defenders that the New Zealand pack was able to recycle the ball and move it quickly into space, creating scoring opportunities for his team-mates.

For his headline-grabbing performances he became pure box office. Crowds flocked to see him play, and in his homeland stewards had to be deputed on match days to protect him from wellwishers and autograph-seekers. Admired universally for his power on the field and his charisma off it, his fame spread quickly and huge offers in rugby's burgeoning professional game came his way. He enjoyed the corporate attention and cashed in on his fame modestly yet effectively to become probably the first player of the professional age to achieve multimillionaire status while still playing.

Lomu was again the man of the tournament when the World Cup circus rolled into Britain, Ireland and France in 1999, but a weak New Zealand side were ambushed by France in a memorable semi-final at Twickenham and his chance of a winners' medal vanished. He had again shown his danger to England with some devastating tries in the pool match at Twickenham, but one man does not make a team and the All Blacks finished fourth after losing the Bronze Medal play-off against their 1995 vanquishers, South Africa.

Yet the rugby public so nearly missed out on Jonah's World Cup talents. In the All Black training camps held before the 1995 event there were serious misgivings about his fitness, commitment and defence in the 15-man game. His undoubted individual abilities made him the star of the New Zealand sevens side, but playing in the extended game demanded more extensive team skills. His mental preparation was questioned. But he made the squad and from the moment New Zealand took the field at Johannesburg's Ellis Park for their opening pool match with Ireland, Lomu became synonymous with the World Cup. Thereafter and when fit, his name was the first on the New Zealand Test team.

Illness, injury and loss of form ruled him out of the 2003 finals in Australia. England (among others) breathed a massive sigh of relief at this news, but rugby lovers the world over mourned the absence of one of the game's greatest icons. In recent years the aura has faded. His private life – two divorces in less than 10 years – tarnished his reputation back in New Zealand, and his attempts to resurrect his career after a kidney transplant were arguably blown out of proportion by the media frenzy he still attracts.

In England Jonny Wilkinson might be remembered in a World Cup context as the man whose winning drop-goal brought home the trophy in 2003. But it is for the unique impact that he had worldwide on the two earlier tournaments that Jonah Lomu will be remembered most. It will be Lomu more than any other's whose name is forever associated with rugby's leading competition.

DAVID CAMPESE
The Wizard of Oz

It might surprise younger readers to learn that, until the 1980s, Australia were regarded as the whipping boys of Test rugby. At a time when membership of the International Rugby Board was restricted to an old boys' network comprising the Home Unions, France and the Tri-Nations, the Wallabies were regularly beaten on tours to the Five Nations and rarely took a series off the All Blacks or Springboks. Even Lions' tours to Australia were only fulfilled as overtures or warm-downs to extended visits to New Zealand, so low down the game's pecking order was the position of Wallaby rugby.

That all changed in the early 1980s under an enlightened coach, Bob Dwyer, who set about building a World Cup-winning team around an exciting back division and athletic forwards. The Ella brothers, Roger Gould and Brendan Moon were among the exciting backs who ushered in the new era in Aussie rugby history with series wins against the All Blacks and France. These high-profile victories provided such a terrific shot in the arm to rugby in the country's eastern states that a whole generation of youngsters were attracted to the union game at a time when league was the dominant force in Australia.

Foremost among the young recruits to the game was a fullback/winger named David Campese, who had left school with few qualifications and little training in the game. But inspired by the Ellas' brand of attacking rugby, he took to union like a duck to water. It was his view that people pay to come and watch something different. Not for him the grinding 10-man rugby and tactical kicking that dominated the game in the Home Unions. Nor the patterned power game of the All Blacks. Campo, the maverick, wanted to entertain and excite the crowds by showcasing his individual talents in the context of a team game. He succeeded spectacularly and, after making his Test debut in New Zealand in 1982, became a trump card for a side that waltzed through a Grand Slam of the Home Unions in 1984, reached the semi-finals of the inaugural World Cup in 1987 and won it in 1991. He was still Australia's first choice in the 1995 tournament and finally hung up his boots, having – he claimed – become the first rugby union player to become a millionaire from playing the then amateur game.

That he remained at the top of a gruelling sport for so long owed much to his dedication to fitness and regular practising of basic skills – certainly Gary Player's maxim about the harder he trained the luckier he became could easily have applied to Campese. He also constantly challenged himself to operate outside the game's comfort zone. The approach was simple. He just wanted to have possession and run with his goose-stepping action past everybody. Perhaps a fault was that he sometimes didn't appreciate how better to use other players. But often his readiness to take risks turned matches in Australia's favour, especially during the 1991 World Cup campaign. It was his audacious diagonal run at a steep angle that brought him a sensational early try at Lansdowne Road in their semi-final tie with the All Blacks. Later in the same game he broke away and, without looking at its recipient, threw a perfectly weighted high pass over his left shoulder for Tim Horan to gather and score the decisive try. It was pure genius, pure Campese. He had sensed Horan's presence like a bat uses its radar.

Sometimes the bold stuff led to spectacular disasters. He ran the length of the pitch playing against the Barbarians in Cardiff in 1988, ball held in one palm and looked certain to score the picture-book try, only for the ball to fall embarrassingly out of his hand without a defender in sight. In 1989, against the Lions, his stray pass to fullback Greg Martin on his own goal-line presented Ieuan Evans with the try that sacrificed the final Test and with it the series. He'd been dropped by Bob Dwyer at the beginning of the rubber on disciplinary grounds, having returned late from his northern hemisphere playing commitments with Milan. His stock wasn't very high with his team-mates after the final Test blunder and, after making an appearance at the post-match formalities, left early to drive home. He was so distraught at letting his mates and himself down that his mind wandered at the wheel and his speed increased, so much so that he was pulled up for doing 104mph. It was the first time since the match that Campo smiled. 'Good job you didn't see me 10 minutes ago,' he told the speed cop. 'I was doing 130 then.' But the joke backfired and Campo was heavily fined. He reckoned that the cop must have watched the match.

Yet for all the criticism he received after the Ieuan Evans incident, and the Aussie press took him to task mercilessly, not a negative word was uttered by the coach Bob Dwyer. In fact he had been the first one to make any consolatory gesture to his winger after the match. He knew that Campo would win more matches for the Wallabies than he'd lose, and the 1991 World Cup demonstrated that. The wizard of Oz was declared the 'Player of the Tournament' and savoured basking in the glory of a World Cup Final win against England, the team he loved to bait most of all with his forthright views on how the game should be played. He could be very outspoken, almost to the point of offensiveness, and even Bob Dwyer was once moved to say that Campo had a wire loose somewhere between his brain and his mouth. But the box-office appeal never waned.

Twice he was talked out of retirement, in 1989 after the disappointment of losing to the Lions and after the 1991 World Cup. Pace alone was not his main attribute, though he did once show his brilliance as a straight sprinter, running the length of the pitch along the right touchline in a fading winter light at the old Arms Park to score against Wales in 1992. He was 30 then, but having sniffed his chance on the Australian 22 he stepped on the afterburners and took off on a glorious run that brought thousands of admirers to their feet. His presence on the field must have been worth untold millions to the various unions around the world and his behaviour off it was always honest. He spent nine seasons plying his wares in Italy and used his name effectively to build up a viable and lucrative business career at a time when rugby union was in the last throes of amateurism.

David Campese was born on 21 October 1962 in Queanbeyan, New South Wales, the son of an Italian migrant father and

Australian mother. He flirted with league at school but never made a commitment to rugby until his late teens. His big chance came after starring for the Australian under-21 team and in 1982 he toured New Zealand with an untried Wallabies side. He went straight into the Test XV where he came up against New Zealand's Stu Wilson. 'Who's he,' Campese asked when told of his prospective opponent. He had no respect for reputations and at his first opportunity on the field stood up to the famous All Black and went past him to score a try on debut. He went on to set a Test record by scoring 63 more in an international career that saw him become only the second man in history to play more than 100 Tests. He finally retired in 1996.

Bill McLaren, the voice of rugby union for 50 years, once called Campese 'probably my favourite player of all time'. As a commentator, McLaren felt he could always expect Campese to lift a game with an unexpected act of genius. For that reason, Campese was many followers' favourite player of all.

IAN SMITH
The Flying Scotsman

Ask the average rugby enthusiast to name the player who has scored most tries in the ancient International Championship and the answer, now that the Five Nations has been upgraded to a Six Nations tournament, is likely to be a distinguished three-quarter of the past decade. One might expect Shane Williams or Brian O'Driscoll to hold the honour – they have many to their names already – but pore over the record books and the name I.S. Smith, the Scottish winger of the 1920s and early 1930s, is the name that stands clear at the head of the all-time lists of Five/Six Nations scorers. He crossed 24 times for his country between 1924 and 1933.

Ian Scott Smith was born in Melbourne, Australia, on 31 October 1903. He came to Britain as a youngster and attended Cargilfield preparatory school in Edinburgh before entering Winchester College, a school with a tradition for soccer rather than rugby. From the post-Great War playing fields of Winchester he progressed to Brasenose College, Oxford, winning a rugby Blue in the university match of December 1923, when Phil Macpherson captained the Dark Blues to victory. Young Smith, running fast and straight, scored two of their tries. His speed and dash made him a formidable opponent, and he could also kick long and straight.

Both his parents were Scottish and during his Oxford days he made it perfectly clear that there was no Sassenach, nor even Welsh blood in his veins. And so, shortly after his blazing start on the Oxford flanks, he was drafted in to appear in a Scottish trial. He was not immediately selected for the opening international match of the season, Scotland's journey to Paris to meet France, but after the visitors were beaten 12–10 in the French capital on New Year's Day 1924, he was brought in to add pace to the Scottish attack for the home fixture at Inverleith with Wales a month later. The Welsh were overwhelmed and Smith, with a hat-trick of tries, helped the Scots establish an unassailable 35-point lead before Wales managed two consolation converted tries in the last six minutes of the match. Scotland's three-quarter line that day comprised Oxford under-graduates: Phil Macpherson, George Aitken (a former All Black Test centre) and Johnnie Wallace (an Australian) joining Smith in what remains Scotland's highest score and biggest winning margin against Wales. One of the visiting Welsh three-quarters made a point of asking to be introduced to Smith after the match. He had only seen the back of him during the game and wanted to make sure he recognised him if they ever met again.

At the end of the season, the Scottish winger was an automatic choice as a member of the British/Irish party that toured South Africa in the summer. It was thought that he would revel in the firm grounds, but he was injured early in the visit and his try-scoring and appearances were restricted to five tries in six games (including the first two Test matches). The year 1925 was to be Scotland's *annus mirabilis*, the Scots winning their first Grand Slam, but the season had an inauspicious beginning for Ian Smith. He lost his place in the Oxford side and missed their big games against the touring All Blacks and Cambridge. He was still at the front of the Scottish selectors' minds, however, and after crossing for five tries in the final trial kept his international place for a season that began with a 25–4 win against France at Inverleith. There was a total eclipse of the sun that afternoon, and on the field Smith was responsible for eclipsing the French, scoring four of Scotland's seven tries. At the post-match banquet, an admiring Frenchman struck up a conversation with the prolific try-scorer and asked him what he'd clocked on the track for the 100 metres. Something must have got lost in translation, for Smith, believing he had been asked how many tries he'd scored, nonchalantly replied, 'Four or five.' The poor Frenchman was speechless. No wonder Smith was known as the 'Flying Scotsman'. A fortnight later he scored another four Test tries, this time against the Welsh at Swansea. Uniquely that scoring sequence included six successive Five Nations tries – back-to-back hat-tricks that included the last three tries of the French match and the first three of the Welsh game.

For most of his long career Ian Smith had Phil Macpherson as his centre. Macpherson was not just an unselfish player with the rare gift of excellent judgement. As a captain, he proved to be a clever tactician with the authority to bring out the best in his teams. Unquestionably Smith – and Scotland – benefited from Macpherson's genius, particularly in the Grand Slam matches of 1925 when the pair formed Scotland's left wing. Macpherson was absent in 1926, studying at an American university, but Smith remained an integral part of the Scottish XV that retained the championship. Smith's two tries against England at the end of the season helped Scotland become the first Home Union to win at Twickenham since the opening of the ground in 1910.

Many are the tales told of his escapades, especially during his rugby career. After Scotland's 20–6 Paris win in January 1926, he and Johnnie Wallace, who had just graduated in law and was about to return home to Australia, decided to take a trip to Switzerland to celebrate Wallace's last match, believing it to be a short train ride from the French capital. They spent a fortune buying tickets to

Davos and eventually booked in to a plush hotel where a friend was staying. They had no money left and relied on the friend for board and sustenance. Next day, they decided to 'do' the Parsenn Run, undaunted by the fact that neither of them had ever skied before. Experts reckon it takes a seasoned skier 25 minutes. Wallace and Smith endured nine hours of danger, pain and grief. But for their bravery they were richly rewarded – dined, wined and entertained by the admiring denizens of Davos at no cost to themselves.

The next season, when Smith and Macpherson were reunited, Scotland headed the championship table once again, losing only to Ireland in a game played in appalling conditions in Dublin. Earlier that season, at Murrayfield, Smith had damaged a foot on an iron railing shortly before the match but, reinforced by a couple of painkilling brandies, he was nevertheless able to take the field. The analgesic was most effective. Smith scored early in the match, running in from his own half, and added a second before the interval. Two more tries, against England at March, brought his tally to 17 from just 14 Tests – a remarkable strike-rate that pulled him into second place on the Test try-scoring roster, one try behind the then record holder, Kid Lowe, the celebrated England winger who had retired in 1923.

In his day it was the custom for wing three-quarters to throw the ball into the line-out. (Hookers weren't deemed capable of the task until the 1970s.) His underarm action, lobbing the ball high into the air, was always judged to perfection and an important source of possession for the successful Scotland sides in which he played. As a try-scorer, he had a particular penchant for running on to diagonal cross-field punts, often waiting for the bounce before outstripping opponents to gather the ball as it rolled at speed towards the goal-line. Smith had a high knee action which made him difficult to tackle when running at full speed.

The Flying Scotsman was out of commission in 1928 but on his return to Test rugby the year after he scored a try against Ireland and surpassed Lowe's record by scoring the two winning tries of the Calcutta Cup match. Playing the 'auld enemy' was a particular pleasure and he crossed for two more against England in 1931 and another the year later, at Twickenham. In 1933, in his last season as a Test player, he was rewarded with the Scotland captaincy and

led them to the Triple Crown. Fittingly at Swansea, in one of
Scotland's rare victories on Welsh soil, the skipper contributed to a
memorable win with the opening score of the match. It was his
24th and last try in Tests for, after leading the side to wins over
England and Ireland (in a postponed match on 1 April), he
announced his retirement. The side had actually been stranded at
sea on its way to the Dublin match originally scheduled for
February of that year. So severe was the weather that radio contact
with the ship carrying the team was lost and prayers for the safety
of the entire Scottish travelling party were offered at Sunday
services throughout Ireland and Scotland that weekend.

His long career, not only for Scotland and the Lions but also for
Edinburgh University, Oxford University, London Scottish and the
Barbarians, was remarkable for his prowess as a try-scorer and, at the
same time, surrounded by enjoyment and fun. On his first
Barbarian tour to South Wales he scored tries in close matches
against Cardiff and Swansea. Indeed, his try in the Swansea game
typified his love of adventure on the field, for it was the climax of a
thrilling move he had started from near his own goal-line. Off the
pitch he was invariably the life and soul of the party and in one late-
night escapade after a Calcutta Cup match was reported as having
driven a car filled with elated team-mates along Edinburgh's Princes
Street . . . on the pavement, horn blowing and headlights glaring.

By profession he had qualified as a chartered accountant at
Edinburgh University, but after Second World War service in the
RAOC he practised law, becoming a solicitor in Edinburgh until ill-
health compelled him to retire in 1964. He later lost a leg through
illness, but his enjoyment of the game he had adorned so brilliantly
in his youth never waned. He retained the cheerfulness of his youth
and even managed to contrive to continue his sporting passions for
shooting and fishing – the River Tweed flowing past the bottom of
his Kelso garden where he and his wife kept an open house for
friends and former players. When he died in September 1972, many
tributes were paid to a man who was described as one of sport's finest
Corinthians, though few then could have foreseen that his wonderful try-scoring record in the International Championship would still
stand nearly 40 years after his death.

MIKE SLEMEN
Famous Lions Try

Mike Slemen threading his way gracefully down the left wing was a sight that warmed the hearts of England and Lions' supporters between 1976 and 1984. The Liverpool winger was an automatic choice for the 1980 Lions' tour to South Africa and wore the England Number 11 shirt 31 times – a then record for an England flyer – between the retirement of David Duckham and the advent of Rory Underwood. He was ever-present in the side that took the 1980 Grand Slam and later, in 1994, took charge of the coaching of the England backs as part of Geoff Cooke's successful management team.

He was born on 11 May 1951 and educated in Liverpool at St Edward's College, where his first loves were cricket and football. He spent three years in the school first XI as a quick bowler while in winter he played Sunday League football in that soccer-mad city before forcing his way into his school's first XV in his last year there.

He was a scrum-half in those days, but soon outgrew the position, reaching 6ft before he left to study pharmacy at Aston University. Even so, the skills that had made him a more-than-useful soccer player were to underpin his emergence as a versatile rugby player who was equally at home at fly-half or fullback.

He spent a year studying at Aston before transferring to St Luke's College down in Exeter. At St Luke's he vied with future England Number 10 Neil Bennett for the fly-half berth, but despite a stunning performance during an Easter tour match at Llanelli he later settled on the wing, the position where he was to quickly become recognised as one of the most promising players in the country. He played for Devon in the County Championship during his student days and gained his first national recognition in his last year as a student, playing for England under-23s against the touring Tongans.

After St Luke's he successfully applied for a teaching post at Merchant Taylors', Crosby, returning to his roots. He resumed his club rugby with the Liverpool club and quickly gained selection for Lancashire and the North. His first full England cap came in 1976 when he was called up to replace David Duckham against Ireland.

Mike learned that he was in the side for that match while he was in the staff-room at school. Terry Cooper, the rugby correspondent of the Press Association, telephoned to inform him of his selection. 'I couldn't stop shaking all week,' Mike said. It was the start of a 31-cap career. At a time when English wingers saw about as much ball as a golfer in a snowstorm, he scored eight tries and established himself as a household name in Bill Beaumont's side, tasting the joy of victory and the despair of defeat.

His first major tour was with the England side coached by Mike Davis and led by Bill Beaumont that visited the Far East and Pacific Islands in the summer of 1979. Mike Slemen had already turned down lucrative offers from Barrow and Widnes to play rugby league before going on tour and appearing in six of the seven matches.

He hit the ground running, scoring two tries in the tour opener against Japan B in Tokyo's Olympic Stadium where the tourists won 36–7. His second try in that match was the result of a clever piece of anticipation. The ball went loose from a long pass into the midfield, but reading the bounce perfectly he stepped in from the left wing, gathered it and sprinted through. In scoring, however, he injured his leg. The in-goal areas in Japan were very narrow and sliding through to score he slipped off the turf and into a running track adjacent to the dead-ball line.

He thus missed the pleasures of downtown Tokyo when the squad ventured on to the bullet train on their first Saturday in Japan, but he did recover quickly enough to play in the first international against Japan on the Sunday. The tourists struggled to win 21–19, only a last-minute Dusty Hare conversion saving England from the ignominy of a draw in a match refereed by Clive Norling, but it was another Welshman's deep voice that cut through the crowd to say (inaccurately as it turned out), as the relieved visitors trooped off: 'You might just about manage this lot, but it'll be 1990 before you beat us.'

Normal service was resumed in mid-week when England thrashed an undersized Kyushu selection 80–3, Mike scoring a handsome hat-trick of tries. That was the occasion on which Bill Beaumont, his side 32–3 up at half-time, told his charges: 'Come on lads, don't let it slip now.' For the second Japan match England redeemed some lost esteem with a comfortable 38–18 win, but the ball did not run Mike's way, a story that was to be repeated in the 19–7 victory over Fiji when the party moved south for the second half of the tour. The visit ended in Tonga with a 37–17 win after a decidedly shaky start.

Tonga led for part of the first half and were only five points adrift with 10 minutes to go before Mike, who had opened the scoring, crossed for his second try of the game. That score heralded a late flurry of 15 points that cemented England's victory.

Although the tourists returned with their 100 per cent record intact, few felt that England had grown sufficiently in stature to pose a threat when the 1980 Five Nations season came round. Confidence, it was true, had been gained on tour, but English rugby had suffered a long period of disappointment since last securing the championship title in 1963 and few predicted that a champagne season was about to follow.

But 1979–80 was to go down as a golden year for English rugby, and the strength of character that had enabled the team to win tight matches and even come from behind in the South Pacific proved a not insignificant factor as the domestic season unravelled. Mike was an integral part of the success.

The nucleus of the England 1980 Grand Slam XV was built around the Northern Division side that beat the All Blacks 21–9 in November 1979. Bill Beaumont was the captain with Slemen on the wing for both the North and the nation. Mike's silken running and subtle changes of pace were assets to a side that coasted past Ireland with a 24–9 win on the opening Saturday of the Five Nations season. He put the world-class mark on everything he did that afternoon, taking his chance brilliantly to capitalise on a Steve Smith blind-side break to put England ahead with a try just before half-time. Defence was his order in the more hard-fought victories over France in Paris and Wales at Twickenham, but he was on the scoresheet again in the Grand Slam decider at Murrayfield in March. Clive Woodward had an outstanding first half that afternoon and put Mike in for England's second try as the champions accelerated into a 16–0 lead. England's final margin was 30–18, a fitting way to round off their first Grand Slam since 1957.

In 1980, the Lions set out for South Africa under the captaincy of Bill Beaumont, the first Englishman to lead the tourists for 50 years. The champion country was well represented, 10 of the Grand Slam side accompanying the Lions. Mike was a first-choice for the tour and was described by the doyen of South African critics, Reg Sweet of the Durban *Daily News*, as 'unquestionably the most talented all-rounder of all'. The visit went down as the unlucky tour, the Lions having to call for eight replacements during their 18-match trip. Mike himself only played in five matches, returning home owing to a family illness after the narrow defeat in the first Test. But in his short time on tour he stamped his class on the team and scored arguably the most memorable try in Lions' history.

The Lions were trailing against the South African Invitation XV at altitude in Potchefstrom as the match entered its dying moments. In a desperate effort to snatch victory from the jaws of defeat the tourists launched an incredible attack that went left to right, back and fore, with the ball eventually passing through 40 pairs of hands before Bruce Hay gave the final transfer to Mike on the left wing, who scored the winning try. He told the *Guardian*'s Frank Keating afterwards: 'We didn't actually realise what we'd done until we trooped off and walked past the grandstand, the crowd cheering us to the echo. It was mesmerising. Okay, I finished it off, but it was the third time I'd had a dash in the whole amazing sequence.'

English rugby, after its *annus mirabilis* in 1980, fell into decline, though Mike scored THE try of the 1981 Five Nations when he was twice involved in a flowing movement on each side of the pitch. The commentator Peter West reckoned 'the try illustrated Slemen's instinct for keeping himself in the game, and not standing waiting in the wings for something to happen'. Mike, who felt that that was the most satisfying try he scored in his England career, was also involved in the memorable try scored by Huw Davies that afternoon.

He lost his place in the England side in 1982–83 but bounced back the next season to become England's most-capped winger. He took part in a famous victory over the All Blacks at Twickenham where the late Maurice Colclough, his old Northern Division chum and another with Liverpool connections, scored England's decisive try. Then, after a defeat at Murrayfield in the opening match of the 1984 Five Nations, he lost his place to Rory Underwood.

Mike always believed in putting something back into the game and his loyalty – to rugby union as well as to his employers at Merchant Taylors', Crosby, where he was a master for 30-plus years – was exemplary. Despite offers, he never felt tempted to follow many of his contemporaries by penning an autobiography, staying with the union code and devoting much of his leisure time to coaching.

He played his last first-class match in May 1986, leading Liverpool against Preston Grasshoppers. Fittingly, it was the last match played on the club's Church Road ground, as the next season they merged with St Helen's. Mike was to give many years to the coaching at LSH's Moss Lane HQ before joining the England coaching set-up in the 1990s. During England's golden era in international rugby Mike's quiet authority and intelligence commanded huge respect among the back division that he directed.

The player once described as 'a winger of resplendent athleticism and polished control' was equally effective at polishing the skills of arguably the most successful England three-quarter line of all time.

TOM GRACE
An Irish Favourite

Nothing endears an Irishman more to his countrymen than scoring tries in international victories against England. Tom Grace, Ireland's tall, rangy right-winger in 25 cap matches between 1972 and 1978, crossed the line in the 1972, 1973 and 1976 successes and was on six successive winning sides against the old enemy, including the 1972, 1974 and 1976 wins at Twickenham.

He was born in Dublin on 24 October 1948 and began his rugby playing as a centre as a schoolboy at Newbridge College in County Kildare before going up to University College Dublin to study commerce and prepare for a career in accountancy. It was at university that his senior career as a winger took off and he graduated via the Leinster inter-pro side to the Irish team that toured Argentina in 1970. Although caps were not awarded, Grace appeared in the two 'Tests' against the Pumas, but remained in the shadow of Alan Duggan, Ireland's automatic choice as right-winger, for another season. At length, he broke into the side for his first full cap, against France, in Paris in January 1972, when Ireland won in France for the first time in 20 years.

He felt lucky to have broken into the side and hung on every word his skipper Tom Kiernan said in the pre-match pep talk, taking consolation from the fullback's promise to cover everything and take the pressure off his wingers if the French halfbacks bombarded them with high kicks. Early in the match Jean-Louis Bérot placed a high ball to land between Grace and his captain. 'Your ball,' shouted Kiernan, and the new winger knew his Test career was under way as he managed to scramble the ball into touch with half a ton of French back-row forwards closing in on him. At the end of his first match he was reluctant to swap jerseys with his opposite number and his captain asked him why. Grace modestly replied that he was afraid he'd never again play for Ireland, to which Kiernan reassured him, saying, 'Jaysus, you've no fear of that.' Jerseys were duly swapped and Kiernan slipped Grace the match ball as a memento of the historic win.

A couple of weeks later, Grace raced on to Barry McGann's angled kick to score in the win against England at Twickenham and a rosy future with the Irish side beckoned. Later the same year, playing for the Scotland/Ireland combination against England/Wales at Murrayfield in a special match staged to celebrate the centenary of the Scottish Rugby Union, he announced his arrival as a winger of true Test class by scoring two of the tries in a 30–21 win. Mike Gibson crossed for three, and the newspaper subs had a field day playing with headlines along the lines of 'Scots win by the Grace of Gibson.'

Blessed with long legs and a raking stride, he used his deceptive speed intelligently on the field. Yet, ironically, few of his six Test tries for Ireland were down to his sheer pace. Grace had to be inventive to make up for a lack of gilt-edged possession and perfected the knack of anticipating where his three-quarters or halfbacks would kick the ball. Like his great Welsh rival, J.J. Williams, he was a brilliant chaser and snapper-up of tries. Apart from his winning contributions to matches against the English, arguably his most memorable try was the last-minute kick-and-chase to earn Ireland a draw against New Zealand in January 1973. That result remains Ireland's best effort to date against the All Blacks. The *Guardian*'s David Irvine described this typical Grace effort: 'The big right-winger produced his speciality of a kick over the fullback's head, and raced over the goal-line, without checking his long stride, to beat both [Bob] Burgess and the dead-ball line by inches for the score.' In later years the myth arose that Barry McGann, Ireland's place-kicker that day, deliberately missed his conversion attempt from the touchline so that he could constantly tease Grace for the rest of his life . . . as indeed he does: 'If I'd kicked that goal your try would have gone down as the greatest scored in Irish rugby history.' Tom had a wicked sense of humour himself and enjoyed the teasing the Irish side gave McGann, who was slightly on the portly side for a fly-half. One of the stories to emerge from the Irish camp was that their coach used to start his sessions with the exhortation to players: 'Right lads, three laps around Barry McGann to warm up.'

In 1974, after featuring on Ireland's championship-winning side, Grace enjoyed an effective tour with the invincible Lions to South Africa. He was the party's top try-scorer, despite badly spraining an ankle shortly before the Lions departed, but missed out on playing in the Test series. Then in 1976, he was appointed captain and enjoyed a run of eight matches at the helm. Though only one match was won – famously at Twickenham in 1976 – his side gave the All Blacks a real fright in Wellington that same summer when Ireland so nearly beat New Zealand in their own backyard. In May 1977 he was forced to undergo an operation on his right knee. Although he recovered sufficiently to retain his place for the opening game of the 1978 Five Nations campaign, he lost form, underwent further surgery and was forced later in the year to announce his retirement from the game owing to injury. Ned van Esbeck, the doyen of Irish rugby writers, described Grace's premature retirement as 'a severe blow to Ireland'.

He went on to enjoy a distinguished professional career with PricewaterhouseCoopers (PWC) working on some of Ireland's most notorious insolvency cases. He retired as a partner from PWC in 2005 after 34 years with the company, having brought the same competitive focus to his professional duties as he had to the rugby field. His business credentials were also in demand by the game's governing body, the IRB, who invited him to oversee the voting procedures that led to New Zealand being awarded the 2011 Rugby World Cup competition. In retirement he became a non-executive director on the board of Paddy Power – horseracing is a relatively recent passion of his – and he has become Honorary Treasurer of the Irish Rugby Football Union.

Tom Grace has also enjoyed the proud privilege of watching his son play basketball for Ireland and he remains a loyal supporter of Leinster Lions. Barry McGann still teases him, but for the older generation of Ireland rugby supporters he remains a favourite for his match-winning feats against the English.

ALEX OBOLENSKY
Prince of Wingers

Alex Obolensky, a fair-haired exiled Russian prince studying at Oxford University, set no special records for England. Indeed he appeared only four times in official Tests wearing the white jersey with red rose. Yet his deeds in a 13–0 win against the All

Blacks on a cold January day in 1936 made him a household name long before the television age.

His two tries against New Zealand on his debut made Obo an overnight star. He was an electric runner who used his acceleration to deceive opponents, but it was his love of the unorthodox that marked him out from the run-of-the-mill wingers of his day. His second try against the All Blacks was a classic. Receiving the ball far out on his right wing, he ghosted through the New Zealand defence to finish off scoring wide out to the left of the posts. Hal Sever, who played on the left wing that day and was, at the time of his death in 2005, the oldest surviving member of that side, recalled that try as 'something rather unique'.

'As [Obolensky] reached the left wing I thought he was about to pass to me, a few yards short of the line, but anticipating that I would probably drop the ball in the excitement, he confounded friend and foe by nonchalantly running round my opposing winger to score near *my* corner flag – to the most tumultuous roar I ever remember hearing,' said Sever. 'It might be said that he virtually ran round the whole of the All Blacks.' Captured on film by Movietone News, it was probably the first famous try to be seen by a broad audience. For most of the following week the news theatres in London had long lunchtime queues of businessmen who wanted to see the unique try that helped beat the All Blacks – the first-ever defeat New Zealand suffered on English soil.

The fascination with Obolensky was heightened by his royal Russian connection. He was born on 17 February 1916 at Petrograd, where his aristocratic father, Prince Alexis Obolensky, was a member of the Tsar's Imperial Horseguard. When the revolution took place the following year, Prince Alex junior, who was just a babe in arms, was whisked out of the country to England. He was educated at Ashe School and Trent College in Derbyshire and went up to Oxford where his uncle, Prince Vadim Obolensky, was Professor of French. 'It is difficult for me to believe that I am anything but an Englishman,' Obo once said, adding that his ambition was to enter the British civil service.

As a schoolboy he had run the 100 yards in 10.2 seconds so his natural position on the rugby field was on the wing. At Oxford he engaged the famous sports equipment suppliers, Elmer Cotton, to design a special pair of lightweight rugby boots for him. He scored countless tries in them for the university in his freshman term in 1935 and was an automatic choice for the Varsity Match. Unusually the match was a scoreless draw, but Obo caught the eye with a spectacular cross-field sprint to cut off the Cambridge winger with a smashing tackle when a try seemed certain. It was that piece of heroic defence that won him a place in the final England trial, where he scored three tries. After that, selection for England against the All Blacks in January 1936 was inevitable.

But the choice of a Russian who was not a naturalised British subject caused eyebrows to be raised among the establishment. His application for British citizenship had been filed at the Home Office, but some said it was scandalous for a Russian to play rugby for England. To their credit, however, the RFU stuck to their guns and stood by Obo, arguing that he had arrived in the country before he could even walk and that there were no strict qualification rules denying his eligibility to play for the country in which he had learned the game. Perhaps his rugby feats accelerated Home Office procedures, for on 16 March 1936 his papers came through and in front of the Sheriff of Derbyshire he swore his oath of allegiance as a British subject and dropped his Russian title. Embarrassed by the publicity, the shy and retiring rugby player kept a low profile before setting off for a tour of South America with a British side in the summer.

It is recorded that he scored 17 tries in a match against a Brazilian XV on that tour and, with his dashing good looks and pleasant personality, was a magnet for attractive female company. He was never a keen one for fitness or training. On the journey out to Argentina, one by one he kicked the bag of footballs out into the Atlantic so that the players could avoid the unwanted interruption of practice and concentrate on enjoying the social side of their long voyage.

Obolensky's fame has never waned, though he rarely set the rugby world alight again in peacetime. He kept his England place for the three championship matches in 1936 – a scoreless draw with Wales, defeat in Dublin and a one-point win against Scotland back at Twickenham, which was his last appearance in a cap match. Injuries kept him out of the reckoning in 1937, and after Oxford he settled in London working for an insurance company and turning out regularly for the Rosslyn Park rugby club. He enrolled for training with the RAF reserve and in May 1938 he was granted a volunteer reserve commission that was the catalyst for more questions to be raised, this time in the House of Commons.

'How many Russians is it proposed to enrol in the RAF?' asked a Labour backbencher, while other members of the Opposition sarcastically demanded that equal consideration be granted to other applicants who might not have carried such distinguished titles. The unassuming Obolensky simply got on with his business and his duties. When war broke out in September 1939 he was gazetted Acting Pilot Officer and stationed in Norfolk. Official rugby matches were suspended, to be replaced by a series of charity games designed to boost the war effort. Obo was much sought after to appear in these games, his presence often guaranteeing to add several thousand to the gate. In December 1939 he scored a try for a star-studded England & Wales team that beat Scotland & Ireland 17–3 in the four home countries match at Richmond. He turned out for Rosslyn Park, war duties permitting, and featured in a series of Red Cross matches, including an 'international' against Wales at Cardiff in March 1940 when 40,000 turned out to see him repeat his amazing cross-field run of 1936 to set up a try in England's 18–9 victory in a game for which no caps were awarded.

Match reports from 1939–40 indicate that Obo had recaptured the flying form that had captivated rugby followers in 1935–36, and he was immediately selected to take part in the return match at Gloucester scheduled for April. The week after the Cardiff game against Wales he turned out for Oxford Past & Present against their Cambridge counterparts in a match played for the benefit of the Army Recreational Equipment Fund at Richmond. His fullback in that match was the former Welsh international Viv Jenkins, with whom and against whom Obolensky had often played. Many years later Jenkins, a great storyteller whose tales were sometimes embellished to such a degree that the line between fact and fiction became blurred, related that he had asked Obo how his pilot training was progressing. According to Jenkins, the winger replied that it was going well but that he was having trouble with his landings.

Barely two weeks later Pilot Officer Obolensky was reported killed in action in a training flight, the first rugby international to lose his life in the Second World War. His Hawker Hurricane overturned while landing at an East Anglian aerodrome on 29 March 1940 and he was killed instantly. Many mourned a man whose name will never die. Indeed, nearly 69 years later, even Roman Abramovich, whose interests lay in a different-shaped-ball game, contributed to the legend of the flying prince by helping to fund a memorial to Obo that was unveiled in Ipswich in February 2009.

THE HARD MEN

WILLIE JOHN McBRIDE
Ireland's Pride

Willie John McBride was the forward who dominated northern hemisphere rugby when he was at his peak between 1966 and 1974. The Irishman was never found to be anything but the solid backbone of his country and the Lions' scrums. On the world scene there were arguably only two forwards who could reasonably call themselves rivals to the title of best lock: the New Zealander Colin Meads and South Africa's Frik du Preez.

He was the first player to tour five times with the Lions and first showed his leadership potential with the successful class of 1971 in New Zealand, where he emerged as their pack leader. He had the respect of his colleagues – a leader whose followers genuinely warmed to his calm control and huge confidence. He was the natural choice as skipper of the 1974 Lions, going on to inspire his team to complete an unbeaten tour of South Africa. The side won the Test series 3–0 against the Springboks, drawing the final match. No British/Irish side of the modern era realised anywhere near such a remarkable achievement.

Immense strength and fitness were the hallmarks of his play. As rucking and mauling became the vogue in rugby in the 1960s, so he applied his strength to the task of winning vital second-phase possession. His tremendous leg drive gave impetus to rucks and he used his mighty arms to prise the ball free in mauls. Then, as the demand for running, handling forwards increased, he even showed that he could join in the frolics of open play with the best of the pack, though his only score in his 63 Tests for Ireland was a try in his last match at Lansdowne Road, against France in 1975.

William James McBride – the 'Willie John' nickname was coined halfway through his career – was born in Toomebridge in County Antrim on 6 June 1940 and brought up on the family's 50-acre farm in Moneyglass. Farming is a physically demanding life but during his upbringing it provided the young McBride with the natural fitness and upper body strength that were to serve him so admirably in his rugby career. It was not until his late teenage years that he discovered rugby, but taking to it like a bird to the air, he developed quickly and progressed from the Ballymena club via Ulster's inter-pro side into the Irish team of 1962, making his debut in a 16–0 thumping by England at Twickenham. It was an inauspicious season for Ireland, but young Willie John was one of the finds of their year and in the summer of 1962 he was chosen for the Lions' trip to South Africa, where he played in two of the Tests. He was to become the tourists' automatic choice on the 1966, 1968 and 1971 tours, building a reputation as a forward who never took a backward step, before taking over as captain for the visit to South Africa in 1974.

Colin Meads, the New Zealand lock that he had famously stood up to in 1963 when the All Blacks had to work devilishly hard to beat Ireland 6-5 in Dublin, respected McBride for his courage and aggression. The pair met again on the 1971 Lions' trip when Willie John became a valued member of the tourists' brains trust – the inner circle that supports the coach and captain in tactical matters – after Ray McLoughlin went home injured. Meads led New Zealand while McBride, as leader of the Test pack, became associated with the rallying cry, 'We take no prisoners', on that tour. His forward expertise and bravery were to help the Lions to their series victory over the All Blacks and his 'minding' of Meads, particularly in the last two Tests of the series, gave the touring backs more freedom in which to dictate tactics. His down-to-earth humour, moreover, was illustrated after the first Test win in Dunedin when the Lions went down to Queenstown for a couple of days' rest and recuperation. A film of the Test had been sent over for the tourists to watch, and as the side assembled around the television set to relive their triumph, it was noticed that McBride was absent. At length he sauntered in, took one look at the film and told the Lions: 'Ah, you don't want to be seeing that, lads. That's history now.'

But the historic tour that etched his name among rugby's eternal greats came three years later. No individual player has ever done so much to ensure the success of a team as Willie John did in 1974. The visit itself was clouded by political controversy before the side even flew out, the British government having made clear that it did not support the trip. Then there was the not insignificant matter of taking on the Springboks in their own backyard. McBride did not pontificate over the moral issues. He simply set about providing strong leadership to a talented group of players. His was a simple approach. Not for him the tactical niceties of how to beat the 'Boks – he left that to his Ballymena and Ireland mate Syd Millar, who was coach of the class of '74. He led by example, took responsibility for his and his team's actions on and off the field and by doing so became a highly respected figure among his team. No one doubted his physical courage in taking the fight to the South Africans, but his tough mental approach inspired his men to achieve the Lions' first series victory in the Republic since the 1890s.

Tales of his leadership off the field on that tour have passed into the game's folklore, embellished a thousand times with each telling. When the side won the Third Test to wrap up the series in Port Elizabeth they celebrated by staging the mother of all parties back at their hotel. The champagne flowed and the party extended to the early hours of Monday morning. Water flowed as well. At one stage in the night every fire hose in the building was gushing. It was a very uptight Alun Thomas, the tour manager from Wales, who sought out Willie John hoping that the skipper would help restore some semblance of order. He found the big-boned captain in his hotel room puffing away on his pipe and relaxing among the jetsam and flotsam of the party. 'Tell me, Alun,' Willie John is reputed to have said, 'Is there anybody dead?'

The Welsh journalist J.B.G. Thomas, who wrote a book after the tour, glosses gloriously over this incident in his recollection of the night. 'Some beer was spilled on the carpets and one fire extinguisher used,' Thomas told his readers. The hotel manager, apparently, took the same calm view as Willie John. 'We are not unduly concerned as none of the damage was serious. We'll welcome the Lions back anytime,' he told J.B.G. Perhaps J.B.G. was just sticking to the old adage that what goes on tour stays on tour?

Willie John's own take on that tour was that there were no stars; only great men whose sole purpose on arrival in South Africa was to win. Dr Danie Craven, South Africa's 'Doctor Rugby' who as player, captain, coach, manager and ultimately president of the South African Rugby Board, was a lifelong student of the game and wanted an insight into the Lions' success. The laid-back McBride had no problem late in the tour allowing him to have a peek behind the scenes and welcomed Doc Craven into the tourists' changing rooms before one of the tour matches. Imagine the shock, then, for the rugby supremo when he entered to find the players in relaxed mood. Chris Ralston, the Richmond and England lock, was even smoking a cigar in his kit, changed and ready to play.

Not everything Willie John was involved in, however, was so successful. After retiring from international rugby in 1975 he remained in the game as a coach and administrator. In 1983 he was the manager of the Lions' tour to New Zealand when the visitors suffered a 3–0 whitewash in the Test series, including a record 38–3 defeat in the final international in Auckland. And when he returned he succeeded Tom Kiernan as coach of an Ireland side that went from heroes to zeros. His squad turned from the vintage wine of 1983 that had shared the Five Nations title with France into water and a Five Nations whitewash in 1984. But for strength of character, sheer physical power and leadership, the only player in the Four Home Unions who has come anywhere near matching his standing as a forward in the past 35 years was England's Martin Johnson. Willie John was that good.

BRIAN MOORE
Pitbull

Too many sweat-bands but not enough sweat. That was the damning indictment of English packs made by the successful

New Zealand forwards in the first 30 or so years after the Second World War. English eights always looked impressive, but in six England–New Zealand matches between 1954 and 1973 they were dismantled up front by mobile, intelligent All Black scrums that neither asked nor gave any quarter in battle. True, England managed to sneak a win over the men in black in a one-off Test in Auckland in 1973, and there was another win at Twickenham in 1983 soon after English rugby had peaked under the leadership of Bill Beaumont, but it wasn't until Geoff Cooke was installed as England manager after the inaugural Rugby World Cup in 1987 that a sea-change swept over English rugby.

Cooke provided the off-the-field drive behind changes in English rugby fortunes that were the foundation for the later achievements under Sir Clive Woodward. Will Carling was the public figurehead of the Cooke era, but the man who epitomised the tough-minded new breed of England forward was the Nottingham hooker, Brian Moore. Quite simply Moore went on to the field full of hatred – hatred of losing that is, for he was never a dirty player. He played within the laws of the game and was expert in all the game's skills: the ruthless efficiency in performance and the new psychological dimension he brought to forward play was a significant factor in helping English rugby to lift its game and embark on the sustained winning streak of the 1990s that culminated in the 2003 World Cup success.

One sensed that to lose a strike on his own put-in or to see the opposition line-out win the ball against his throw was taken as a personal affront. Dominance up front was the platform of England's successes in the early 1990s and Moore was the catalyst who whipped the tight five into a unit that was capable of subduing any pack in the world. He had no superior for sheer commitment or energy. So often he was the player who held the England pack together at critical moments in matches, leading by disciplined example and exhorting his team-mates with a thoughtful mix of encouragement and advice.

He also had the knack of getting in the faces of opponents, particularly the French for whom he became their *bête noir*. Facing them 10 times in his career he lost only twice: 10–9 in his first match against them in 1988 and again in the meaningless 1995 World Cup bronze-medal game that turned out to be his final Test for England. In between there were wins in a Grand Slam decider and World Cup quarter-final in 1991. His very presence in the England side was a distraction to the French, and when two of their front row were sent off in Paris in the 1992 Five Nations match Moore's niggling, nagging demeanour was thought to be a contributing factor to the dismissals. He was nicknamed the Pitbull for very obvious reasons.

The life of Brian began on 11 January 1962 in Birmingham. He was brought up in Yorkshire and it was during his schooldays at Crossley & Porter in Halifax that the first signs of his mental toughness were seen. He joined the Old Boys club from Halifax Wednesday in 1979, turning out as a centre for the school in morning matches and packing down in the front row for the Crossleyans in afternoons. Then, while studying law at Nottingham University, he joined the town's club, and early representative honours were won with England Students and Under-23s. He captained England B against Italy in 1985 and was called up for his first full cap against Scotland in the final match of the 1987 Five Nations. He was fiercely proud of his England position and battled hard to keep Graham Dawe and later John Olver, his nearest rivals, on the bench. All told, Brian won 64 England caps – a then world record for a hooker – played in the World Cup Final against Australia in 1991 and was the automatic choice as hooker for the 1989 and 1993 Lions. His courage and stamina meant that he was never dropped and never once required replacement during a major international match.

Apart from establishing himself as the ace hooker in the victorious 1989 Lions' pack against Australia, he perfected a mean aeroplane imitation in the lighter moments of that tour. The motorists on Sydney Bridge discovered this almost to their peril after the tourists' long night of celebrations at winning the Test series. It was Brian's good fortune that his antics on a busy highway were spotted by a kindly British journalist, who picked him up and taxied him for a safe landing.

Work took him to London in 1990 and he became a fixture in

the Harlequins side that won the RFU Cup in 1991 and were runners-up in 1992. By now he was a busy solicitor with a London legal firm and when he wrote his autobiography in 1995, his journalist collaborator was overawed by the volume of briefs and work that Moore took on. He had played hard on the field but seemed to work even harder at his professional duties off it.

Nowadays he has become a regular member of the BBC's live rugby coverage, forming with former Welsh international Eddie Butler an entertaining commentating double-act. Butler sometimes assumes the air of a confused, benign bear while Moore fills him in with pitbull assertiveness. At other times the roles are reversed: Moore can't believe what he's seen while Butler provides the rational explanation. One recent amusing exchange of banter came during the 2008 Wales–South Africa game when 'Beast' Mtawarira, the Springbok prop, had to change positions when another prop, Mujati, came on as a substitute. Moore asked: 'Does Mujati have an animal name as well?', to which Butler drily but accurately replied: 'No – only Brian.'

Old Moore's views on rugby, the universe and life in general are much in demand. He writes the thinking man's rugby column in the *Daily Telegraph* and has appeared on the panel of the BBC's current affairs programme, *Question Time*. The edginess is as sharp as ever. 'I used to be a solicitor until I discovered I had a conscience,' he recently told David Dimbleby, during an answer to a topical question. Long may the pitbull entertain us.

JAMMY CLINCH
They shall not Pass

Few flankers between the wars were as intimidating as James Daniel Clinch, an Irish and Lions' legend who terrorised back divisions between 1924 and 1931. He was unique among loose forwards, using his strength and considerable ball skills as a defensive flanker at a time when back-row forwards were developing as destroyers in set-piece play and skirmishers in the loose. His mode of play involved dropping back in defence to anticipate the direction of an opposition attack. It was a very brave player who decided to take him on: 'If you've got the ball, he'll get you,' it was said. Clinch's motto was 'They shall not pass'.

He was a rib-shaking tackler, had flypaper hands and could kick with the accuracy of a fullback, a role he was pressed into filling twice for the British/Irish Lions in 1924 in South Africa where the hard grounds took their toll of injured tourists. A raw-boned, no-nonsense player, he struck fear in opponents because of his uncompromising hardness. He enjoyed mixing it on the field, where his intimidating presence earned him the respect of the hard men from the Home Unions, France and the Dominions, but he was fair in his courage, expecting as good as he got. Mark Sugden, his scrum-half and captain in many club matches for Trinity and Ireland, reckoned there was only once that Clinch used his aggression illegally and that was in retaliation. 'Never did I know him to do anything unsporting, but at Swansea in 1926 I was laid out by a Welsh forward and Jammy quietly enquired who was responsible. A few minutes later the Welsh forward had to leave the field for repairs.'

Sugden described Clinch as 'a man of enormous strength – of muscle and character – entirely unflappable, and his serene composure under any conditions had much to do with our successes during the 1920s.' Indeed, his toughness on the field passed into legend and was handed down in fiction by that much-praised Irish novelist of the 1970s, Aidan Higgins, who referred to Clinch in a novel depicting the adolescence and early adulthood of a Catholic lad brought up in rural Ireland. In *Scenes from a Receding Past*, Higgins wrote, admittedly with artistic licence, '. . . Jammy Clinch, who in India killed a man with his bare hands because he had crossed his path, my father said. Clinch certainly looked capable of anything. Once he had set fire to a train.'

Jammy Clinch was born in Clondalkin on 28 September 1901, the son of Dr Andrew Clinch, who had played for Ireland as a rumbustious forward in the 1890s. It was at Catholic University

School in Dublin that the 'Jammy' soubriquet was given by a form tutor who always seemed to be taking the young Clinch to task for eating jam sandwiches. It wasn't until he went up to Trinity College to study medicine and play with the Wanderers club that his rugby career took off. He appeared in a talented college side that included Irish internationals Mark Sugden, Terry Millin and Bob Crichton and won his first cap, against Wales, in 1923. On his debut he fell for one of the oldest sucker-punches in the game when, at the first line-out, a Welsh forward told him that his bootlace was undone. As Clinch bent down to tie it up the Welshman took him unawares and floored him with an uppercut. Clinch did not complain and came through a baptism of fire in a winning Irish side to become a regular on the Irish XV the next year. He was to be an automatic choice, when fit and available, for the next seven years, winning 30 caps to equal the then record for an Irish forward.

He quickly became one of the team's great characters, off as well as on the pitch, where he was always conspicuous wearing a white, elastic headband instead of the orthodox scrumcap favoured by most forwards of the day. He found the band less restrictive and less likely to tear. During Jammy's long career Ireland twice shared the Five Nations Championship and in 1926 only a narrowly missed last-minute drop-goal against Wales denied them the Grand Slam. In fact, he always appeared to play his best rugby against the Welsh and the legion of stories told about Jammy's Ireland career invariably involve his exploits against the Celtic cousins. In 1928, at Cardiff, his opposite number in a typically rough encounter was Tom Hollingdale from Neath, who had recently left the police force to study for the Church. The match was a tight one in which a number of controversial offside decisions went Wales's way, Hollingdale giving his opponent the run-around for most of the game. At the end, however, the better side prevailed and Ireland managed to win 13–10. As the sides left the field Hollingdale congratulated Clinch, saying, 'The Lord wasn't on our side this afternoon,' to which Jammy quickly replied: 'No, but the ref was.'

Two years later a Welsh spectator at St Helen's, remembering the boisterous match Jammy had played there in the narrow Grand

Slam failure in 1926, welcomed him on to the field with the shout of, 'Send the bastard off, ref!' Typically, he took it as the highest accolade of his long playing career. Indeed, Jammy loved the Welsh and their rugby so much that when he qualified as a doctor he spent many years in general practice in Gwent, first at Newport and later in Pontypool, where the rugged forward displays of the eastern valleys club struck a chord with his own playing exploits and yielded a long list of patients for his Monday morning surgery.

Once, during a game against the French in Paris, he and the rest of the Irish pack were given a torrid time during the first half of a very rough match. At half-time the Irish pack leader exhorted his men to keep their powder dry and not retaliate. 'Play like a gentleman and uphold Irish honour,' Jammy was told. Whereupon he asked the pack leader if the referee could delay the restart for 15 minutes. He needed a quick briefing on the subject, he claimed, because he didn't know anything about playing like a gentleman.

Besides his great wit on the field, away from rugby he was the subject of many tall tales, several of which he himself originated. One of his own stories concerned his anatomy viva, where he was asked to identify a bone. Jammy correctly recognised the fibula, but when asked to discriminate between the left or right bone politely told his examiners: 'Sirs, I would like you to know that I am not going for honours.' Although he left Trinity in 1925, he did not qualify as a doctor until 12 years later. In the interim he took up a commission in the British army where he became heavyweight boxing champion. He also did a stint in the insurance industry.

Jammy, moreover, was a born prankster whose escapades were the stuff of coarse rugby. Prized trophies were smuggled from other clubs, Parisian gardens were plundered on New Year's Day expeditions after Ireland's traditional holiday matches with France, and even colleagues' dress-suits were commandeered when Jammy was hard up. As a penniless student on the 1924 Lions' visit to South Africa, he bought secondhand evening dress from Ian Stuart, a contemporary of his in both the Trinity and Ireland XVs. He paid Stuart half the cost for the tails but for one reason or other never got round to paying off the debt. Five years later, after Ireland had beaten England at Twickenham for the first time, while Jammy and the Irish side celebrated their maiden victory the tails were torn in half. Stuart promptly reclaimed his half of Jammy's longstanding debt, walking off with the left half of the torn tails, which he kept as a souvenir for years.

In 1967 Jammy returned to Ireland from Wales and died in Dublin aged 79 on 1 May 1981 following an operation. His old captain, Mark Sugden, led the tributes. 'He was many players' hero, certainly he was mine, and those of us who are left and who played with him are the sadder for his going. I can see him now with his headband with two or three opponents trying to bring him down.'

DICKIE JEEPS
The India-rubber Man

Resilience of both mind and body has always been the prime quality required of an England scrum-half. In the past their national selectors were famed for fickle ways, and arguably no other position suffered the slings and arrows of outrageous fortune to such an extent. An England scrum-half was lucky to last more than one international, let alone a whole championship season, so had to have the strength of character to be indifferent to the constant threat of demotion. And it goes without saying that an English scrum-half was always a target for opposition loose forwards hell-bent on disrupting line-out and scrum ball. English forwards have always managed to win their fair share of set-piece possession, but often needed a real nugget to tidy up behind them and act as a ninth forward to put on the pressure around the fringes.

Competitive, courageous, stroppy even, Dickie Jeeps was the little tough guy type of scrum-half England's forwards loved to have aboard. He never hesitated to stick his oar into the tide of players bearing down on him and made life awkward for his adversaries. His uncanny sense of anticipation, whether popping up to make a covering tackle or supporting a breakaway, was second to none. Moreover, the lack of fuss with which he made light of the batterings he received while pitting himself against bigger rivals gave him an air of indestructibility. Press and colleagues called him the 'India-rubber man' on account of the bouncy manner in which he took his knocks. He invariably emerged unscathed and the only outward sign he ever showed of any damage was an occasional plaster on the forehead to protect the odd stitch.

Dickie Jeeps was born on 25 November 1931 in Willingham, Cambridgeshire, into a family of fruit farmers. He was fair-haired and chunky, with a ruddy complexion to match the apples he harvested. Moreover, he possessed the natural fitness and physical toughness of a man brought up to work the land from dawn till dusk. His early rugby education was at Bedford Modern School and he quickly graduated via the Cambridge club to Northampton, one of the top British club outfits of the 1950s. He was fast-tracked into the England trials but had to understudy Johnnie Williams for the 1955 Five Nations before unexpectedly getting the call to tour with the Lions to South Africa that year as the third scrum-half. Williams went as the Number One and was expected to partner Welshman Cliff Morgan in the Test series. But Dickie's short passes delivered at the perfect height and speed – distance was never a feature of his service – were to Morgan's liking and he was promoted to the Test side for the opening match of the series in Johannesburg, becoming one of the rare band of international players to play in a Test for the Lions before winning his cap for his country. The Lions were a successful band of players, holding the Springboks to a shared series, and Dickie played in all four Tests before returning to win a place in the England side for the opening match of the 1956 Five Nations. The selectorial curse on English scrum-halves struck again, however, and in the aftermath of a defeat by Wales in a battle royal at Twickenham, Dickie was banished to the sidelines for the rest of the season and left to contemplate a future as one of England's many one-cap wonders. He deserved to be dropped, he said, confessing to being overweight, and had to be content as travelling reserve when Johnnie Williams regained the berth for the rest of the season. He took the disappointment stoically. Like several of England's 1955 Lions, he had looked jaded and slightly out of touch playing in difficult conditions against the Welsh, despite his bravery standing up to the opposition wherever trouble brewed.

When the trials came round for the 1957 Five Nations, he had to withdraw from the first match but was promoted to the Probables to partner Harlequins' Ricky Bartlett for the second. The pair hit it off like friends reunited. Dickie was the man of the match, serving his consort with plumb-accurate passes that encouraged taking the ball on the burst without check. That way Bartlett was able to engage a flying three-quarter line that unlocked the Possibles' defences and laid the platform for a convincing 30–6 victory. The win and manner in which it was achieved created the template for a wonderful Grand Slam for England. Led by Eric Evans and with Dickie at their heels, the forwards carried all before them. The immaculate service from the scrum was the stuff of dreams for an attacking fly-half like Bartlett during a period when tight marking was the norm in international matches. Dickie was also on top of his individual game, going down suicidally to snuff out oncoming rushes, mixing it stroppily with anyone who dared to challenge him in the loose and popping up to tackle like a thunderclap in support of his forwards. He never wilted.

His finest hour came in the match against Scotland, when England wrapped up all the silverware the championship had to offer. He bobbed about the field like a cork floating in choppy waters, at first bearing the brunt of Scottish back-row attacks and several times saving England's line with defensive covering before settling to take a hand in all three of England's tries. In 1958 he appeared in all five of England's internationals during another unbeaten season, becoming the first English scrum-half to play throughout two successive seasons since the legendary Cecil Kershaw in the early 1920s.

Not surprisingly for one so exuberant on the field, Dickie enjoyed a lark. Raw eggs in colleagues' pockets, water pistol shoot-outs and catapult practice were as much a part of the Jeeps routine as his dive pass or blind-side break. On tour, big forwards walking close to a swimming pool were seconds away from a soaking when he was around, especially South Africans. He even got so bored with a French official's long-winded speech at a post-international banquet in Paris that he crawled under the top table and exploded a firework. Popular with players for his determination on the field and his endless practical jokes off it, he was considered natural leadership potential by the selectors.

In 1960 he was appointed England's captain for a championship season which brought another Triple Crown and a share with France of the Five Nations title. Open government was his style. He had a nucleus of experienced forwards, many of whom had been fixtures alongside him in the team for four years, and he confidently turned to them for advice. England received a setback on the eve of their Five Nations campaign when fly-half Bev Risman withdrew and had to be replaced by a rookie named Richard Sharp. The plan hatched by the old campaigners was to get Dickie to break more often from the scrum to tie in the Welsh flankers and give the new fly-half breathing space in the early exchanges of the match. The ruse worked a treat. When Sharp was eventually given possession, the Welsh back row were caught unawares and he ran rings around the defence to set up two brilliant first-half tries that helped England establish a match-winning 14–0 interval lead. This was heady stuff, for the Twickenham crowd that had not seen England score a try for two years, and Dickie's team were promptly installed as favourites to win the championship. He was an inspiring leader who shrugged off the clattering tackles from a rampaging French pack in Paris where a 3–3 draw deprived England of a Grand Slam – poor old Don Rutherford having missed a sitter trying to convert Mike Weston's try.

He retired from international rugby in 1962 after leading England in 13 successive matches and playing in 13 Tests for the British/Irish Lions. At the time he was England's most-capped scrum-half and the most capped Test player in Lions' history. A Transvaal horse owner even named a racehorse Dickie Jeeps. Like his namesake, the horse was a frequent winner.

Dickie enjoyed a couple more seasons of first-class rugby with Northampton before returning, as he had always promised, to his local junior club in Cambridge to see out his playing days. If international recognition had come relatively late in his playing career, he was to achieve everything else in his public life several years earlier than normal. He was a JP at 28, RFU committee member at

30 and Chairman of the Sports Council at 46, where he was the driving force behind the 'Sport for All' campaign. To these public offices he brought all the tenacity and sense of fun that had attended his brilliant playing career. After attending a press conference given by David Lord in 1983, publicising plans to launch a breakaway worldwide rugby circus, Jeeps, wearing his Sports Council hat, announced to the assembled gathering, 'The way England played last season I hope they've all signed for Mr Lord.'

In his mid-40s he served as president of the RFU, introducing regular press conferences and lifting English rugby out of the doldrums. The side had suffered a whitewash in the 1976 Five Nations and results since the early 1970s had been in decline. A new spirit of urgency filtered through the entire organisation with Dickie at the helm, and international results began to improve. In his year of office, the season opened with wins against Scotland and Ireland at the start of the 1977 campaign. France and Wales were the main forces in the championship at this time and England gave gutsy performances against both of them, going down by the slim margin of one point to the French before losing 14–9 in a Triple Crown decider with Wales in Cardiff.

The determination and spirit within the RFU in general and the international side in particular, had improved beyond recognition. Arguably it was Dickie Jeeps who, during his presidency, set England on the course that ultimately led to the Grand Slam three years later, in 1980.

MARK PEREGO
One Man and his Pig

Had he been born 10 years later, it is doubtful whether Mark Perego would ever have contemplated playing top-class rugby. It was a game that he played for enjoyment, but as rugby moved inexorably towards its professional destiny in the mid-1990s, he came to resent the intense hours of practice and training that were expected of players. Fitness was important to him. Indeed, he showed extraordinary commitment to keep himself in the highest of conditions in order to play the game. But organised training he viewed as an intrusion on his spare time, and as a result he often withdrew from the game for long periods, choosing to follow his own leisure interests instead. Welsh rugby followers should count themselves lucky that for most of his prime years he was available for national selection. After the 1995 watershed when rugby union relaunched as an open game, Perego and others of his ilk would never have wanted to become professional players and would never have entered the higher echelons of the game.

Born in Winchester on 8 February 1964, Mark Angelo Perego was the son of an Italian father who had played rugby for Llanelli and the army. Mark showed as a schoolboy that he had the credentials to make it at the highest level, captaining Graig Comprehensive School (formerly Llanelli Grammar School) in 1982, when it was awarded the *Rugby World* 'School of the Year' title for winning all 23 of its fixtures. He was also an outstanding forward in Welsh Schools representative teams at Under-15, Under-16 and Under-19 levels, playing alongside future senior caps Aled Williams and Alun Carter. After winning Welsh Youth honours, he joined Llanelli and quickly impressed in first-class rugby as a flinty flanker. He quickly made people sit up and take notice of his all-round back-row play. With his lack of inches – he was barely 6ft 1in – there was little pressure on him to win line-out ball, but as the Scarlets had a big pack with plenty of line-out alternatives, Mark was left to concentrate on becoming one of the most effective destroyers in Welsh club rugby.

A career move into the South Wales Constabulary led to his joining the police club in the late 1980s but a later transfer to the fire brigade in west Wales brought him back to Llanelli. At the time the national side was in considerable turmoil and in 1990, after Wales suffered a hiding at Twickenham, John Ryan tendered his resignation as national coach and was replaced by Ron Waldron, the Neath supremo. Waldron turned to his Neath club side, ringing the changes for his first international match, and also called up Mark, who made a sound debut in a side beaten but not disgraced by a Scotland team that went on to win the Grand Slam. Even Waldron, however, was taken aback after the match to find that, instead of getting showered and changed, the young Llanelli star bolted off into the Cardiff streets for a warm-down run. It was his way of doing his own thing, being his own man, but the somewhat eccentric behaviour was too much for his coach and there was no place for him in the Welsh team for the last match of the season.

Indeed, there were to be no more matches for Mark in a Welsh jersey for another three years. Fire service in Milford Haven, in Wales's far west, meant a 100-mile round trip to Llanelli for training and the youngster became tired of the journey. In 1990, regular competitive rugby in the form of a national league was launched in Wales, but Mark shied away from the limelight, fearing that competition would breed a new type of player. He was determined to keep his perspective on what was still supposed to be an amateur game and, sensing that his hobby would turn into a profession, took a sabbatical from playing. Indeed, for the best part of a third of his career during his prime he actually withdrew from playing – 'I've chosen not to play rugby because the things which come with playing have stopped me,' he told the *Daily Telegraph*'s John Mason. But when the most reluctant flanker in Wales did return to first-class rugby in 1992, his fitness, speed and devastating tackling showed that he had lost none of his skills. This was hardly surprising in one whose training regime involved cutting down trees. Indeed, he cut opponents down like a lumberjack. He starred for Llanelli in their defeat of the Wallabies in November 1992 and for his outstanding contribution as one of the Scarlets' runners who ruled the roost in Wales that season he regained his Welsh place in the side that toured East Africa in the summer of 1993.

He still enjoyed his post-match runs. Fans streaming away from the National Stadium after watching Llanelli beat Neath 21–18 in the SWALEC Cup Final were taken aback to find Mark pulling up for breath near the city's civic centre . . . barely 20 minutes after competing in one of the club's most passionately fought matches. What a contrast to the post-match routine of most of today's players, whose priority on coming from the pitch is a shower and gel before a night out. For Mark, the priority was to get away for his warm-down run, accompanied by his constant companion, an ornamental pig. It went everywhere with him, tucked into the top of his backpack whether he was out river-running or yomping through the forests of the Cefn Sidan beside the Carmarthenshire coast where he had been brought up. Richard Webster, his Swansea rival for the blind-side position in the Welsh side, once grabbed the pig during a training weekend in Lanzarote and threw it in a swimming pool. There was an animated discussion between the two flankers before Mark dived in to rescue his companion.

Llanelli were without his services for the early months of the 1993–94 season and with Webster having turned professional, Perego's place in the Welsh side went to his club-mate, Lyn Jones for the autumn internationals. He had suffered with hamstring and neck injuries, the legacies of his uncompromising tackling and mauling. However, when Mark was persuaded to rejoin the Welsh squad for its preparations for the 1994 Five Nations, he showed that he was still the fittest and strongest player in Wales, surprising many by cruising home ahead of the entire squad in a 3 kilometre training run just a week ahead of the opening match of the championship. He was promptly recalled to play a full season of Five Nations rugby and it was perhaps no coincidence that the year turned into Wales's most successful in over a decade, only a defeat in the final match of the campaign at Twickenham denying Wales the Grand Slam. It was their first outright championship title for 15 long years. Critics often talk about flankers who are first to the breakdown. Mark Perego was the flankers' flanker who invariably was the cause of the breakdown: the man whose all-enveloping tackle broke down the designs of opposing teams in the 1994 Five Nations.

He was 30 then and with the game on the brink of becoming fully professional he once again faded into the background. After taking part in Wales's World Cup qualifying match against Spain in May 1994, he did not play again, for club or country, walking out on Llanelli saying he had lost his enthusiasm for playing rugby at any level. He was persuaded to make one appearance in late October and played for the club against the touring Springboks, but there was to be no Wales recall – not that he expected or even wanted one – and the man who said that he preferred to be judged by how he performed on the field faded from the first-class scene.

For his style on and off the field Mark Perego was half Tarzan, half Action Man, but he will be remembered as an international player who did not conform – arguably the last of the breed for whom top-class rugby was a game to be enjoyed as a relaxation and not viewed as a way of life.

CLEM THOMAS
Carpe Diem

Those born with common surnames in Wales have often needed as many as three Christian names to distinguish them from the crowds of Davieses, Thomases and Williamses who overrun the principality's telephone directories. Rugby football, for example, has had its W.J.A. Davies, J.B.G. Thomas and J.P.R. Williams, men whose initials alone uniquely identified them to the game's followers. The parents of Richard Clement Charles Thomas, however, need never have worried about their son's need for three initials. He was to become a household name through-out the rugby world as a player, journalist and broadcaster simply as Clem.

Born in Cardiff on 28 January 1928, Clem Thomas was raised on a farm in Brynamman and always regarded himself as a Swansea 'jack'. His father was in the wholesale meat trade and the fruits of the land gave Clem an early taste for business. He was never one to hold back, either closing down an opponent on the rugby field or seizing an opportunity to make a fast buck. As a teenager he sold farm produce to GIs stationed in the Swansea area in the war-torn summers of the early 1940s. Then, in the autumn, when term began at Blundell's School in Tiverton, Devon, the profits of Clem's hard work satisfying American cravings for wholesome food were shared among his schoolmates. The traits of the boy were to become the hallmark of the man, for throughout his life he was gregarious, generous to his friends and acquaintances, and boyish in his enthusiasm for his many interests.

His rugby career blossomed at Blundell's, where he became the first schoolboy educated in England to captain the Welsh Secondary Schools. He led the side in France in 1947 when future Welsh fly-half Carwyn James, who was later to become a senior team-mate and press-box colleague, was in the side. The young Clem instantaneously fell in love with the French way of life, especially their food and style of rugby, and had he later chosen to live there he would undoubtedly have been warmly welcomed. As it was, he went up to Cambridge University soon after the end of the war and won his first senior Welsh cap, also against France, in Paris in 1949 before he had even won his Blue.

As a flanker he brought weight and presence to the open side, but Wales were beaten, left holding the wooden spoon and Clem had to wait another three seasons before returning to national colours. His vitality and drive stood out for Swansea in their fixture against the Fourth Springboks in 1951–52 and his performance that day alerted the Welsh selectors to his maturity. He was recalled in March for the Triple Crown game in Dublin, where his impetus in the loose and tight marking of Dr Jack Kyle were valuable assets to a side that carried off a famous 14–3 win to nail the championship. He scored one of Wales's tries and made another that day, and kept his place for the Grand Slam clincher with France on his Swansea home ground at St Helen's a fortnight later. His ability to bottle up opposing fly-halves at the highest level and the steely, uncompromising way he managed to obstruct opponents when minding his own fly-half, Cliff Morgan, made him an automatic choice thereafter and he went on to gain 26 caps.

Against the All Blacks in 1953 his inspirational cross-kick, when hemmed in on the touchline, brought Wales their most famous win of the 1950s and guaranteed him a place among the legends of Welsh rugby. The scores were deadlocked at 8-all when Clem, finding himself isolated, grasped the situation in an instant. He reacted instinctively and dropped his kick with precision into the fast track of Newport's Ken Jones out on the right wing. Jones darted inside the New Zealand defence for the winning try. A story emerged after the match questioning whether Clem had actually seized the day for Wales or had simply acted on instructions from the wily Welsh touch-judge, Ifor Jones, who claimed that he had shouted the advice to kick wide. Clem's friends felt the story couldn't possibly be true. He would never have obeyed anyone! Indeed, years later his friend Geoffrey Nicholson of the *Observer* told the tale of how Clem once parked on a double yellow line on the busy Queensway roundabout in Swansea. A local policeman stepped forward to book the driver when, realising who it was, reputedly said: 'Oh, it's you Clem. Don't be too long, please – I'll keep an eye on the car for you.' It typified the standing he held in his own community, even when he was stretching the law.

His finest hour on the rugby field, he always contended, was touring South Africa with the 1955 Lions. Never one to overlook an opportunity – *carpe diem* might well have been his motto for life – he recovered from appendicitis early on that visit to force his way into the back row for the important third Test of that summer. He was magnificent in an important Lions' victory, proving a scourge to the Springbok backs as a rampaging destroyer of attacks. The tourists won 9–6, putting them 2–1 up with one match to play. The rubber was eventually split 2–2, but had Clem been available for the earlier Tests the Lions might well have won that series.

His great playing adversary was Peter Robbins, the English open-side of the 1950s, and through their shared interests in rugby, journalism and French cuisine they became bosom pals. It was Robbins who used to introduce him as 'Thomas the butcher – the only man who practises his trade on the rugby field'. Clem loved that, reacting in character with a wicked chuckle that hinted at the possibility that Robbins' comment contained more than a grain of truth. He always admitted to enjoying the edgy stuff but usually knew where to draw the line between hard, vigorous play and gratuitous violence.

Once, though, he did overstep the mark. In 1957, in the early days of live televised international rugby in Wales, he was captured on camera swinging a haymaker at the England winger, Peter Thompson. The selectors omitted him for the rest of the season but finally recalled him in 1958 to lead Wales in nine consecutive Tests before he retired. Fittingly, his final Test was against his favourites, the French. Although his team were beaten, he was pleased that the match sealed the first ever outright Five Nations' title for his Gallic friends. There was no better man to congratulate and share in their achievement than Clem, for few players of any generation ever mixed so amiably and formed so many lasting friendships among opponents.

In 1960, he became the Welsh Rugby correspondent of the *Observer*, where his sport editor was Chris Brasher, an old friend from Cambridge days. Clem was as successful as a forthright writer on rugby as he had been as a player. Never one to sit on fences, he was outspoken, particularly against the game's establishment if he perceived injustice or plain stupidity, fair in his criticism of players and always in tune with a sport that developed rapidly in the 1980s and 1990s. The contacts he had made in his playing days stood him in good stead journalistically. He was never short of a good story and constantly in demand to contribute worldwide. Indeed, on the morning of his sudden death at home in Swansea on 5 September 1996 he was revising proofs of his classic history of the Lions and, very much in harness, had just completed a radio broadcast for BBC Wales on the state of the game in the principality. To him journalism and broadcasting, like his business interests encompassing the meat trade, wine bars and publishing, were seen as a sport; a constant competition to survive on his wits and exploit openings that funded his wonderful capacity to enjoy life to the full. For all that, though, he was also generous to young journalists, often sacrificing some of his own opportunities to advance the careers of friends and former players anxious to break into the rugby media.

Throughout his life Clem retained a distinctive accent, whether speaking in English or Welsh, a combination of rural west Wales with a faint English public school intonation. His ability to speak French fluently extended his capacity to engage with people from all walks of life, from princes to players, young or old. Even Prince Albert of Monaco was a guest at the Swansea family home when Clem's son, Mark, was the brakesman in the Prince's Winter Olympic bobsleigh team.

Celebrities from all over the United Kingdom were among the 600 mourners who attended his funeral. Clem's circle of friends had a large radius and featured pop stars, politicians (he had stood as a Liberal candidate in west Wales) and players, but it was Tony O'Reilly, his fellow Lion of '55 and frequent Irish adversary in the Five Nations, who perfectly summed up the feelings of many when he wrote: 'I will treasure him in my box of memories as will so many more. They don't come better.'

RICHARD COCKERILL
Incredible Journey

The man with the biggest smile on his face in English domestic rugby in May 2009 was the former Leicester and England hooker, Richard Cockerill – Cockers to his Tigers friends. He served a stormy apprenticeship as a player, gaining the reputation for being the loose cannon who was discarded from Sir Clive Woodward's England squad after making unwise comments about the manager in an autobiography that some called the longest suicide note in rugby history. Later, he turned his hand to coaching, starting out as a no-nonsense assistant working wonders with the forwards at his former club. Then, when he unexpectedly picked up the reins as head coach in the New Year of 2009, in the space of five months he fired Leicester to an English premiership title and runners-up in the Heineken European Cup.

Born in Rugby on 16 December 1970, Richard Cockerill took to the hard graft of the front row of the scrum like a duck to water. He was put there because 'I was short and fat' but he fell in love with the combative side of pack play as a youngster when he was training for a career in the antiques restoration business. His rugby calling came while watching the Welsh and English packs make an explosive start to the X-certificate-rated Five Nations match of 1987. The teenager was instantly hooked on the sport's physical aspects – not, perhaps, the induction that the game's authorities would wish for an impressionable young recruit – but he developed rapidly with the Warwickshire village club, Newbold-on-Avon, before joining Leicester from Coventry in 1992.

One of those players who enjoyed jabbering his way through a game and winding up the opposition, he knuckled down to training with zestful exuberance. Leicester's forward workouts were notorious for their violence. If there was plenty of claret spilt on the mid-week training ground and the needles were worn out applying stitches in the changing rooms, the Tigers' management was happy that all would go well in the competitive matches at weekends. After one particular dust-up before the 1997 Heineken European Cup Final it was reported that Dean Richards was so incensed that he chased Cockers around the ground. Not surprisingly, the belligerence he showed to crowds and opponents earned him notoriety. Indeed, there were times in his career before senior Test honours came his way he was not on speaking terms with two of England's best hookers, Brian Moore and Mark Regan.

Even so, Cockers modified the 'Jack-the-Lad' image and quickly established himself as a fearless competitor who could look after himself squaring up in the tight, while his mobility and good hands made him a storm of energy in the loose. One contemporary, complimenting him on his versatility, described Cockers as having the potential to be an international flanker. But at 5ft 10in, and despite Neil Back showing that a good little 'un could be as good as a six-footer in the back row, Leicester were never likely to field two pocket battleships at the back of their line-out. Anyway, Cockers always regarded himself first and foremost as a hooker, and it was in that position that his consistent all-round performances in a very successful Leicester side brought him to the attention of Jack Rowell during his stewardship of the England team.

Cockers was promoted to the England squad that visited Argentina in the summer of 1997 while the senior England players were touring South Africa with the Lions, and came off the bench to win his first cap in the opening Test in Buenos Aires. He started in the second Test, but when England's returning Lions became available for the one-off international celebrating the centenary of Test rugby in Australia, he was overlooked. Jack Rowell stood down after that match and when Sir Clive Woodward became the new head coach for the autumn internationals, Cockers was promptly installed in an experimental squad for a demanding run of home matches against Australia, New Zealand (twice) and South Africa.

He immediately impressed, showing that he was up for any challenge, particularly when England faced the All Blacks for the first time at Old Trafford. The new coach had urged his team to 'find your opponent and stand opposite him' during the pre-match *haka*. So Lawrence Dallaglio and his team stood shoulder to shoulder in a line to await the traditional New Zealand challenge, but Cockers, shaven-headed and eyes popping, responded by interpreting the face-up challenge as an invitation to get in his opponent's face. Norm Hewitt was the All Blacks' hooker and happened to be leading the *haka*. As the war-cry progressed, he and Cockers edged closer and closer to each other until eventually they stood snarling eyeball to eyeball at one another, 55,000 spectators and 28 players on the field all focusing on the pair as the confrontation developed. The hookers were clearly very fired up and referee Peter Marshall from Australia made a token gesture at trying to get the hookers to back off. The *haka* ended, bringing the confrontation to a temporary close, but the sight of the England hooker aggressively fronting up to the traditional challenge had the All Blacks and the crowd at fever-pitch even before the match had started.

Even his England colleagues were surprised by his antics. Martin

Johnson, his Leicester clubmate, walked past him as the England team retreated to receive the kick-off and muttered under his breath: 'Cocker, what have you done?' And Will Greenwood, another Tigers team-mate who was then a rookie in the England set-up, later wrote of the incident: 'If you want proof that backs and forwards come from a different planet, you need look no further than this little episode.' That was Cockers. Instinctive, courageous and a bit of a nutter. But there was no doubting his commitment and it cemented his place as England's automatic choice as hooker through to the 1999 Rugby World Cup.

If his sense of direction when it came to challenging the *haka* was questionable, he had no such problems beating a path to opponents' goal lines, scoring three tries in the 27 Tests he played between 1997 and 1999. One of those tries came against the All Blacks in 1998 on England's tour of the Tri Nations. England were demolished by New Zealand but Cockers and Norm Hewitt did not actually have to face up to each other that day, Hewitt warming the bench while Anton Oliver was the New Zealand hooker. That didn't stop the old enemies from continuing their confrontations off the field in a late-night dust-up in Dunedin, an incident that Cockers later described as a 'bit of fun . . . horseplay'. The tour itself was a disaster for England. An inexperienced team was thoroughly overwhelmed four times in as many weeks, but for his defiance and bravery under fire he emerged as one of the successes, proving himself in difficult circumstances.

His form dipped inexplicably during the 1999 World Cup. It was a great disappointment for him to be demoted to the bench for the quarter-final against South Africa in Paris, where Phil Greening was given the vote as hooker, and his poor form resulted in his losing his place in the Leicester squad to Dorian West. Shortly afterwards, his autobiography was published. It was a typical Cockers effort, straight from the gut and hard-hitting. He took swipes at the press, the England management and the Leicester club. Everyone, it seemed, was in his firing line, and there were repercussions.

Most serious of all was that he was omitted from the England squad and never again played Test rugby. But he didn't apologise; he never backed down in his play or his actions. Only two of

Cockers' England caps had been won before Sir Clive Woodward's tenure began, but look through *Winning*, the coach's inside story of how England flourished between 1997 and 2003, and there is no mention of the Leicester hooker in the text. Search the index and there is no reference to him. Ironically, where the reader would expect to find Cockerill listed there is an entry for 'code of conduct' – the key to Cockers' fate. For as part of the squad's teamship rules set out in their so-called Black Book, members had promised that no one – management, back-up team or players – should be adversely criticised by another member of the squad through the media. Cockers had committed the cardinal sin and it cost him his Test career. Years later, with the benefit of hindsight, he saw the error of his ways and admitted that he wouldn't be too pleased to read criticisms of his own coaching style.

Although his Test career was over, he did regain his form at Leicester as the middle man of the famous A-B-C club in the front row with Graham Rowntree and Darren Garforth when the Tigers used to wear letters instead of numbers. Yet for all the success he enjoyed at Welford Road, the feeling was that Richard Cockerill was a case of talent gone to waste. All the graft and bravery were still there but representative rugby was a wilderness to him.

In 2002, he departed for France, signing to play with Montferrand and settling with his young family in a village to the south of the city. He relished the heavy-duty scrummaging that is part and parcel of the French Championship and enjoyed every minute of matches against former British and Irish hookers when his club faced them in European ties. He reckoned the two years spent in France rounded him as a person, broadened his horizons and completed his rugby education. He returned to Leicester in 2004 to begin a coaching career as a junior in the Tigers' management team. Starting as assistant forwards' coach, he was acting head coach in 2007 before Marcelo Loffreda was able to take up the full-time appointment, and he filled the same role a year later when Heyneke Meyer had to return unexpectedly to South Africa. Then in April 2009 he was officially named as permanent head coach at the club where he had made 229 first-team appearances and where Sir Clive Woodward now sits on the board of directors. One month later, his strong work ethic and determination to succeed brought immediate rewards in the form of the Guinness Premiership title. Now, wiser and more mellow as his incredible journey turns a new corner, it will be interesting to see how the next stage of his rugby career evolves. Richard Cockerill, your moment has come.

REACHERS AND ACHIEVERS

COLIN MEADS
Pinetree

New Zealand's Colin Meads was the biggest name in world rugby in the late 1950s and throughout the 1960s. The very mention of the All Black forward sent shivers down the spines of opponents, who were in awe of the toughness, skills and bravery of an unassuming giant who, for his hardness and implacability, was appropriately known as the 'Pinetree'. The veteran South African journalist, Fred Labuschagne, described him as 'a muscular superman who terrorises the rugby world', adding that even Boris Karloff would run for cover were he to meet Meads in the heat of rugby battle. Even today, nearly 40 years after he retired with a then world-record haul of 55 Test caps, the Pinetree commands the undying affection of the rugby-mad population of New Zealand. A recent unofficial poll which drew on the experiences and knowledge of a highly regarded mix of New Zealand journalists, ex-All Black captains and respected historians totalling more than 200 years' first-hand knowledge of the rugby scene ranked Meads as the greatest All Black of all time. Quite simply, Meads was, and still is, a rugby legend. A great achiever.

Born on 3 June 1936, in Cambridge, New Zealand, he put his physical strength down to the demanding outdoor life of his hillside stock farm at Waitete in the King Country. Images of him trudging across the land with sheep tucked carefully under each arm fuelled the legends about his tremendous strength. And a parade of the world's leading lock forwards who played against him, including Rhys Williams and Brian Thomas of Wales, Johannes Claassen and Frik du Preez of South Africa and Willie John McBride of Ireland, could testify to the huge upper-body strength Meads exercised in rucks. His arms were longer than average, enabling him to apply a more effective torque on the ball when wrenching it from opponents in the mauls, and his hands were the size of shovels. He was a fearsome figure on the hoof, and in his younger days his speed around the field meant that several of his early Tests were as a flanker or Number 8. When he ran with the ball, invariably held in one hand the size of a dustbin lid, it resembled a peanut in a giant's palm.

At 6ft 4in and weighing 16 stone, he was a big forward for his time and naturally dominated at the line-out. When he pitched up for his first New Zealand trial, in 1956, his winger, Ron Jarden, asked him how he wanted the ball at the line-out. (Wingers used to throw in in those days.) The big, raw recruit was lost for words: he couldn't appreciate that anyone could throw the ball accurately enough to pinpoint a player. Such niceties had never previously bothered him: he was used to winning the ball in most free-for-alls.

Inevitably the buffetings that went with his work as a lock demanded aggression; he certainly knew how to look after himself and was an intimidating presence to opponents. Even the toughest of opponents, however, had the utmost respect for him. When Brian Thomas, the hard man of Welsh rugby, toured New Zealand for a series against the All Blacks in 1969, he was asked by a journalist if he had come to sort out Colin Meads. Thomas reputedly replied: 'Certainly not. I intend to die in my native Wales.' The Welsh flanker John Taylor was also on that tour and tells a story about hooker Jeff Young, who had his jaw broken by a punch thrown by Meads in retaliation at having his shirt tugged. Young was admitted to hospital to have his jaw wired up and while there told his team-mate that the New Zealander had warned him that he'd thump him if he continued to hold his jersey. Taylor asked Young if he had replied. 'Yes, I said bugger off – the trouble is I didn't say it very loudly,' the hooker said.

It's true that Pinetree was no saint and at Murrayfield on the

1967 All Blacks' tour he became only the second player in Test history to be sent off. There were no red or yellow cards in those days, but he had been warned by referee Kevin Kelleher earlier in the match for foul play when trampling on a Scot who was lying on the wrong side of a ruck. Cleaning out players in the path of the ball as it was recycled was part and parcel of rugby in New Zealand and Meads was an acknowledged expert at this aspect of the game. Then, three minutes from the end, he was caught aiming a kick at the ball when it was about to be gathered by Scotland's fly-half, Dave Chisholm. The incident looked reckless, as if the kick was aimed at the player. At least, that is how the referee viewed it and he sent the New Zealander to the changing room for dangerous play. Meads took his punishment and was suspended for the next two matches, but many felt that he had been unjustly punished simply for playing the game in what was acknowledged to be the uncompromising All Black way.

On another occasion his enthusiasm for removing bodies on the wrong side of a ruck led to controversy in Australia. In 1968 he dragged the Wallaby captain Ken Catchpole from a ruck with such force that he inflicted such a severe groin injury that the Australian had to prematurely end his brilliant rugby career. But Meads could also take the tough stuff when he was sinned against on the field. When his head was lacerated by a French boot in the 1967 Test in Paris he played on, heavily bandaged. And when his arm was broken by a kick during an early tour match in South Africa in 1970 he again played on. He sat out five weeks of the visit patiently waiting for the injury to set and heal before resuming and playing nine of the last 10 tour games, including two Tests, in a specially designed armguard. Arguably no man ever bore such a high pain threshold.

Pinetree's presence in a team invariably added 5,000 to the gate and was said to be worth a six-point start to the All Blacks. Indeed, at his peak in the late 1960s he was the workhorse at the heart of a side that set a world record by winning 17 Tests on the trot. He would do anything for the team. He set high standards of physical fitness on tours and also relished the social side of touring, enjoying nothing better than a beer with friend or foe, pint mug looking like a thimble cupped in his huge hands. He was always a good tourist.

Colin Meads retired from international rugby in 1971 after leading New Zealand in their series against the Lions and played his last provincial game in 1972, when it became known that the projected South African tour of New Zealand for the year after would be cancelled for political reasons. Without the Springboks, he said, there was no incentive to continue playing. Apart from 55 Tests, 14 of which he played in the engine-room in partnership with his brother Stan, he played 133 games for the All Blacks, a national record that is unlikely to be surpassed in the near future. He was, moreover, an automatic choice for the World XVs that were invited to landmark celebrations staged by the South African Rugby Board (1964) and the Rugby Football Union (1971).

Below Test level, he fondly remembered leading his province to their famous 12–6 victory against the 1966 Lions in Wanganui. It took him more than 15 minutes to reach the dressing-room after the final whistle had blown. Meads, a modest man, respectfully signed autographs for hundreds of youngsters and shook hands with wellwishers from all over King Country before reaching the dressing-rooms. He continued to serve his native province as coach and selector, and from 1992 to 1996 served on the New Zealand Rugby Football Union council. For his great rugby achievements, he is looked up to as probably the greatest living New Zealander and certainly the greatest All Black of them all.

PETER STAGG
Reticent Giant

Big Peter Stagg provided rugby players, journalists and followers of the game with the greatest mystery of the 1960s: exactly how tall was the man mountain who stood head and shoulders above every other lock forward of his generation? The noise a man generates is usually inversely proportional to his size. That was certainly true of

Stagg because he was extremely reticent about his height. When he went up from St Paul's School to St Peter's College, Oxford, in the early 1960s he admitted to 6ft 7½in when he won his Blue in 1961, but even then many who played against him suspected that he was even taller. The biggest man who had played international rugby up to that time was England's David Marques, who was around 6ft 5in, so the intake of breath that Stagg caused among spectators when he first arrived on the first-class rugby scene was like the effect Bob Beamon had when he broke the world's long-jump record at the altitude-assisted 1968 Mexico Olympics.

At Oxford he was long remembered for his size and exceptional feats. His impressive standing jumps were talked about by college scouts at St Peter's long after he graduated and his party trick on the rugby pitch was to stand beneath a goalpost before jumping to clap his hands together above the crossbar. But he always remained guarded on the subject of his real height. He passed the six-foot mark as a boy and reckoned that he stopped growing when he was about 23. But he never made a point of measuring his increasing height against the wall at home; he just made sure that he remembered to duck when he walked through the door.

When he entered the Scotland team in 1965 his team-mate Brian Henderson was assigned the task of measuring him for the press release to the media, and it was said that he was the only man who knew Staggy's true height for he was sworn to keep the true result a national secret. The programme for his first match, against France in Paris, showed his height as 202cm – the first two-metre player to appear in an international – and caused eyes to pop out of the heads of French fans. One French journalist was reported as referring to him as '*L'interminable Stagg*' in the press box.

Peter Stagg was born on 22 November 1941 a stone's throw from Twickenham rugby ground and attended Colet Court prep school, where he played as a hooker before going on to St Paul's. He always said that the biggest influence on his rugby career was his captain during his Oxford days, John Willcox, the England full-back. Stagg came on literally in leaps and bounds under Willcox's coaching methods and soon developed into an outstanding line-out lock. After Oxford, where he read chemistry, he went to work for

ICI in Manchester and played his club rugby with Sale, turning out in the County Championship for Cheshire.

Through his father's ancestry he attracted the attentions of the Scottish selectors. They had first noted his potential during a Scotland team practice at St Paul's School before a Twickenham Calcutta Cup match several years earlier. His size, of course, meant that he was a natural target for barging, holding and pulling – any kind of obstruction or interference that reduced the height advantage. When he first played he was something of a stripling, weighing in at between 14 and 15 stone. But he dealt with the various buffetings he received in his own quiet way, never one to moan or retaliate unfairly when he was tipped over or chopped at a line-out, though he did once confide to a journalist that he wished for higher standards of refereeing. He just got on with his game and his best line-out work was seen when the ball was thrown high so that it dropped slightly as he reached the top of his jump. His sheer size made him a most difficult forward to play against.

He was a laid-back giant and team-mates warmed to his dry sense of humour. There is a story that he arrived in the changing rooms at Cardiff for the 1970 Wales–Scotland Five Nations match and, unravelling his playing kit, discovered that his navy blue Scotland socks had several large holes in them – badges, maybe, of his courage in a difficult and close-fought struggle with France at Murrayfield four weeks earlier when he stood out like the Eiffel Tower. The Scottish Union in those days expected their players to keep their socks from match to match, so when Stagg not unreasonably asked for a new pair he was given short shrift by a Union official. There was no argument from Stagg, who quickly turned his mind to solving his sartorial problem. He quietly returned to his peg in the changing room, saw his neighbour cleaning his boots and politely asked to borrow the polish. Then he proceeded to black his bare shins and calves before putting on his socks – problem solved.

Stagg was a first choice for Scotland for five years, only missing out when nursing shoulder injuries. To minimise obstruction the Scots wisely employed the four-man line-out to get the best out of him in their international matches, and when he was on the field

Scotland invariably dominated possession. The last of his 28 caps for Scotland came in the summer of 1970 when he toured Australia with Scotland. By now he had bulked up considerably, so much so that his 18-stone-plus mass was thought to disturb the balance of the Scottish scrum when he packed in the second row. That eventually cost him his international place. Even so, the Australian press were obsessed by Stagg's height and couldn't resist publishing a photograph of him standing beside the smallest player on the Scottish side, that man of many rugby parts, Ian Robertson. The moustachioed Stagg dwarfs the diminutive fly-half, whose nose is at Stagg's elbow level in the picture of the pair taken at the Sydney Cricket Ground on the eve of the Test.

The final word on the most endearing rugby mystery of the day came from the late John Reason, the *Daily Telegraph*'s forthright rugby correspondent who had a tenacious character and a good nose for a story. Stagg was a member of the 1968 British/Irish Lions' tour party that visited South Africa, where his biggest problem was finding hotel beds tailored to his size. He played 11 games on the tour, including three of the Test matches where his height published in tour guides and programmes was alleged to be 6ft 10in. The player himself claimed that he had no idea where that figure had come from, evading constant enquiries from nosy journalists. Finally, Reason provided the answer. He found Stagg asleep in the sun outside the tourists' seaside hotel one afternoon and surreptitiously drew two lines in the sand, effectively topping and tailing his man. After Stagg had moved on and before the tide came in Reason went back out and measured the marks, They were 6ft 9in apart, making Peter Stagg at least five per cent taller than any of his international contemporaries.

Only Martin Bayfield (at 6ft 10in) and Richard Metcalfe (just over 7ft) have 'outgrown' Stagg on the international scene in the 40 years since, but because they played with forwards who themselves were relatively closer to their heights in percentage terms they never seemed to quite dominate the line-out to the same extent as Stagg.

BILL MULCAHY
Unsung Hero

One of the most honest line-out jumpers and toilers in Irish packs of the late 1950s and early 1960s was Bill Mulcahy – 'Wigs' to his colleagues. Never a spectacular or flashy forward, he nevertheless played with a reasonable consistency of sound judgement to become the most admired of tight forwards in the era between Karl Mullen and Ray McLoughlin when chaos theory ruled Irish rugby.

Mulcahy was an inspirational player. He was a solid, hard-working forward and a sturdy scrummager. At the line-out, either as jumper or supporter, he worked with tireless enthusiasm. He revelled in the carefree days of the old amateur game, when a rugby coach was nothing more sophisticated than the transport that took teams to their matches. He operated in the days when wingers threw the ball into the line-out and Tony O'Reilly, as Ireland's winger, was well-acquainted with the terse instructions for line-out calls. 'OK Riley,' he reported Mulcahy as saying. 'Let's have it the usual way. Low and crooked.'

Bill Mulcahy was born on 7 January 1935 in Rathkeale near Limerick and while attending St Munchin's College played his first club rugby with the Newcastle West RFC as a 16-year-old. His first experience of senior rugby was in the Limerick Bohemians side. Modest, calm and dependable, he quickly acquired a reputation as one of those players whose achievements are greater than their promise. He was an intelligent student, too, going up to University College Dublin to study medicine and later becoming medical officer to the Aer Lingus airline company based at Dublin Airport. He quickly became the mainstay of the college's pack and representative honours soon followed when, in the autumn of 1955, he began his 16-years' service as a lock in the Leinster inter-provincial side. His resolute performances for UCD, his Dublin club Bective Rangers and Leinster impressed the Irish selectors and in 1958, alongside several others who would become fixtures on the Irish side, he gained his first cap in Ireland's 9–6 defeat of the touring Wallabies. He became a stalwart of the team and after a series of shining displays in the 1959 championship went with the Lions to Australia and New Zealand.

Injury curtailed his appearances Down Under. He had started the visit in a blaze of glory in Australia, where he was singled out as the Lions' outstanding forward in the early games. He partnered big Rhys Williams in the first Test in Brisbane, but a couple of days later, in a mid-week match at Tamworth against the New South Wales Country XV, he was tipped over at a line-out near the end of the game. He fell and tore the muscles in his shoulder so severely that the injury sidelined him for six weeks. Still, every cloud has its silver lining and the medical student put his unexpected rest time to good use, swotting up his injury and other medical matters for his forthcoming degree examinations. The attitude he subsequently showed in resuming light training was an inspiration to the rest of the tour party. He overcame the injury with a steely determination to win back his Test place and by the end of the tour he had proved himself to be of such nuisance value to the Lions that he returned for the final international at Auckland. There, he showed that he could jump and catch as well as provide protection for his second-row partner. His unfussy contribution was a telling factor in the Lions' 9–6 win.

Three years later, by which time he had become a popular choice as captain of his country, he was an automatic choice for the Lions' tour of South Africa. As first-choice lock, his experience was invaluable to a side that struggled to keep parity with a much-vaunted South African pack in the Tests. Tellingly, the South African critics assessed him as the equal of any Springbok forward – praise indeed. Like many an Irish forward of the amateur era, the day-to-day round of fitness training and set-piece practice that were features of touring improved his fitness. Certainly he brought a very professional attitude to his approach to touring and commentators felt that the best of Wigs Mulcahy was seen as a Lion.

With him on the 1962 Lions' tour was a young Willie John McBride, who had made his Irish debut earlier the same year partnering Mulcahy, one of his boyhood heroes, in the second row. Even Willie John, however, admitted to being underwhelmed by Wigs's approach to captaincy. Ireland had lost their earlier championship games to England and Scotland when Mulcahy rose to address his troops in the changing rooms at Stade Colombes before the French match that year. McBride was filled with expectation as he prepared to listen to his captain speak. 'Any ideas how to beat this lot?' Mulcahy asked almost desperately. McBride's expectation turned to confusion and then to total bemusement when the team's senior player, a back-row veteran, said: 'I suggest that we spend the next 80 minutes kicking the s*** out of them.' This remark was followed by a long silence until Mulcahy stood up and thumped his chest saying, 'Bejaysus! We have a plan, men' and led his side out.

Ireland lost with honour (11–0) against a French side that retained the Five Nations' title that day. Even so, Mulcahy felt justifiably satisfied with the team's performance when he travelled into Paris and prepared to make the customary captain's speech at the top table for what he thought was the traditional post-match banquet. Wine flowed freely and Mulcahy quietly enjoyed himself awaiting the arrival of his colleagues. It was only after returning to the reception after a comfort break that he realised that he had become totally confused with his directions and was, in fact, attending a wedding.

All told, he won 35 caps for his country and captained Ireland 11 times between 1962 and 1964, leading them in the epic match at Twickenham when victory was Ireland's reward for the first time in 16 years on English soil. He retired from international rugby the following year, having handed the captaincy on to Ray McLoughlin for the 1965 Five Nations. In his last international match, in April 1965 at Lansdowne Road, he enjoyed the satisfaction of avenging the series defeat he had suffered playing for the Lions by taking part in Ireland's first ever defeat of the Springboks. The Ireland career of one of its unsung heroes thus ended as it had begun: with a win against a major tour side. After his playing days were over he devoted his leisure time to the Skerries club in Dublin and took pride in seeing the team develop from a junior outfit into a respected force. There he worked tirelessly as an unsung coach and administrator whose prime motivation for rugby was the fun and fellowship that the game engenders.

WAVELL WAKEFIELD
Wakers

Wavell Wakefield was the dominant personality of English rugby during its golden era in the early 1920s. Although a forward of immense strength and all-round ability, it was his intellectual and physical energy allied to a strong personality that made him stand out as rugby's most innovative and natural leader of his day. His legacy was that he changed the shape of British forward play; he was the father of the modern game. Nicknamed 'Wakers', in keeping with the time and his public school background, his clear, booming tones were to be prominent in English rugby's corridors of power for more than 50 years, first as a player, later as an administrator and ultimately as president of the RFU. 'Off to rugger for sippers of champers with Wakers at Twickers' was the clarion call to England's ruling classes on international days. There might have been a touch of irony to the catchphrase, but its reference to Wakefield was a mark of respect to his standing in the game.

William Wavell Wakefield was born into a Quaker family at Beckenham, Kent, on 10 March 1898 and educated at Sedbergh School and Cranwell, where he learnt to fly. Schooldays in the Lake District inspired a love of outdoor pursuits that were fuelled by unbounded enthusiasm and gave him an exceptional zest for life that remained the striking aspect of his personality into retirement. He served with the Royal Naval Air Service during the Great War, later transferring to the Royal Flying Corps (forerunner of the RAF), where he demonstrated his intellectual and practical abilities. When they were wrestling with the problem of landing an aircraft on HMS *Vindictive* while at sea, it was Wakefield who derived the appropriate calculations to side-slip a biplane on to the deck. Having checked his relative velocity calculations, he practised his theory successfully up at Scapa, heralding the age of the aircraft carrier.

When organised rugby resumed after the armistice, he joined Harlequins and became a prominent member of the England pack. Wakers was an ever-present in a side that lost only five Five Nations matches in the first seven postwar seasons. He was a skilful line-out jumper and a brilliant dribbler – a key skill in the 1920s when forwards perfected a method of attack by wheeling the scrum and breaking away with the ball at their feet. But it was his tremendous pace, which brought him six Test tries, that marked him out as an exceptional forward. The caricaturists of the day always showed him scrumcapped, body thrust forward at an impossible angle with his shoulders hunched. He had once been pushed in the back while racing with the ball in a school match and to maintain his balance realised that leaning forward increased his speed. In his England days, nothing could be more certain to raise a roar from a Twickenham crowd than the sight of Wakefield emerging with the ball from a maul, careering headlong for the line like a runaway train. As a sprinter he was around the 'evens' mark (in the days of imperial units, this meant that a sprinter could run 100 yards in 10 seconds) and while at Cambridge, where he had arrived on an RAF scholarship in 1921, he gave the future Olympic gold medallist, Harold Abrahams, a run for his money in the final of the 100 yards at the university sports.

It was the ability to think about his rugby that underpinned England's Grand Slam wins of the 1920s. He brought his analytical mind to the mechanics of forward play at a time when 'first up, first down' was the scrummaging norm in Britain. This simply meant that front rows of scrums were invariably formed by the first three forwards arriving at the scene. As England's pack leader in 1923, Wakefield set about developing fixed positions for his forwards at scrums, with specialist props, hookers, second rows and flankers performing their respective duties at the set piece. He felt that it was more efficient to specialise in this way and persuaded the England selectors to support his idea. The critics greeted the experiment with guarded praise after England opened their season with a narrow 7–3 win against Wales. But the way their forwards improved, and particularly the way the players adapted to their duties in the scrum, was impressive. 'The great strength of the team lay with the forwards,' wrote one critic after the Grand Slam was achieved against France in Paris on Easter Monday.

Several distinguished members of the England side retired after that match and Wakefield, now promoted captain, led a side that contained five new caps at Swansea in the opening game of England's 1924 campaign. The nucleus of the previous season's pack remained intact, however, and played methodically to provide a young back division with plenty of possession. In a new development, Wakefield encouraged his forwards to join in the open play and a lively brand of 15-man rugby evolved. Whereas the emphasis in the 1923 victories was limited to the pack, the entire class of '24 brimmed with the confidence of youth and ran in tries with sweeping movements all over the pitch. England crossed for 17 tries in winning a back-to-back Grand Slam. Sixteen were scored by their backs and the other Home Unions were so impressed that they, too, adopted Wakefield's plans, with the result that scrummaging began to resemble its modern format.

He led England for two more seasons before winning his 31st and final cap – an English Test record that stood until 1969 – in Paris in 1927. During his playing days he captained every side he played for – Sedbergh School, the RAF, Harlequins, Cambridge University, Leicester and England. Moreover, in 1930, three years after his last international appearance, he was invited to lead the British/Irish Lions to New Zealand and Australia, an offer he had to decline owing to his business commitments.

After retirement, Wakefield went on to make a valued contribution to the RFU as an outstanding administrator. He had been elected to the committee while still a player at the age of 23 and served on it for 40 years, becoming president in 1950–51 and representing the RFU on the International Board, rugby's ruling body.

There, his thoughts on the laws were influential in bringing about much-needed change to the shape of the game. His forthright views regarding the tackle area and the differential penalty were both subsequently incorporated into the rule book. One of his most interesting proposals was to make all penalty offences a straight kick at goal from the offending team's 22-metre line, no matter where on the field the infringement took place, thereby ensuring three points to the non-offending side. Rugby's closest approach to soccer's spot kick, however, has yet to take effect. Rugby football, he once wrote, 'should be predominantly a running and handling game, and the side that runs and best carries the ball should win'. The laws, he felt, did not promote such a view.

Throughout his long association with rugby he maintained an active interest in many other sports, most notably skiing and water-sports. In an incredibly crowded life he was also a successful businessman and even found time to enter Parliament as the member for Swindon in 1935. Later he represented Marleybone and was a Conservative MP continuously until 1963, when he was made the first Baron Wakefield of Kendal and became an active member of the House of Lords. In all his interests, as with his rugby, his achievements were outstanding.

Sir Carl Aarvold, whose England rugby career began soon after Wakefield's ended, became a close friend and never ceased to be amazed by his energy and enthusiastic commitment to many causes. One of Wakers's business interests was the Rediffusion Company – an enterprise that was to the early days of terrestrial television what cable is to today's satellite broadcasting. Returning together by train from an international match in Wales, Sir Carl asked him about the business. Wakers set out to explain. Aarvold spoke no other word, listening spellbound until two hours later the train pulled into Paddington, whereupon Wakers left him, saying, 'Sorry, must dash. I will tell you more about it when we next meet.'

Lord Wakefield died on 12 August 1983, aged 85, in Kendal. The former international and veteran critic, Vivian Jenkins, described him as 'the outstanding rugby personality, worldwide, of the 20th century. It will be a long time, if ever, before the game sees his like again.'

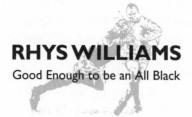

RHYS WILLIAMS
Good Enough to be an All Black

There is no new thing under the sun, according to the Good Book. While controversy rages worldwide over experimental law changes to the set-piece in rugby's good book, particularly relating to the maul, it is true to say that feelings ran just as high 55 years ago when radical alterations to the rules governing the line-out were first introduced. The result of the changes in 1954 was to nullify the effective technique of Neath's salmon-leaping line-out ace, Roy John, whose modus operandi depended for its success on the patterned blocking of his props and lock partners in the second row. When the International Rugby Board outlawed this so-called wedge method, a new breed of line-out expert who could hold his own in the absence of minders was sought.

Step forward Rhys Haydn Williams – or 'R.H.' as he was always affectionately known. Williams was the player who admirably succeeded Roy John as lock for Wales between 1954 and 1960. A beefy forward from Cwmllynfell who graduated with a science degree from Cardiff University, R.H. brought the systematic, intellectual approach of the research chemist to his tight-forward work. At the height of his career for Wales and the Lions, he was the master of all the forward arts: line-out catching, scrummaging and mauling, and even the ancient skill of dribbling. He was the real pack professor in Welsh rugby and, at a time when the line-out had a tendency to develop into a standing maul, his middle-of-the-line strength was priceless. It was said of him that when he hit a ruck or maul it moved – visibly. He would have been invaluable in today's first-class game.

Wales prospered after R.H. entered their side midway through the 1954 Five Nations campaign. He replaced Roy John and helped them to wins against Ireland, France and Scotland, Wales finishing the season joint champions with France and England. 'Rhys Williams added vigour to the Welsh eight,' noted one correspondent after the new lock had made his debut against Ireland in a match won through a last-minute drop-goal by his former Ystalyfera school chum and Llanelli club colleague, Denzil Thomas. By the end of the season, R.H. was being hailed as the find of the year in Wales. A newspaper pen-picture of him on the morning of the Scotland match at the St Helen's ground in April stated: 'Williams is one of the best of the younger school, expert in the loose and line-out play, and has helped improve Welsh scrummaging.' His versatility about the field that day confused the editor of the *Playfair Rugby Annual*. Admittedly there were four Williamses in the side that defeated Scotland in Swansea's last-ever Five Nations match, and two of them – Ray (a winger from Llanelli) and Billy (the Swansea prop) scored tries. But Owen L. Owen in his summary of the game for the *Annual* somehow managed to attribute the first Welsh try to big R.H. The player cleared matters up years later, emphasising with typical modesty that he had never managed to score a try for Wales in his 23 international appearances.

He was at the heart of his country's efforts again in 1955, another championship-sharing season, and his line-out prowess for the Lions in South Africa that year was a vital ingredient of the tourists' winning recipe in the third Test in Pretoria – that city's first ever international match. Through his expertise, the Lions won the decisive line-outs by a ratio of 2:1, giving Dickie Jeeps and Cliff Morgan, the halves, sufficient ball for them to exercise a tight tactical grip on the Test. Their forwards held their own in the scrums and line-outs, with Tom Reid and Williams continually prominent. The two forwards were at their fittest on that tour, though comparisons with the modern training regimes the Lions' parties follow when preparing for tours makes interesting reading. Big R.H. had 'trained' with bricks as improvised dumbbells when the Lions assembled at Eastbourne before leaving for the Cape.

In 1956, a fresh challenge to Welsh supremacy was launched by a new-look England pack that included the young second-row pairing of Oxbridge and Harlequins giants, John Currie and David Marques. R.H., showing no signs of fatigue after the long tour of

South Africa, stoked the engine-room of a Welsh pack that, despite struggling to hold its own against the coltish exuberance of the English, managed to set up a narrow 8–3 victory at Twickenham and went on to win the Five Nations title outright. Several barren seasons followed for Wales, but there were plenty of rugby honours still to be collected by R.H. He captained Llanelli and took them behind the Iron Curtain to play a trail-blazing game in Moscow.

He was greeted as a 'blood-brother' by the magnificent New Zealand pack against whom he toiled in 1959 on his second Lions' tour. The tourists played their best rugby in the final Test at Auckland to win 9–6, but it was thanks to the Welshman's all-round strength that they held their lead in the closing stages of the match. Williams played a vital part at a critical period in the second half by winning six line-outs in a row. The All Blacks rated him good enough to play for New Zealand and paid him the great compliment of inviting him to their farewell party for his famous second-row opponent, 'Tiny' Hill, who retired at the end of the series. The *New Zealand Rugby Almanac* for 1960 – New Zealand rugby's *Wisden* – named him as one of its five 'Players of the Year', the citation calling him 'the outstanding forward of the Lions' side. He had as much energy at the end of the tour after 17 appearances as he did at the start.'

After 10 successive Lions' Test appearances between 1955 and 1959 – a then record he came home from New Zealand and was named captain of Wales for the start of the 1960 Five Nations Championship. Wales, with a host of returning Lions, were expected to defeat an inexperienced England side at Twickenham. But sadly R.H., the fair-haired colossus who always played fair, found his side 0–14 down at half-time. He rallied his charges in the second half, but Wales could only manage two Terry Davies penalties before finally going down 6–14 – a whipping compared to the low-scoring norms of the day. He was dropped, never capped again and retired at the end of the season.

R.H. was born on 14 July 1930 at Cwmllynfell and made his Llanelli debut as a teenage student in 1949–50. Playing for Cardiff University against Pontyberem, he had impressed the former Llanelli and Wales forward Ossie Williams, who encouraged him to join the Scarlets. R.H., a proud Welshman and a proud Welsh-speaker, never looked back and relished the company of a side that was predominantly Welsh-speaking. In later years he disclosed that the achievement that gave him the greatest satisfaction as a Scarlet was leading the club to four victories over Swansea during his season as captain in 1957–58. Those from west Wales who remember the epic matches between these great rivals in the pre-Welsh Region days will know exactly what he meant.

Apart from his beloved Scarlets, he also had a soft spot for South African rugby and many of the landmarks in his notable playing career were to involve the Springboks. His first taste of the big time came in the autumn of 1951 when he turned out for his club against Basil Kenyon's tourists. Llanelli were beaten 20–11 but J.B.G. Thomas, in the *Western Mail*, had noted the young second-row's promise. 'In the Llanelly pack,' he wrote, 'R.H. Williams was always going well.' It was on the strength of his performance against the tourists that he was invited to play for the Whites (the junior side) in the first Welsh trial, but he couldn't oust Roy John, the established Welsh line-out jumper, from the side that was subsequently chosen to represent Wales against South Africa in December.

R.H. meanwhile had entered the RAF on National Service as an education officer after graduating from Cardiff University and it was for the Combined Services team that he again tasted representative rugby playing against the South Africans on Boxing Day at Twickenham. Further highlights of his career involved the 1955 Lions' trip there, where his reputation was confirmed, and a return visit with the Barbarians in the summer of 1958. He also toured Canada with the famous club in 1957 and later served as a Barbarians committee member and selector.

For many years he was a production superintendent with the Steel Company of Wales, but despite his strong roots in west Wales he moved to Cardiff in the early 1970s, returning to the education world to work as an education officer at County Hall. He later became assistant director of education for Mid Glamorgan before taking early retirement and spending part of his leisure time in the company of old rugby pals at Cardiff Athletic Club, regaling them with an unending stream of rugby stories told with humour and wit. He also put plenty back into the game he loved, serving the Welsh Rugby Union as an administrator for more than a dozen years. After cutting his committee teeth at Llanelli and then with junior clubs in Cardiff, he joined the WRU advisory coaching committee before being approached to stand as a national representative in 1975 when his former Wales second-row partner, Rees Stephens, stood down through ill-health.

A strong candidate, R.H. became a selector, managed the Wales B team that visited Spain in 1983 and later succeeded Keith Rowlands as chairman of the WRU's Big Five. But in 1989, a few years before the abolition of apartheid in South Africa, he resigned amid bitter controversy. He had been invited to take part in the centenary celebrations of the South African Rugby Board, but after telling his Union that he would not be going he finally accepted the invitation. As the junior vice-president of the Union he was in line to act as its president in 1991, but the recriminations that surrounded the fallout from his visit precipitated his resignation, depriving him of that final honour.

He died, aged 62, on 27 January 1993 and was widely mourned. Numerous Lions of the 1950s vintages turned out to pay their final respects to the man whose selfless deeds in the engine-room of the pack enabled others to shine.

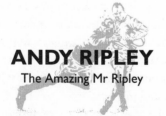

ANDY RIPLEY
The Amazing Mr Ripley

Andy Ripley charging down the field like a stallion was a rare sight to warm the hearts of England fans during the Five Nations campaigns of the early 1970s. The Rosslyn Park Number 8, who stood 6ft 6½in in his size 13 boots, was one of a few standout players available to England's selectors at a time when the national side's fortunes were at their lowest ebb in the International

Championship. He played 24 times for his country between 1972 and 1976, starting and finishing his career in seasons when England were whitewashed in the tournament. But colleagues and opponents alike had nothing but admiration for the instinctive ball-handling skills that made him the perfect example of the all-round back-row forward.

At the beginning of his career he also caught the eye for his off-beat appearance. The shoulder-length hair, John Lennon spectacles and unconventional dress sense marked him out as a noncon-formist at a time when English rugby appeared to be a game run by and for the benefit of England's public school classes. Ripley, revealing a left-wing leaning, once famously said: 'I enjoy the company of Tories: their arrogance, built-in contentment, burning sincerity is hard to take but amusing. Some people in rugby are that way.' He nevertheless held the utmost respect for Sandy Sanders, England's chairman of selectors at the time of his debut, for never reprimanding him or commenting on his appearance. 'We all go through phases,' Ripley said later, 'and Sandy must have looked and wondered when I joined the squad, yet not once did he tell me to go and get a haircut.'

When he went on the 1974 Lions' tour of South Africa, how-ever, he did not find his manager quite so easygoing. Admittedly there was much opposition to the tour in Britain. Welshman Alun Thomas had a difficult PR course to navigate as manager during what turned out to be the most successful Lions' tour of modern times. He naturally wanted everything to appear to run perfectly, but clearly had not reckoned with Ripley's lively and wicked sense of humour, which was invariably aroused by what might be called 'establishment ways'. The poor manager did not always see eye to eye with his players, occasionally overreacted in dealing with prob-lems and by doing so seemed to inspire the quick-witted Ripley's love for the unconventional. When he was ordered by the manager to obey the strict Lions' dress code of blazer, grey trousers and tie for a formal drinks reception, one of many of the tedious functions tourists were expected to attend, an indignant Thomas was forced to send Rips from the room for literally doing as he had been told and turning up wearing no socks, no shoes and no shirt.

A popular tourist, Rips was noted for his flip-flops, love of taped jazz and wide variety of T-shirts, including one proclaiming: 'I'm so perfect it scares me.' On another occasion he found his manager's treatment of England centre Geoff Evans harsh. The Lions were leaving for the airport to fly up to Rhodesia for some rest and recuperation prior to preparing for the second Test in Johannesburg when Mr Thomas directed Evans to change his blue shirt for a white one as part of the tour party's regulation flight gear. Rips thought this was over the top so, during the flight, 'transferred' the manager's regulation tour blazer to his own hand luggage. Poor old Mr Thomas had to step off the plane wearing a battered white raincoat to meet the various Rhodesian dignitaries while his team were immaculately dressed in their blazers.

Rips went on that tour as understudy to Wales's Mervyn Davies but played his part in keeping the Lions' unbeaten record with a series of brilliant performances for the mid-week team, the dirt-trackers. He was effective at disrupting the recycling of opposition ball at second phase, a useful strike force picking up from the back of the scrum and a human battering ram softening up defences with his charging runs in the loose. The only weakness in his game was a slight lack of concentration trying to offload the ball in the tackle. It was that minor flaw that prevented him challenging Davies for the back-row spot in the Test side, for the Welshman, although nearly two inches shorter than the giant Ripley, was as brilliant a player with the ball in hand as he was in all other aspects of Number 8 play.

Andy Ripley was an individualist. While many were happy to sunbathe on the glorious South African beaches, Rips took to his surfboard, indifferent to shark warnings, and while other forwards were content to relax in soaring temperatures he was happy to showcase his considerable skills as a track athlete by competing against Irish scrum-half, Johnny Moloney, in 400-metre sprints. Mad dog and Englishman: the entire squad thought Rips and Moloney were utterly bonkers.

Although his Five Nations career had few highlights, he enjoyed his part in three famous English victories against Tri Nations sides. In 1972 he played in the England side that beat South Africa 18–9 in Johannesburg, a year later he was a member of the side that shocked New Zealand by winning 16–10 in Auckland and in November 1973 he took part in the 20–3 demolition of Australia at Twickenham, scoring one of England's three tries. John Pullin, the Bristol farmer, was England's captain in all three games and a leader Rips enjoyed playing for. 'We've got to do something for Pullin,' Rips said on the eve of the 1974 Five Nations, but the only win of a disappointing campaign came at the end of the season when Rips himself had one of his best games for England, driving over from a scrum to score in a 16–12 defeat of Wales. That match turned out to be England's only success against the principality between 1960 and 1980. He finally lost his place after the defeat by Scotland at Murrayfield in 1976 when his opponent was an old adversary, Alastair McHarg. The two old campaigners enjoyed a battle within the battle that day, forming a friendship that has lasted a lifetime. Calcutta Cup reunions were not the same when one or other of the dynamic duo were absent. On one occasion, when McHarg was away on business in the subcontinent, it was said that only McHarg could go to India for a Calcutta Cup celebration.

Andrew George Ripley was born in Liverpool on 1 December 1947 and raised in Bristol by his headteacher mother. He was educated at Greenway Comprehensive School before putting his sharp mind to the study of economics at the University of East Anglia, where his interest in rugby was inspired by the former Welsh winger and 1955 Lion, Haydn Morris, who showed him the short cuts to getting through a rugby match. He joined Rosslyn Park when he was studying at the London School of Economics for a postgraduate degree, and subsequent work as a City high-flier working for a number of leading merchant banks enabled him to retain his allegiance to the club. He easily shed his hippie image for pinstripes to build a successful career in business.

Cycling, canoeing and track running all came naturally to him and his love of competition has never waned. He was the ideal candidate for the BBC's *Superstars* series, which pitted top performers from different sports against each other. He became a charismatic champion, giving the appearance fees to charity in order to retain his treasured amateur status and thus continue his rugby connections, first as a player until his 40s and later as president, with Rosslyn Park, long after they had ceased to command a place in the game's spotlight. Even he, though, admitted that he might have had second thoughts about donating his proceeds had he netted the *World Superstars* prize. It was typical Ripley whimsy rather than sour grapes when he confessed that losing the *World Superstars* competition was the best thing that had happened to him. It meant, moreover, that his beloved Rosslyn Park enjoyed the benefit of his unique brand of leadership as its president, the club surviving to this day as the standard-bearers for grass-roots rugby.

His constant search for challenge extended to his business life. He gave up his City salary in the late 1980s to go freelance, starting his own financial services company. Charitable causes remained a high priority, with royalties from a number of books going to good causes and, at the age of 50, he came to within a whisker of rowing in the Boat Race, having enrolled at Cambridge University on a post-graduate course. More recently, his well-chronicled fight against the scourge of prostate cancer has been a source of both amusement and encouragement to fellow sufferers. He has gone about coping with the illness with the same determination dashed with humour that characterised the manner in which he faced sporting and business challenges in his prime. The Amazing Mr Ripley, who was one of rugby's great reachers, is one of life's great achievers.

LEADING BY EXAMPLE

JEAN PRAT
Monsieur Rugby

D own the years the French club championship as well as the French international team has regularly been dominated by players from Toulouse and Perpignan. But for one purple patch in French rugby history between 1945 and 1968 the great clubs were upstaged by a small town side from the remote pilgrimage centre of Lourdes. It was like St David's becoming the hub of Welsh rugby. During that period French rugby enjoyed maiden victories on Welsh, English and Scottish soils, beat the mighty Springboks and All Blacks, claimed their first share of honours in the Five Nations Championship and even secured a first Grand Slam. The men from the miracle city also went on to win six French Championship titles and were runners-up three times. The individual whose name became synonymous with the spectacular rise of Lourdes and French rugby – first as a player and later as a coach – was Jean Prat.

He was born on the family farm in Lourdes on 1 August 1923. The farm adjoined the land where a century earlier Sainte Bernadette had tended her sheep, and in 1948 Jean Prat married into the blessed Bernadette's family, the Soubirous. During the war the French Government of Occupation had outlawed 13-a-side rugby and the then Minister of Sport, Jean Borotra, decreed that the only form of rugby that was acceptable was the game played between teams of 15 men. The *treizistes* of the nearby Tarbes club switched codes and moved en bloc to join Lourdes, and thus was born one of the great teams of French rugby union history. As a teenager young Jean quickly became a star of the town's team and for his skills and courage he became a local legend. Esteem for him was so high that when he opened a bar – '*Le winger*' – it rapidly became a much sought-after watering-hole and a successful business venture for its owner.

In appearance he had the olive skin and clear eyes that go with an outdoor upbringing in the Pyrenees. His chin was firm, nose slightly crooked and his body framed by shoulders like swing-doors. 'He is not a particularly tall man, but his build is heroic,' wrote a British rugby critic in the 1950s. As a flanker he won 51 caps for France between 1945 and 1955, scored 139 Test points (a then world record for a forward), including nine tries, and was remarkably adept at dropping goals from the fringes of scrums and mauls. All told, he led France 17 times and was at the helm when French rugby shared the Five Nations Championship title for the first time – in 1954, with Wales and England – and again in 1955, when France shared the title with Wales.

French national sides before the Second World War had lacked leadership. Flair and skills there were aplenty, but these were left raw and unharnessed; French rugby cried out for a captain with the wit and generalship to transform the side into potential champions. The Agen Number 8 Guy Basquet had given the side impetus as a much-respected captain in the early postwar seasons, but it was not until Prat succeeded him in 1953 that the call was properly answered and honours materialised.

Jean Prat's credentials for leadership were impeccable. He had already led his side twice to the French Championship and had been instrumental in making Lourdes a forcing-ground for open, attacking rugby before taking over the national reins after Basquet's retirement. He had missed only one French international match since the war and his courage, determination and stamina – the legacies of his rural life and prowess as a cross-country runner – were outstanding features of his personal game. Moreover, he had been a member of the French sides that had won for the first time on Welsh soil (at Swansea in 1948), at Twickenham (in 1951 when he scored a try, converted one and kicked a towering drop-goal in an 11–3 victory) and at Murrayfield in 1952, when he scored 10 of his side's 13 points. But Jean always maintained that the huge 25–3 setback against Hennie Muller's Fourth Springboks in Paris in 1952 was his cathartic moment. He was absorbed by the way the Springboks' pack operated as a unit and began considering how he might harness the natural abilities of his countrymen to the forward methods adopted by the South Africans.

By 1954, Jean Prat's strong personality had become firmly fixed over a young and inexperienced French team that included his younger brother Maurice and several other Lourdes clubmates. 'Jeannot', as he was known among his rugby friends, ruled with an iron fist, instigating a tight-marking policy with an attacking base off the back of the scrum that immediately paid dividends. His side went on to claim their first ever share of the Five Nations Championship and the same season also brought him one of his most treasured moments when he scored the only try of a 3–0 win in Paris against the Fourth All Blacks – France's first victory over New Zealand. The year 1955 was to be his last in the French side and brought joy and disappointment. France won their two opening matches of that season's Five Nations comfortably and came to Twickenham in search of a third victory that would ensure at least a share of the championship's spoils. Prat was the focus of attention in London that weekend, with many of the British rugby media building their match previews around profiles of the skipper. The side stayed in Victoria's Grosvenor Hotel, where Monsieur Prat came over as a modest, unassuming man. Asked if he thought Twickenham's famous swirling currents of wind would pose a problem, Prat politely replied: 'That is a question for a philosopher rather than a rugby player.' Jeannot was so down-to-earth and realistic that a journalist overheard a colleague remark: 'According to my ideas, that chap [Prat] is the sort of man they need as Prime Minister of France.'

Prat was never particularly forthcoming in interviews, preferring his efforts on the field of play to do his 'talking' for him. Rugby was like life to him: a simple game to be played in the plain yet honest spirit of his rural roots. During the match against England, though, he was transformed into a warrior leader, exhorting his troops to do this, that and everything as France strove to win at Twickenham. It was all a bit too much for one of the young French props who, finding himself unexpectedly in possession, tossed the ball like a hot potato to his captain with the throwaway remark: 'Here – see what you can do with it.' Prat promptly dropped a goal, one of two he kicked that day as France sealed a 16–9 victory that was only their second at Twickenham. Never before had any forward dropped two goals in a major Test and for his fantastic leadership and efforts on the field that day he was nicknamed 'Monsieur Rugby' by the British press.

In the match with Wales a month later Prat became the first rugby player to appear in 50 Tests. A first Grand Slam was at stake for the *Tricolores* while victory for Wales would guarantee the Red Devils a share of the championship's spoils with France. The match attracted a record crowd to Stade Colombes, the rickety old Paris stadium that had staged the 1924 Olympic Games 30-odd years earlier. Odds on a Welsh win were quoted as 15-1 against, but off they went like a rocket at the start and the French found themselves bereft of the perfect timing and control that had characterised their three earlier championship matches. The traditional uncertainty had returned to the French game and they trailed 11–0 at the interval. Then 'Monsieur Rugby' lifted his men in the second half. French teamwork returned and some brilliant technique in handling excited the huge crowd as Prat's men staged a roaring comeback. But Wales had established too big a lead and held on to deprive France and Jean Prat of a first Grand Slam. It was a tribute to the French captain's standing in world rugby that at the final whistle the Welsh forwards carried him off shoulder high and at the post-match dinner in honour of the teams the Welsh captain, Rees Stephens, expressed the sympathy of his team at Monsieur Rugby's failure to realise his lifelong ambition of a clean sweep against the Home Unions.

At the same dinner Prat announced that he would retire from international rugby at the end of the season. 'I am leaving the game with some sorrow,' he said. 'I have experienced great satisfaction from leading a very good French side, but sadness from today's failure to win [outright] the championship. The match proved to me that I still had something to learn!' He carried on learning, putting his thoughts to good use as player–coach with Lourdes. In

1958–59, after retiring from club rugby, Lourdes provided the nucleus of the French side that secured a historic series win in South Africa and carried all before it in the Five Nations. It was a huge tribute to the influence Jean Prat had exercised as mentor to his beloved town club. Later, between 1963 and 1967, he coached the national side with the same effectiveness and was a selector when France eventually won the Grand Slam for the first time in 1968. Truly he had been an important factor in the rise of French rugby.

'Monsieur Rugby' died from cancer of the throat in Tarbes on 25 February 2005, aged 81. Michel Crauste, who succeeded him as flanker and captain for both Lourdes and France, paid tribute to Prat's leadership: 'He could make his team-mates put their bodies on the line because he always did it himself. He had inside him all the rugby values.'

CLIVE ROWLANDS
Top Cat

Early in the winter of 2008 a presenter on BBC Radio Wales's weekly rugby magazine programme had cause to reflect on the 1963 Scotland–Wales match at Murrayfield. It was an infamous game that went down in history as the match of 111 line-outs. The tyro radio presenter cast doubts on the figure, arguing that with only 80 minutes to a match it would have been impossible to have reached such an unlikely figure – more than a line-out a minute.

Well, he should have asked the 1963 Welsh captain Clive Rowlands about the game. Rowlands was the scrum-half and tactical controller who was responsible for more than half of the throw-ins that statistician Tommy Thompson carefully logged that cold, Arctic afternoon in Edinburgh. Unlike today, where a whole cottage industry of statisticians attend and analyse matches, back in the early 1960s Thompson was the sole operator whom the national press consulted as the oracle on such details. All the leading reporters of the day were happy to quote Mr Thompson's figures – 55 line-outs in one half; 56 in the other . . . and 42 scrums, too. Certainly the tactical pattern of international rugby was very different then compared with today, with far less formality, particularly at line-out time. Rowlands kicked every bit of posses- sion he had, figuring out that his forwards could outmuscle the Scots and force victory from a game of attrition. His plan worked. He hardly passed the ball all afternoon and Wales went on to win 6–0 and record their first victory in the Scottish capital for a decade.

Welsh wits in the crowd had a field day. 'Clive's got six different signals for his backs,' said one spectator, 'and every one means he's going to kick to touch.' A desperate Scot was heard to shout midway through the first half: 'Come in number nine, your time's up.' And years later Rowlands himself, on his way to the media centre on another Scotland–Wales occasion, made a wonderful remark when asked by a stadium steward about his pass. 'Pass?' queried Rowlands, 'I've never passed at Murrayfield in my life.'

Clive Rowlands was born on 14 May 1938 at Upper Cwmtwrch and grew up in the rich, fertile rugby crescent that arcs through the Tawe valley down to Swansea Bay. He developed his game as a back-row forward in schoolboy rugby before serving a hard appren- ticeship as a fly-half in the rough-and-tumble of the former West Wales Leagues. After qualifying as a teacher at Cardiff Training College, he settled in as scrum-half for Pontypool, where his sturdiness and resilience provided the perfect support for the forward-dominated game that his club traditionally played. He was elected Pontypool's captain in 1962 and revelled in the responsi- bility. Never the nippiest of scrum-halves around the field, he never- theless possessed a convincing dummy and used it sensibly to create chances off the base of the scrum. Yet it was as a kicking scrum-half that he really made his name. With no law restrictions on touch- kicking in the early 1960s, his slightly bowed legs equipped him perfectly for the hook kick back to touch over his forwards from a line-out.

It was for his tactical abilities as leader that Rowlands was surprisingly named as captain and one of six new caps in the Welsh team to face England in January 1963. He was disappointed after Wales lost in Cardiff to an English side that went on to win the Five Nations Championship, but his determination was undimmed and, exercising an iron grip over his team, he went on to direct them to that Murrayfield win three weeks later. For his dominance that day he was forever nicknamed 'Top Cat' after the popular TV cartoon alley-cat who bossed it over his gang.

It's true that there was never any doubt about who was Wales's captain during his three-season reign. For sheer character he had no postwar equal. His appeal to enthusiasm and love of country imbued his teams with a mighty corporate spirit, and in 1964 his side shared the Five Nations title with Scotland before eventually regaining the Triple Crown and outright championship the season later. By then he had played 14 times for his country and uniquely had led them in every game. Then he was dropped as quickly and as mysteriously as he had been originally selected.

Between the 1965 Triple Crown and the start of the 1966 Five Nations campaign he changed jobs, leaving the hustle and bustle of the teaching profession to become a salesman. In the run-up to the new international season there were criticisms that he had become slower around the field. Moreover, there was a clamour for a more attacking emphasis from a Welsh side that, with backs like David Watkins and D. Ken Jones, was well equipped to win matches by scoring tries from open play. Rowlands was viewed now as a bit of a one-trick pony and the Welsh selectors felt that a more expansive approach from their backs was needed. Even so, it came as a bomb-shell to the Welsh public when 'Top Cat' was dropped for the Twickenham visit that opened their 1966 campaign.

Clive Rowlands was there at Twickenham as travelling reserve and, extreme loyalist that he always was, delighted in seeing Wales win. Victories against the old enemy always warmed his heart. Years later, after managing a Welsh touring side that had been heavily defeated by New Zealand, he was asked what he thought the future held for Welsh rugby. 'We'll just have to go back to beating England,' he replied.

He was never selected for Wales again, but after retiring from playing in 1968 his popularity was immediately recognised with his election as a Welsh Rugby Union vice-president and he quickly reinvented himself as a coach. In this capacity he once more became Welsh rugby's 'Mr Motivator' and showed that he was far from the dull, kicking tactician that had characterised his playing days. In 1968, the International Board finally caved in to demands to brighten up rugby and introduced the so-called Australian Dispensation law that restricted direct kicking to touch. Teams could no longer gain ground through the simple expedient of winning the line-out and hoofing the ball upfield to the next touch throw-in. Many said that the match of 111 line-outs had sounded the death-knell for touch-kicking tactics.

Ironically, it was Rowlands who was among the first to appreciate the different tactical nuances that the dispensation law offered. Installed as Wales's new national coach in 1968, he took a party away to Argentina for a tough tour on the eve of the 1968–69 season. It was on that visit that Rowlands envisaged the opportunities of using an attacking, running fullback and in the young J.P.R. Williams found the perfect role model. Here was a player with all the traditional solid virtues of the position, but he could also launch counterattacks. With touch-kicking restricted, fullbacks suddenly became very important weapons in attack and the young Welsh Number 15 was to become the prototype when the international game adopted the new laws in the New Year. Rowlands went on to stir a mix of youth and experience into a Welsh team that won the Triple Crown and Five Nations title.

Later the same year the coach persuaded Gerald Davies, then Wales's centre, that his skills were better suited as a wing three-quarter. Thus, in fewer than 12 months in his new post, Rowlands had made two of the most important positional decisions that were to serve Wales handsomely for the best part of a decade. Tactical nous, though, wasn't his only strength in the coaching job. Rowlands was a brilliant orator who raised his Welsh teams to fever pitch with famously inspiring pre-match appeals to their patriotism, yet he also possessed a cool and calculating tactical mind that prepared players thoroughly during a series of extracurricular weekend training sessions at the Afan Lido centre near Port Talbot. His trailblazing methods became the envy of the Five Nations.

Clive Rowlands's stint as Wales national coach ended in 1974. He had added a Grand Slam (1971) and share of the championship (1973), while in 1972 an unbeaten Welsh side had been unable to meet Ireland for the championship decider owing to political troubles. 'Top Cat' had paved the way for his successor John Dawes to lead Wales to greater achievements in the second half of what became known as the 'Decade of the Dragon' . . . the outstanding era of Welsh rugby in the second half of the 20th century.

He continued to serve the Welsh Rugby Union for many years in a variety of administrative capacities and was always in demand for interviews after Welsh matches, particularly Welsh victories. Wherever he went he attracted an excited following. When Wales temporarily decamped to Wembley Stadium to play their home matches while the Cardiff ground was redeveloped in the late 1990s, he was always surrounded by wellwishers and friends – a reflection of the high regard the Welsh people had for his talents and the power of his magnetic personality. Even hardened old hacks from rugby's press media wanted a slice of his opinions when he entered the old Wembley press bar. 'Top Cat' would oblige with his quick wit, lightening up a soulless place that more closely resembled a 1950s railway station buffet bar than a press centre.

KARL MULLEN
Alone he Stood

Alone he stood: Karl Mullen, the man who led Ireland to their only Five Nations Grand Slam until Brian O'Driscoll's men repeated the feat 61 years later. Before 2009, Irish rugby's *annus mirabilis* was 1948 when Mullen became one of the first captains in the Five Nations to think deeply about the tactical preparation of an international team. Touring sides to Britain had had their influential thinkers – men like Dave Gallaher of the first All Blacks and Bennie Osler of the 1931–32 Springboks, skippers who planned matches with attention to detail and enjoyed the spoils of success. But it wasn't until the early postwar years that any attempt to think deeply about tactics arrived in the domestic Five Nations competition. Mullen was the man who persuaded Irish players to abandon their happy-go-lucky reliance on the rub of the green and, instead, take their lead from a general who commanded his campaigns with military precision. To this day he is hero-worshipped in Ireland for his Grand Slam achievement.

The perennial failing of Irish rugby between the wars had been its tendency to run out of steam in the closing stages of matches. Under Mullen, Ireland played a patterned forward game based on ball retention. His expert hooking was an important cog in the team's wheel of fortune. For without possession in defensive situations Ireland could not shut out their challengers. Nor could they let loose their star outside-half, Jack Kyle, to create tries when attacking in their opponents' halves. The strategy was simple and extremely fruitful. Dr Mullen's prescriptions worked a treat for Ireland, with a further Triple Crown in 1949 and a third championship title in 1951 as the men in green became a very awkward hurdle for other teams to overcome.

Born on 26 November 1926 in the pleasant coastal town of Courtown in County Wexford, he was educated at Dublin's Belvedere College, where he played his school rugby in the backs. He was converted to a hooker at the age of 17 when the Old Belvedere senior club were short of a specialist in that position and 'auditioned' several members of the school side for the role. On account of his physique, it was always argued that Mullen had been born to hook. Now he had it thrust upon him and he took to the part with relish. His style in the loose was captured perfectly by the colourful prose of the veteran English critic R.C. Robertson-Glasgow of the *Observer* who described him running around like a terrier that had swallowed a grenade.

He was still a teenager, studying at Dublin's College of Surgeons, when he first made the Irish selectors sit up and take notice of his talents. He caught their eye while playing for Leinster against the 'Kiwis', the famous New Zealand Expeditionary Forces side that toured Britain and Ireland in 1945–46, and later on during that chaotic first postwar rugby season he featured prominently in the series of unofficial 'Victory' internationals that paved the way for normal cap matches to be resumed in 1946–47.

Measuring 5ft 9in and weighing 13 stone, he was a robust figure in the loose. But it was for his expertise striking the ball at the scrums that he won his spurs. Contemporaries said he could win a strike against the head even when the ball was in the opposition's back row. He was nimble on his feet, tough as teak and benefited from the support of rock-solid prop forwards. It was no wonder that, during his run of 24 successive cap matches for Ireland, he rarely conceded a strike against the head. As a hooker in the immediate postwar seasons he had no superior, and to many he had no equal.

Captaincy came naturally to him. He was only 21 and the youngest player on the side when he took charge for the first time, at Twickenham in 1948. Years ahead of his time in his thoughtful approach to leadership and team preparation, he also had the priceless gift of being able to adjust his tactics depending on the state of a game. He called team meetings before matches where the strengths and weaknesses of his own side as well as the opposition's were considered. Even his half-time assessments were perceptive, often leading to a change in approach that swung the course of a match Ireland's way. That's an art that has eluded many distinguished rugby captains of modern times. But Mullen's capacity to detach himself from the hectic fray of the front row, not the ideal position from which to lead a team, and calmly reappraise playing options was a vital element of Ireland's successes. He complemented his strong organisational powers with shrewd psychology. The ability to have absolute faith in your colleagues is a strength of effective leadership. Mullen had this quality in bucketloads. He told his players of his belief in them; he really didn't think they could lose if they played to their best. They did play to their best and rewarded him by raising their game to become masters of the Five Nations.

The closeness of Ireland's championship title wins in 1948, 1949 and 1951 underlined the value of Mullen's steely nerved stewardship: 11–10 v. England and 6–3 v. Wales in 1948; 5–0 v. Wales in 1949; and 9–8 v. France, 3–0 v. England, 6–5 v. Scotland and a 3–3 draw v. Wales in 1951. Not surprisingly, he was nominated captain of the Lions for the 1950 visit to New Zealand and Australia.

Without his intelligent lead in 1952, when the captaincy passed to Des O'Brien, Ireland became less difficult to beat. Mullen bowed out of the side the same year, still relatively young, in order to devote more time to developing his professional career in medicine. But he retained a high profile in Irish rugby, becoming a national selector between 1961 and 1964 (when Ireland next won at Twickenham) and running the Irish Wolfhounds, the well-known Irish invitation side based on Barbarians' lines. Recently he was named Ireland's most successful captain of all time, and in the early years of the 21st century, whenever Ireland came to within a match of winning an elusive second Grand Slam, the kindly Karl Mullen was happy to recall the simple but effective tactics that took the boys of '48 to their clean sweep.

He left the world of rugby to mourn his passing in the year that his great Grand Slam achievement was finally equalled. He died on 26 April 2009 at his home in Kilcullen in County Kildare, just a month after Brian O'Driscoll's men had beaten Wales to win the Grand Slam. It was estimated that, as a doctor, he had helped deliver more than 40,000 babies. Many of them were probably among the 82,300 record crowd at Croke Park where, a couple of days after his death, there was a moving minute's applause in remembrance before his beloved Leinster rose splendidly to the occasion and defeated old rivals Munster in a memorable Heineken European Cup semi-final tie.

RAY McLOUGHLIN
The Thinking Prop's Prop

Ray McLoughlin was the thinking prop's prop. He applied the analytical powers which brought him first-class honours and a doctorate in his academic studies at University College Dublin and Newcastle University to solve the essential mechanics of scrummaging. Later, he was just as thoughtful in his approach to captaincy, though if there was a criticism of his manner it was that he was a little too analytical and intense for his colleagues. The state of Irish rugby when he arrived on the scene was often described as desperate, but never serious. McLoughlin's legacy was that Irish (and Lions) rugby would become a serious force to be reckoned with ever after.

Irish rugby had drifted aimlessly and without a Five Nations title during the decade or so that followed their 1951 championship win under Karl Mullen. By the early 1960s, McLoughlin's growing reputation as a successful club captain with Gosforth in Newcastle attracted the interest of the Connacht selectors in his native province. Connacht has always been regarded as the Cinderella of the Irish provincial set-up, but under McLoughlin's leadership the players were persuaded to plan more carefully and prepare more seriously for matches.

His strategy worked wonders with the province. Could his methods be transferred to the national side, wondered the Irish selectors? The answer was a resounding yes. He injected the spirit of purpose into the Ireland team. At a time when the word 'coach' in a rugby context meant nothing more sophisticated than a mode of transporting teams to matches, Irish international players were summoned by their new captain to team meetings at which tactical options were explored. He caused something of a stir on the eve of his first game as skipper, against France in Dublin in January 1965, when he demanded that *all* members of the side, even those who were resident in Dublin, stay the night at the team hotel.

Senior players were invited to contribute to discussions and even the opinions of selectors were sought. McLoughlin succeeded in motivating his team to concentrate on victory and, in the psychological and physical preparation of an international side, he was probably five years ahead of his time. France had walloped Ireland 27–6 in Paris in their previous international nine months earlier. McLoughlin's plans were so effective that the Irish forced a creditable 3-all draw, derailing French hopes of the championship.

Born in Ballinasloe on 24 August 1939 and educated at the local Garbally College before going to the northeast to read for his degree at Newcastle University, he first appeared in the Irish jersey on the same day that Willie John McBride made his debut: against England at Twickenham in 1962. By March 1965, as his country's captain, he was seeking a first Ireland Triple Crown since 1949. That draw with France and victories over England and Scotland had set up the showdown of the season when Ireland visited Cardiff to meet an unbeaten Welsh XV.

Ireland's failure to kick their goals early in the match cost them dearly and Wales went on to win 14–8. Though many were satisfied with the huge improvement Ireland had made in moving from 'wooden spooners' to championship contenders, shrewd critics felt that their captain should have manipulated the tactics more subtly to give his side the edge when Wales were reduced to 14 men early in the first half of the big match. A month later, however, he was the toast of all Ireland after leading the men in green to their first ever victory over the Springboks. Fullback Tom Kiernan summed up: 'It's been a wonderful season, marvellous to play under Ray McLoughlin,' he said. 'The discipline, the feeling that now we know what we're at, has made all the difference.'

But the next season McLoughlin was relieved of the captaincy after Ireland disappointingly lost at home to Scotland. He had played with a temperature of 102°F while fighting off a flu bug, but the leadership passed to the more extrovert Kiernan for the match with Wales, which Ireland went on to win. Even so, his propping skills were retained and he was an automatic choice as prop on the

1966 Lions' tour of Australia and New Zealand before a knee injury and increasing business commitments kept him out of the Irish side thereafter. His influence on Irish rugby was made, however, and in the seasons that followed Noel Murphy and later ·Kiernan were to lead Irish sides that challenged vigorously for championship honours. Irish rugby had become a considerable force to be reckoned with and it was undoubtedly McLoughlin's professional approach that had moulded what was substantially the same squad of players from the early 1960s into the formidable unit that played to its strengths in the later years of that decade.

Five years later, McLoughlin made one of the most astonishing comebacks in international history. He had switched to loose-head but all the old scrummaging expertise was still there. The strong back, aligned low and parallel to the ground, put opponents under tremendous pressure. As a senior player, he was an integral part of the 1971 Lions' tour squad that made such an impact on the New Zealand leg of the tour, and he proved to be effective in passing on his rugby insight. Injuries sustained in a brutal match against Canterbury, where he broke his thumb, robbed him of a part in the Test series. He had learned that for a team to be successful against New Zealand it must never take a backward step. Individuals, moreover, could not afford to be overawed by their opponents. The points were well made to the 1971 Lions, who had enormous respect for his ideas. He formed an important alliance as forwards' adviser to coach Carwyn James, though even the scholarly Welsh coach had difficulty keeping up intellectually with the Irish genius. 'What's it like discussing tactics with Carwyn?' McLoughlin was asked before returning home after the Canterbury match. 'It's hard to say,' replied the Irishman, 'he always falls asleep when I start talking.'

Enjoying a new lease of life, he confirmed the maxim that good props really do come of age in their 30s. For five more seasons he burrowed away conscientiously, becoming the cornerstone of the Irish scrums that paved the way to championship honours in 1973 and 1974. In 1972, when Ireland were deprived of the chance of a tilt at the Grand Slam because of the cancellation of the Scottish and Welsh matches, he scored the only try of his Test career in the Paris win against France. Ireland had not won in Paris since 1952, but the prop's try just before half-time was the decisive score. Barry McGann, resident funny man on that Irish side, described the try afterwards: 'He was in the wrong place at the wrong time and fell over the line with the ball.' McLoughlin finally quit at the top in 1975. Having started his Ireland career with the great Willie John, he ended it against Wales on the same day his famous compatriot retired.

After 40 caps as a prop – a then world record he shared with David Rollo and Hughie McLeod of Scotland – he had earned his rest. Certainly his international opponents welcomed the respite that his retirement brought for them. He became a well-known businessman and continued to take an interest in the trials and tribulations of Irish rugby, especially in 1976 when his younger brother Feidlim won his only cap for Ireland, propping against the touring Wallabies. Feidlim, terribly proud of his brother's achievements, would subsequently relish telling new acquaintances how he and his brother had played 41 times between them for Ireland!

BILL BEAUMONT
British Bulldog

Bill Beaumont was the player who more than any other was responsible for England's rugby revival in 1980. The Fylde and Lancashire lock entered the side in the mid-1970s and soon commanded a regular place through his technical expertise and special skills as a front-of-the-line jumper. It was the quality of his captaincy, however, that was to drive up England's rugby stock. He stepped in as leader in 1978 and quickly showed his knack for player management. Never one to bawl out his players, Beaumont set about establishing a good team spirit in the belief that mutual respect on the field grew from trust and good relations formed off it. After enforced premature retirement from the game in 1982, he made a smooth transition to popular television sports personality and became a national institution, serving a long stint in the captain's chair on the quiz programme, *A Question of Sport*. Today he is a wonderful ambassador for English rugby and serves the RFU as its highly respected representative on the International Rugby Board.

Bill Beaumont was born in Preston on 9 March 1952 and began his rugby as a raw eight-year-old fly-half at Cressbrook prep school in Kirkby Lonsdale, where John Spencer, another future England rugby captain, was then the head boy. At Ellesmere College, he spent a couple of years as a fullback before he joined Fylde – it was to be the only senior club he played for during his entire first-class career – and graduated from flanker with the sixth XV to lock for the firsts. Fylde have never been a particularly fashionable club (though one of their highlights was a 33–3 thrashing of kingpins Gloucester in the mid-1970s while Bill was in his prime) and Beaumont's loyalty to them was typical of his love for the game, from the grassroots at club level to the international stage. He had excellent ball skills and, for a heavy man, was remarkably adept at kicking and passing, but early on some critics felt that he was too small to play lock yet too slow to feature in the back row and doubted whether he had the physique to make it at representative level.

His big break came in the early 1970s when he was chosen to play for Lancashire and came under the influence of John Burgess, an inspiring and knowledgeable coach. Burgess moulded him into a world-class lock and Bill's consistent performances for a side that regularly vied with Gloucestershire for the County Championship title brought him to the attention of the England selectors. His first cap came in Dublin against Ireland in 1975, by which time Burgess had become England's coach. Bill got his chance as a late stand-in for Roger Uttley, who had ricked his back in the most unlikely of circumstances, eating a slice of apple pie on the train down to London to join the team for the flight to Dublin.

After touring Australia with the England team in the summer of 1975 he commanded a regular position in the second row and enhanced his international reputation with a series of impressive technical displays, both for England and the 1977 Lions. Arguably the 'find' of the British/Irish tour to New Zealand, he was the outstanding scrummager in the party and made an impact as an effective mauler who used his upper-body strength to wrest the ball from the All Blacks. Players from all four of the Home Unions spoke highly of the spadework the Englishman put into his forward play, duties that were largely unseen from the stands and terraces.

When he returned he was given the England captaincy and went on to lead his country 21 times – a record that stood until the Carling era. Yet he had no track record as a skipper and there were several more senior members of the England team who could quite reasonably have felt miffed at having been overlooked for the job. That none did was tribute in itself to Bill's standing among his peers – he was held in such high regard by his colleagues. Everyone warmed to his leadership and likeable personality. One of his greatest strengths was his readiness to seek advice and listen to other colleagues. Although quiet by nature, his dealings with the media and the relaxed manner in which he delivered speeches at after-match functions were a revelation. His secret was to be himself – a down-to-earth realist. Once, when arriving at Cardiff to lead the side against the all-conquering Welsh team of the late 1970s, he was greeted by a wellwisher with the words, 'May the best side win,' as he led his men off the team coach. Bill, in bluff Lancastrian tones, turned to his team to say: 'I bloody well hope not!'

England's results steadily improved. With the nucleus of his successful Lancashire county side he led the Northern Division to a famous victory over the 1979 All Blacks before his rebuilding work reached its peak in 1980. A national side bursting with the confidence instilled by Beaumont carried off its first Grand Slam for 23 years. In the summer he led the Lions to South Africa, where the tourists were unlucky to go three Tests down with just one to play. But so loyal were the members of that British/Irish tour party to their captain that sheer determination not to let him down spurred them to register a resounding victory in the final Test and so spare Bill the stigma of a whitewash against the Springboks.

He remained as England's captain for another two years. In the opening match of the 1981 Five Nations he had to give a young Clive Woodward a piece of his mind when the centre strayed offside late in the game at Cardiff and presented Wales with a last-minute narrow victory. England probably deserved to win that match, but the defeat only temporarily pricked the bubble of confidence that Bill had helped inflate, and strong wins followed against Scotland and Ireland – only the second by England in Dublin in a decade. The next season began with Bill leading his side to victory over Australia, despite the spectacular half-time distractions of a half-naked Ms Erika Roe. The substantial Beaumont backside – his outboard motor some called it – had been a source of humour among his England sides and the sight that distracted the players as they gathered around Bill to hear his interval pep-talk was perfectly described by Peter Wheeler, who announced: 'Turn round Bill, a bloke has just run on with a backside like yours on his chest.'

Before the month was out he had played his last game of rugby. He was forced to retire with an injury while leading Lancashire to the County Championship title against the North Midlands at Moseley. He had received a bang on the head – the third such injury he had suffered in 12 months – and after consultation, he accepted medical advice to take early retirement. It almost certainly deprived him of the honour of becoming the first player to captain successive Lions' tour parties, for he would have been the leading contender for the position on the tour to New Zealand in 1983.

It was a disappointing way for one of England's finest rugby servants to depart from the game he deeply loved. His Lancashire and England colleague of long-standing, Steve Smith, represented the views of players and followers from the four corners of the rugby-playing world when he wrote later, 'We all miss you Bill. Thanks for all you have done for us, for Fylde, Lancashire, the North, England, Lions and most of all for rugby.' Bill was awarded the OBE for his services to the game in 1982, after which his well-known successful involvement in the media was complemented by his conscientious efforts as an RFU administrator when rugby became an open game in 1995. In 2008, he was made a CBE, prompting Francis Baron, the Chief executive of the RFU, to pay further tribute to him on behalf of the Union: 'I'd like to congratulate Bill on his honour, which is thoroughly deserved. Bill has put so much back into the game he loves at a playing and administrative level and he remains one of the most easily recognisable faces in our sport.'

JEAN-PIERRE RIVES
Renaissance Man

Jean-Pierre Rives inspired the loyalty and respect of players and supporters throughout his rugby career. When he first entered the French team he found the emphasis on organisation and pattern oppressive, but toed the line to channel his enthusiasm into winning. Then, on becoming captain, he cast asunder the heavy chains of discipline that he felt were shackling the French game and encouraged his sides to play with the elan that had characterised the rise of his nation's rugby fortunes in the 1950s and early 1960s. He totally committed his sides to playing expansive, 15-man rugby, and for his vision and faith in reinventing the attacking game he became the toast of France when they carried off the Grand Slam under his leadership in 1981.

Jean-Pierre certainly brought something refreshing to French rugby when he erupted on to the Test stage at Twickenham in 1975. Until then, French selectors had developed a taste for picking converted Number 8s to play on the side of the scrum – mobile giants who could win ball at the tail of the line-out and strike the fear of God into opponents as they broke away in the loose. Jean-Pierre did not fit this category. Not big enough to be a tight forward, nor fast enough for a three-quarter, Jean-Pierre had concentrated on becoming a flanker, but even for this role was considered by some to be on the short side for international level. Fortunately for France the selectors did not share the view.

With his prominent helmet of flaxen hair, Rives gave a good approximation to perpetual motion. From the start of his Test career he stamped his strong personality on the game with his particular brand of talent. He had the knack of cropping up in the right place at the right time. Shrewd and strong, he had the ability to save his side from a dangerous situation or create rucks and mauls from which scoring opportunities arose. He was French rugby's bionic man and the shining reputation he built in his younger days was the basis of his success as a leader. He filled his team-mates with a desire to run the ball in the style cherished by the French public, even if results did not always win prizes.

He was born in Toulouse on 31 December 1952 but spent his early years in Morocco, where his father served with the French Air Force. Tennis was an early love, but under his father's influence he became interested in rugby as a teenager, warming to the game quickly. The sturdy independence, travel and lasting friendships that the game engendered appealed to his laid-back personality, and after joining Toulouse he earned national Junior and B honours before leaving university. With his average build, student appearance and handsome looks – he was one of the few forwards of his day who received as much mail from lady admirers as rugby fans – he was the complete antithesis of the traditional rough, tough Test forward. Even when his university days studying medicine before switching to law were over, he cultivated a bohemian manner. He was a real romantic who carried that spirit on to the field. If he had been born in England 80 years earlier, he would have been a staunch upholder of the Corinthian and Barbarian ideals of fair play. Indeed, the British Barbarians, recognising the joy he derived from playing in their traditions, had no hesitation inviting him to turn out for them in their centrepiece match against the 1977 Lions to mark the Queen's Silver Jubilee.

Throughout the 1970s and 1980s, followers of the game in Europe felt France had the potential to carry off a Grand Slam every season. Yet a misguided approach to tactics polarised rugby opinion in the country. Jacques Fouroux, as captain when Rives entered the side, restrained the natural tendency of French players to play a genuine running game. The upshot was that the national side adopted a stodgy style of forward-oriented play that, despite appeals from those who wanted to see a more instinctive form of rugby based on flair, was highly successful. When he joined the

French XV, Jean-Pierre went along with his captain and coach and was an effective part of a team that did indeed lift the Grand Slam in 1977. But when he became captain in 1979, he immediately railed against win-at-all-costs tactics to take France back to their natural position as the most exciting team in world rugby. He had the power of body and mind to inspire a renaissance of the French game during a five year stint.

His first success as leader was against the All Blacks in 1979, where he invested in his followers a spirit of adventure that paid thrilling dividends in the Test staged at Auckland. He wanted to move the ball about, for as he pointed out, 'taking New Zealand's pack on was like trying to push elephants with matchsticks'. The French were transformed in spirit and method. In the best display of open rugby seen in New Zealand for years, Jean-Pierre's team ran in four tries to record their first ever Test victory in the country. They exuded fun and panache, though when they tried to copy that approach in the 1980 Five Nations, success turned to disastrous failure. Starved of possession, the French were unable to bring their refreshing outlook to a championship that was dominated by forwards, marred by accusations of foul play and bereft of memorable attacking football. The next season, however, saw France – and Jean-Pierre – at their best. The wooden spoon of 1980 was traded in for the Grand Slam in 1981 when Rives tackled like a bulldozer all season and was unanimously declared the 'Player of the Year'. One of his senior forwards paid tribute to his leadership that year, saying: 'You follow Rives because where Jean-Pierre is, there is the ball.'

Twickenham was his favourite ground. Its Englishness, the politeness of its crowds and the fact that he won there four times in his distinguished career moved him to call it 'the English temple of rugby. It feeds on emotion, steals your heart, chews it up and turns it inside out.' Indeed, soon after he played his last international there he said, 'I hope there will always be a small corner left for Jean-Pierre – in the crowd with my mates who really love our great game.' One sensed that in another life he might well have been a philosopher. His last Test appearance in England was in 1983, when his side opened the Five Nations with a typically swash-buckling 19–15 win at Twickenham. His team went on to share the championship honours with Ireland and in 1984 won its first three matches playing sublime rugby before facing Scotland at Murrayfield in a winner-takes-all battle for the Grand Slam.

It was probably his worst day as a Test player. Petty squabbles and indiscipline in the ranks saw a 6–3 French half-time lead disappear. Jean-Pierre himself was not without blame for France's second-half decline. His side had threatened to submerge the Scots in the opening 40 minutes, but frustration at France's inability to establish a clear lead was compounded by some eccentric refereeing decisions and left the captain remonstrating endlessly with match officials. It was an unsavoury spectacle, the only time that the sportsmanlike Rives ever blotted his copybook and a sad way to finish his career, as nine months later, plagued by shoulder and neck injuries, he announced his retirement from international rugby. He had won 59 caps for France, the last 34 of them as a captain who practised a philosophy of enterprising, direct rugby that many in France and the Home Unions warmed to. The president of the RFU that season was Ron Jacobs. He called Rives 'an extraordinary ambassador who has graced the game'.

After withdrawing, he steadfastly refused to become involved with the coaching or administrative side of the game, turning down offers with characteristic languorous charm. He was a player first and last. 'I very much regret not to be playing for my country any more,' he once reflected, but nothing could entice him to bring his inspiring ideals to bear in any official supporting capacity. 'I have nothing to pass on,' he modestly felt, adding that the game changed very quickly after his retirement. Instead, he channelled his considerable creative and physical energies into sculpture, eschewing the pinstripe suit of the corporate world for the crumpled jacket and rimless spectacles of the more bohemian existence that somehow reflected his offbeat approach to playing rugby.

It is hard to imagine a Jean-Pierre Rives playing in the professional game of today and rugby is manifestly the poorer for that.

DAVE GALLAHER
New Zealand Legend

Dave Gallaher's name is as indelibly stamped on the psyche of the New Zealand rugby player as W.G. Grace's is on the English cricketer. Each bestrides the history of his country's sporting achievements, a legend whose name will live for ever.

Gallaher was the captain of the Originals, the first All Black team to make the round-the-world voyage to play rugby in Britain, Ireland, France and North America in 1905. His team's wonderful record of 35 wins in 36 matches and dazzling style opened the eyes of the rugby establishment to the effectiveness of supreme fitness, tactical awareness and mastery of the game's basic skills. The tourists stunned the cream of northern hemisphere rugby, scoring 205 tries in their 830 points in Britain and Ireland, and conceding only seven tries and 39 points. Their line was crossed only once in their first dozen matches and their only defeat was against Wales in a match surrounded by controversy.

The man who held this talented group of rugby footballers together was David Gallaher, a foreman at the Auckland Farmers' Freezing Works. He was born on 30 October 1873 in Ramelton, County Donegal. His family came to New Zealand from Ireland in 1878 with the Vesey Stewart immigrants and young Dave grew up in Katikati near Tauranaga before moving to Auckland. He was a noted athlete in his youth and developed his rugby with the crack Auckland club, Ponsonby, winning his provincial honours in 1896.

In 1901 he joined up with the flower of New Zealand youth to serve in the Boer War, where his leadership qualities were quickly recognised by the army authorities. He enlisted with the New Zealand Mounted Rifles and was promoted to the rank of corporal before returning to New Zealand when the war ended. He quickly resumed his rugby career and first represented his country at the age of 29 in 1903 in their maiden Test against Australia. He was an automatic choice for the first ever All Blacks v. Lions meeting the year later, before winning selection for the groundbreaking tour to Britain in 1905.

Rugby had evolved slightly differently in New Zealand, where a diamond-shaped scrummage comprising seven bound forwards in a 2–3–2 formation was favoured. Their front row used two hookers and no props, but the ball tended to be heeled back very quickly in this arrangement. It was impossible, therefore, for the same player to feed the scrum and gather it as it emerged from the back row. To accommodate this difficulty, New Zealanders stationed a loose forward adjacent to the scrum. This player's duties were a mix of the scrum-half's and the wing-forward's. He fed scrums when his side had the put-in or aimed to disrupt attacks when it was won by opponents. The New Zealanders gave the term 'rover' to the dual-purpose position and it was in this role that Gallaher excelled.

He was not an automatic choice to lead the 1905 team. The story is told that during the voyage to Britain there was dissent among the tourists, who early on split into a North Island/South Island divide. It was the mark of the man that Gallaher openly offered to resign as skipper, forcing a vote among the factions. Both Jimmy Hunter (the standing North Island captain) and Billy Stead, who had led New Zealand in the winning Test against the Lions the year before, had their proponents, but it was Gallaher who carried the day by a ratio of three to two over his challengers. Stead became vice-captain and was to prove an able lieutenant, with the bond formed between captain and his deputy resulting in one of rugby's classic textbooks when they jointly authored *The Complete Rugby Footballer*, the manual which set out the blueprint that has arguably been a key to the All Black approach for more than a century.

Gallaher's openness and strength of character engendered trust among his charges. He was also one of the oldest players in the party and his outstanding war service meant that the younger players looked up to him in awe. As a disciplinarian he was able to command the unquestioning respect of the entire team. It was said his standing was so great that even the appointed coach, former New Zealand captain Jimmy Duncan, had to play second fiddle to

Gallaher in tactical and selection matters. He enjoyed poring over the theories of the game; moreover, he set very high standards in his physical preparation, for he was committed to fitness and led by example in the conditioning sessions as well as on the field.

The New Zealand methods were greatly admired by the sides that fell to their superior physical fitness and wonderful grasp of the game's basic skills. A vociferous minority, however, perhaps through jealousy or sheer poor grace, were highly critical of New Zealand's tactics and especially of Gallaher's role as the rover. He was criticised for imparting spin on the ball when he fed the scrummages while opinions were expressed among members of the press that the wing-forward was 'an abomination', the view being that technically his positioning rendered him either offside or obstructing play. British referees, unused to the unusual tactics employed by the colonials, were inconsistent or plain unsure in their interpretations of the laws.

Yet Gallaher took the criticisms in his stride, never publicly uttering a bad word. E.H.D. Sewell, the leading critic of the day who followed that tour, admired Gallaher for his sphinx-like inscrutability. Not once, according to Sewell, did the skipper lose his temper, on or off the field. A man of few words, Gallaher was described as 'the personification of silence'. Yet he was adept at raising his team's spirits before matches. To a man, the All Blacks of 1905 remembered his few simple words of encouragement: 'Give nothing away; take no chances.' Quite simply, his own fitness, strength and style of play were his preferred ways of communication, actions that spoke louder than any words. That he was so highly regarded among British and Irish opponents spoke volumes for his standing as a man, player and captain of the tourists.

There were times when the actions of opponents annoyed him. In the dressing-rooms before kick-off in the first Test of the tour against Scotland, where the New Zealanders received the frostiest welcome of their entire visit, he was offered two rugby balls by the referee. The match was to be staged on a frosty, bone-hard ground, but both balls had been so deliberately over-inflated that, for once, the captain was exasperated as he pondered his choice. 'They'll bounce like hell and spoil our passing,' he feared. Whereupon Ernest Booth, one of the All Blacks' reserves on the day, took them into the baths and gave them a good soaking. The beaming captain was delighted by his colleague's ingenuity and led his side to another victory.

The only defeat suffered by his team was 3–0 to Wales at Cardiff near the end of their tiring tour. The All Blacks' centre, Bob Deans, was denied an equalising try in the second half, and while the press blew the controversy into a debate that is talked about to this day, Gallaher conducted himself graciously. He congratulated the Welsh captain on his team's outstanding performance, sincerely adding that the better team had won. The Deans incident wasn't mentioned by the captain. It is interesting to add that all of the Home Unions paid the All Blacks the compliment of copying their rover system (though not the 2–3–2 scrum formation) for their Tests with the tourists. Indeed both Wales, where the criticisms of New Zealand's methods had been most intense, and Ireland continued to experiment with the seven-man scrum in their subsequent Five Nations campaigns before finally abandoning it in 1907.

Shortly after the 1905 expedition had finished, the New Zealand manager, George Dixon, published a diary of the visit. His final verdict on the tour was: 'It is to be hoped that the result of this pioneer tour will be an interchange of visits between the Colony and the Motherland, with increasing popularity and stimulus to good old Rugby.' More than a hundred years after those words were written, the fact that Dixon's prophesies have been so fully realised is greatly to the credit of the Originals' captain. For from 1905 down to the age of current incumbent, Richie McCaw, New Zealand captains have led their teams with the immense pride in the black jersey that Gallaher originally inspired.

When the 1905 side returned to New Zealand, he retired from playing and devoted his recreation to coaching in Auckland. He was later a selector for both the province and national side before enlisting again during the Great War, serving in France and Belgium as a Regimental Sergeant-Major with the New Zealand Reinforcements. He was in his 40s and didn't have to volunteer, but was eager to return to the service of King and Commonwealth. He died, aged 45, on 4 October 1917 of wounds received leading his men at Passchendaele. His grave at Nine Elms cemetery in Poperinghe, Belgium, has been the scene of moving visits by All Black teams for more than 80 years; and since 2000, to mark his memory, France and New Zealand have played for the Dave Gallaher Trophy.

CHEEKY CHAPPIES

PERCY BUSH
Will-o'-the-Wisp

With the possible exception of Barry John, who wowed opponents and followers of the 1971 tour to New Zealand, few players have stood out for their individual performances on a Lions' tour Down Under more than the Cardiff and Wales outside-half Percy Bush, who was the star attraction of the 1904 British/Irish team. Bush was pure box office in Australia where most of the tour matches were staged, and it was for his cheeky and devastating displays that the Antipodean press nicknamed him the 'will-o'-the-wisp'.

He hadn't even played for Wales when he embarked on that tour, but his reputation after the visit was so considerable that it was later to influence the outcome of the most famous game in Welsh rugby history. Bush impressed the Australian and New Zealand players with sidesteps that left opponents grasping at thin air, and his tour colleague Rhys Gabe, who was to play centre to him for both Cardiff and Wales, later confided that there were times on tour when not even Bush's own team-mates knew what he was going to do next. 'When he was really at his best and in the mood,' Gabe recalled of that tour years later, 'he could run through the whole team, as I have seen him do from a kick-off.' Bush had been fascinated by drop-kicking as a schoolboy and practised assiduously to become almost infallible at the skill. On tour he amassed more than 100 points, a colossal feat in those far-off days, and his haul included four drop-goals and five goals-from-marks kicked with drops. On the long train journeys between match centres he used to make bets with fellow travellers that he would drop-kick a goal in the next match. By all accounts he acquired a wonderful collection of umbrellas and walking sticks as the result of winning his wagers. During the visit he was also a popular speaker at public occasions. Once, in Bathurst, he made the outspoken pronouncement on Australian sport that: 'Australian Rules will never overtake rugby in popularity.' He was, it seems, as impudent off the field as on it.

In 1905 he featured twice in famous matches against the Original All Blacks. The New Zealanders held him in such respect from the 1904 visit that they feared his every move on the field. Bush was the only new cap in the Welsh side that beat the New Zealanders 3–0 – the All Blacks' only defeat on that tour – and he played his part in the famous decoy move that led to the only score of the match. His halfback partner that day was Dickie Owen of Swansea, who was halfway through a record-breaking career of 35 matches for Wales. The partners didn't really get on, being too similar in personality and style of play to complement one another. Both wanted to dictate tactics and revelled with the ball in their hands. But Bush and Owen's part in the winning move became part of Welsh rugby folklore.

Wales won a scrum in the New Zealand half and Owen gave the signal for the famous decoy move. This involved the scrum-half feinting to pass to Bush for an orthodox open-side move. The All Blacks, mindful of Bush's genius, bought the dummy and set off to snuff out the threat. Owen, seeing the opposition committed, threw a smart reverse pass to the blind side, where slick Welsh passing created an overlap for winger Teddy Morgan to exploit and sprint over for the winning try.

Ten days later, Bush was exposed as a wayward genius who cost his Cardiff club the opportunity of defeating the All Blacks. The scores were tied at 5–5 when a New Zealander kicked the ball into Cardiff's in-goal area. Bush had dropped back to cover and it seemed a foregone conclusion that he would touch down and restart on the 25 with a drop-out. A sudden rush of blood went to his head and, inexplicably, he dallied, with the ball near his fingertips. He said afterwards that he wanted to tease the following up New Zealanders and tire them out. But the ball was new and slightly more pointed than a used one. It bounced on its vertex and away from Bush for a New Zealander to rush in and claim a try. New Zealand went on to win 10–8 and Bush, Cardiff's captain in an otherwise unbeaten season, was left to rue the error of his ways for the rest of his life.

Percy Bush was born in Cardiff on 23 June 1879 and educated at St Mary's Hall School, Penarth Collegiate and Cardiff University, where he often played soccer on Saturday mornings (once playing in an inter-university match against future Wales goalkeeper Leigh Richmond Roose, who was a student at Aberystwyth University) before appearing for the rugby team in the afternoon. He began his first-class rugby career with the Penygraig club before entering the Cardiff first XV in 1899–1900 and was a fixture in the side for 10 years, captaining them for three seasons. From Cardiff University he went into teaching, but evidence suggests that the call of schoolmastering was not loud enough for him. He was as much a will-o'-the-wisp to the Cardiff Schools Management Committee as he was to opponents on the rugby field. Now you see him, now you don't. In February 1908, after Bush had starred in Wales's two opening matches of their maiden Grand Slam season, the headmaster of Cardiff's Wood Street Board School, where Percy was an assistant master, was compelled to complain to the Committee about the international rugby player's absences. '[Mr Bush] is constantly unable to attend school owing to illness and injuries received playing football,' the head wrote. 'This makes the seventh occasion on which Mr Bush has been absent through illness or injuries since September 1st last, and his absences [for the half-year to February] have been equal to 42 days.' In other words, Percy had been teaching for approximately 53 of the 95 teaching days in that half-year – an attendance record of just over 50 per cent at a time when he was turning out regularly for Cardiff and Wales! When the Board Committee convened to discuss the matter, Mr J.J. Thomas, the director of education, reported that Bush's absences totalled 58 term-time days in the previous 18 months, equivalent to 11 weeks and three days. The Board resolved to write to Percy to draw his attention to his shocking record and to point out that the Committee were unable to allow it to continue.

Within two years he had left both the teaching profession and Welsh rugby for good. Having been dropped in 1908, he was recalled to play in Wales's matches with Scotland and Ireland in 1910 but left Cardiff in March of that year for a new life in France. He joined a commercial firm in Nantes and, apart from a brief return to Cardiff for a month in the autumn of 1913, remained abroad until the beginning of the Second World War. In between, he worked for the French government during the Great War, and from 1918 was the British consul in Nantes. French rugby historians credit him with helping to develop back play in their country, for he kept his game up when he first emigrated there and became the backbone of the Nantes University club. He once scored the staggering total of 57 points in one match with the club, running through the card of scoring actions to clock up seven tries, seven conversions, two penalty goals and four drop-goals (at a time when tries were valued at three points and drops four).

Percy Bush won only eight caps for Wales owing to the uneasy halfback partnership he formed at international level with Swansea's Dickie Owen, the outstanding scrum-half of what has been called a golden era for Welsh rugby. Bush expected his halfback consorts to deliver the ball quickly to him so that he could dictate the play. This wasn't part of Owen's game. The Swansea man regarded the quick service to the fly-half as cramping his own style, a relinquishment of the tactical control that he relished and applied most effectively for Wales, who won three Grand Slams and five Triple Crowns during his career.

All told Bush and Owen played only three times together for Wales. Their last game in harness was the 11–0 defeat by the Springboks at Swansea in 1906. It was Wales's only home defeat between 1900 and 1913 and Bush was scathing of his partner's play that day. 'I had the extreme misery of assisting in that calamity,' he wrote many years later, 'by catching cold waiting for passes which never came.' Bush's partners in his other internationals for Wales were his Cardiff club colleagues Dicky David against Ireland in 1907, Billy Morgan against Scotland in 1910, and Newport's

Tommy Vile in the 1908 matches that launched the first Grand Slam. He and Vile had also been the British halves in the 1904 Tests in Australia and New Zealand, so knew each other's play inside out. These three were scrum-halves who, unlike Owen, saw their first duty as providing an efficient link between forwards and backs. Their quick service provided Bush with the time and space to concoct his cunning strategies. His favourite match, he once recalled, was the 1907 rout of Ireland at Cardiff, where Wales won 29–0 and Bush had a field day. He had a hand or a foot in almost every one of the Welsh scores that afternoon, and contributed a try and, inevitably, a drop-goal. But his reason for recalling the game so fondly, he once confided in a radio interview, was because 'this was the very first time that I had been given a scrum-half (Dicky David) who was content to *be* a scrum-half and from whom I could, therefore, expect to get a pass now and again.'

Bush had been unwell in the week leading up to the match but showed his craftiness at the first scrum. Dicky David, in his only international, was anxious to feed his partner with a careful pass and as a result sacrificed speed for accuracy. David's passes usually arrived speeding like a bullet to Bush in club matches. But on this occasion the service was more like a velvety spring breeze – a hospital pass that Bush looked as if he was going to receive at the same time as being hammered by the Irish halves, centres and entire back row. So the artful dodger kept stock still and went through the motions of throwing the ball back to his scrum-half as if the whistle had blown. His actions had the desired effect, for the advancing Irishmen stopped dead in their tracks. Bush then scooted off upfield and started a round of passing that culminated in the Cardiff winger Johnnie Williams crossing for the first try of the afternoon.

Another of his favourite days for Wales was in the fog at Bristol's Ashton Gate ground against England in 1908. Even the players couldn't see each other at more than a few yards' range for much of the game. Bush reckoned that on one occasion he smuggled the ball to Rhys Gabe in the centre and carried on running, pulling a number of English players in his shadow trying to grab him. Gabe went through virtually undetected, the fog lifting temporarily to reveal him scoring at the posts. Gabe's take on the story was slightly different: 'You didn't smuggle the ball,' he told Bush: 'You tried to steal the ball from me before making your run. But you certainly put your pursuers off the scent.'

After returning to Cardiff, where he worked as a factory welfare officer during the Second World War, Bush was always ready to talk rugby. In peacetime he found himself in great demand for newspaper columns and regularly contributed articles to the Welsh media as well as the *News of the World*. Wales's will-o'-the-wisp died, aged 75, in Cardiff in 1955.

BARRY JOHN
The King

B arry John was rugby's first popular idol – a sportsman whose appeal transcended the sweaty, muddy, beer-swilling confines of the rugby game. He had the boyish good looks, the stylish hair and, above all, the sporting superstar reputation to make him rugby union's equivalent of soccer's George Best, a player whose fame reached far beyond his sport. Successful sides need a catalyst that can take a tight game by the scruff of the neck and, with insouciance, turn it in their favour. Best did it for Manchester United; Barry John filled that role on a history-making Lions' tour and in the Welsh team that dominated the Five Nations in 1969 and the early 1970s.

His game was near-perfect. Defenders were left for dead as he jinked, sidestepped or subtly changed pace to drift through heavy traffic. His scores against Scotland and England in the 1969 Triple Crown season were typical John efforts. He was a Number 10 who exhibited ghost-like qualities as he wafted his way to the line, quite unlike the quicksilver outside-halves Cliff Morgan, David Watkins and Phil Bennett who came before and after him. A television reporter awaiting him for an interview was relieved to see him walk through the door of the studio – from the press hype he'd expected John to spirit himself through the walls!

He was born on 6 January 1945 at Cefneithin, a little village between Carmarthen and Llanelli that was also the home of Carwyn James. Barry followed Carwyn to Gwendraeth Grammar School and was a student at Trinity College, Carmarthen, in 1966 when he was given his first Welsh cap against Australia. He was playing club rugby at Llanelli in those days, catching the notice of the headline writers with his match-winning drop-goals and wraith-like running. For most of his international career he was blessed with an outstanding scrum-half partner in Gareth Edwards, but the pair did not play together until selected for the Probables in a Welsh trial at Swansea in January 1967. Beforehand, the uncapped Edwards called John to suggest they meet for a practice on the Sunday ahead of the match. They duly arranged their workout on a wet pitch west of Carmarthen and after hitting it off straight away, Barry felt there was little point in prolonging the exercise. Keen to enjoy the rest of his Sunday he said to Edwards: 'Gareth, you throw them – I'll catch them. Let's leave it at that and go home.' But the trial a week later was a disaster. John gashed his knee after three minutes and missed the rest of the match; and the Probables – featuring Gerald Davies, John Dawes, Dewi Bebb, Delme Thomas and Brian Price, as well as Edwards and John – were beaten 5–3 by the Possibles. They would not begin their Wales partnership for another 10 months, by which time Barry was working in Cardiff and playing for Edwards's home club.

John was an exquisite kicker with the ability to land a tactical punt on a sixpence. Legend has it that he honed this skill when he and Edwards were playing club friendlies for Cardiff. If either of the cheeky pair spotted a pretty girl on the sideline Barry would be instructed to find touch near her. The boys could get a better look and show off their talents. He rarely missed. Then there was his penchant for the drop-kick, which brought him a then record eight goals in his 25 appearances for Wales. Once, playing for Cardiff against Llanelli in November 1970, he dropped four in a match to give his adopted club a 12–10 victory over his home team. Peter Walker, reporting that match for the *Daily Telegraph*, described them as 'classics of intelligent positioning, instantaneous reading of the given situation [and] smooth manoeuvring'. It was relatively late in his career that he was invited to take place-kicks for Wales, but his nonchalant round-the-corner style enabled him to become the then leading Welsh points scorer, racking up 90 points in next to no time.

An unlikely aspect of Barry's game helped Wales to the 1971 Grand Slam in the showdown match with France in Paris. Even his best friends would be the first to admit that tackling wasn't his strength, but in taking out big Benoît Dauga as France threatened to score he underlined his bravery. His effort earned him the respect of the most gnarled of Welsh forwards. He even suffered a broken nose for his troubles and had to go off briefly to receive attention. Typically, he complemented his defensive part soon afterwards by making a classic outside-half break for the try that paved the way to victory.

A story that did the rounds of south Wales when he was in his prime illustrates his standing. The joke of the day was that the Heavenly Welsh were playing the Heavenly English in a tight game on the Elysian Fields. The Welsh fly-half was showing off but achieving very little. A recent arrival supporting the Welsh team turned to a fellow spectator to ask: 'Who's the Welsh Number 10?' 'Ah,' began the reply, 'that's God, but he thinks he's Barry John.'

He had been a Lion in South Africa with Gareth Edwards in 1968, but a broken collarbone in the first Test curtailed his appearances. In New Zealand with the 1971 tourists, however, he was the standout player among an outstanding team. His tactical alertness and brilliant kicking – from out of the hand as well as place-kicking – had the All Blacks on the run throughout the series. The Lions became the only British/Irish side to date to win a rubber over there and for his efforts the New Zealand public christened him 'The King'.

But the hero-worship, in New Zealand as well as back home in Britain, was not to his liking. The hordes of backslappers and the excesses of their praise embarrassed him. Everyone, it seemed, wanted a slice of him. The pressure to maintain his high playing standards and the incessant requests to fulfil public engagements disillusioned him and less than a year after the Lions' tour he left his followers wanting more when, aged only 27, he suddenly retired.

STEVE SMITH
The Smiler

Steve Smith's big smile was the happy face of English rugby in the 1970s and early 1980s. It was not a barometer of England's form but, through thick and thin, it epitomised the happy spirit of a team that had few pretensions to greatness yet managed to climb the Five Nations' peak by winning the Grand Slam in 1980. It was said of that mercurial decade for English rugby that its players arranged two big parties for every international weekend. One a celebration for those who were still members of the team; the other a reunion for those who had just been ejected from it. Whatever his playing status, Steve Smith would have been at the heart and soul of any gathering. Naturally gregarious, he was one of the most popular players of his generation.

Born in Stockport on 22 July 1951, he went from Kings' School Macclesfield to Loughborough Colleges to study PE and history with the initial aim of becoming a teacher. Coming under the coaching influence of Jim Greenwood, one of Britain's most influential thinkers about rugby, Smith's career blossomed in a successful Loughborough Colleges team that included future England internationals Fran Cotton and Dick Cowman. Smith was also a talented soccer player and cricketer, but with his love of touring and enjoyment of rugby's 'third-half' his future in the 15-a-side sport was secured. At 5ft 10in and 13 stone when fighting fit, he was big for a scrum-half. Indeed, his size 11 feet actually matched Cotton's, the big prop to whom he once lent a pair of boots in an emergency. Smith is still waiting for a new pair from his old pal – he said Fran was so much heavier that he'd squashed them beyond further use.

He was noticeably left-handed in his play, making him an awkward scrum-half to defend against. The natural break for the right-handed player is to his right off a scrum, moving anticlockwise from the put-in. Smith confounded opponents, however, by swinging back from the scrum feed and darting away to his left. His blind-side breaks on that side of the field often caught defences on the wrong foot and brought many tries for his left-winger, Mike Slemen. Yet the natural passing direction for the left-hander is to his right, so when he chose to break to that side of the scrum he was just as effective, with his long spin-pass making tries for his other winger, John Carleton.

Steve was cool and resourceful under pressure and always one to keep his head up before choosing his options. He had a smooth service, kicked shrewdly and was tactically aware. Intelligent and physically strong, he was well able to protect his fly-half and had all the requisites for a Test scrum-half. His strong performances for Wilmslow, his first senior club, attracted the attentions of the England selectors and in 1972 he went to South Africa as a replacement. He joined Sale on his return and was a member of the North-Western Counties side that overcame Ian Kirkpatrick's All Blacks 16–14 at Workington in 1972 – the first ever defeat experienced by a New Zealand side against an English provincial team. Smith won his first cap against Ireland in Dublin the same season, and when England went on to share in a unique Five Nations quintuple tie he was hailed as one of the finds of the year. English scrum-halves of the 1970s were called the butterflies by the critics – their lifespan was very short. Steve was no exception and he failed to nail down his position in the side. As a succession of scrum-halves passed through the selectors' notebooks, he put on weight, ballooning close to 15 stone, lost motivation and fell out of favour. There was also a perception that he was unpopular with selectors, that his smiling face, cheerful banter and informality, which was in keeping with the 1970s, gave the impression that he was complacent. Moreover, with his flowing hair and sharp line in wit, he was regarded by some members of the England selection committee as something of a rebel.

It's true that he often needed a strong personality to push him, someone to coax him through training. It was the arrival at Sale in the late 1970s of Fran Cotton, the straight-talking former colleague from his Loughborough and North-Western Counties days, which gave Smith the spur to raise his game. He set his sights on regaining his place alongside Cotton in the England side. In 1979, the pair set themselves the task of reaching peak fitness for the Northern Division's match with the All Blacks at Otley scheduled for November. For six months Cotton, a fitness fanatic, cracked the whip and had Smith out training daily. At about the same time a switch of county allegiance from Cheshire to Lancashire saw Smithy fall under the inspiring coaching guidance of Des Seabrook and his game was revitalised. The scrum-half scaled down by a stone and a half to match the weight he was when he played at Loughborough.

He successfully relaunched his career in the North's 21–9 victory over the New Zealanders, reclaimed his place in the England side led by Bill Beaumont and showed all his old sharpness to fire the England backs to a Grand Slam season in 1980. His reading of the game was better than ever and his distribution at Murrayfield, where England ran riot to win 30–18, was an important factor in his side's five tries – all scored by the backs, including one by Smith himself. Many felt that he was unlucky to miss out on selection for the 1980 Lions to South Africa, and it was little consolation to him later in the summer when the injury-stricken tourists called for him as a late replacement. He was effectively the fourth-choice scrum-half and sat on the bench without being called for the final Test in Pretoria. When he was presented with his Lions' blazer and tie afterwards, he felt unable to wear them. That was not as an act of disrespect; he felt that he had not deserved the honour.

The England playing set-up at the time was well led by men such as Budge Rogers and coach Mike Davis, and with Beaumont at the helm on the field, Smithy at last enjoyed a 'run' in the England side. Maybe wine turned to water in 1981 when England slumped after the Grand Slam, but the management kept faith in the players and in 1982, when Beaumont was forced to relinquish the England captaincy, the selectors turned to Smithy to lead the side. He maintained his extrovert smile but beneath it there lurked a streak of competitive ruthlessness. Making him captain was a popular decision. He had been an able lieutenant to Beaumont for Lancashire, the North and England before and he went on to skipper the side five times. Smithy was fired up, worked on his fitness to keep at bay the scrum-half challenge of the young pretender Nigel Melville, and helped England play with zest and enterprise in recording excellent wins against France and Wales.

He went on to become England's then most-capped scrum-half before surrendering his place to the young Nigel Melville in 1983. Even so, he finally earned what he saw as the right to wear the blazer and tie of the Lions when, in New Zealand in 1983, he captained the tourists to a much-needed win against Hawke's Bay. After retirement from the game, he went on to smile his way through a successful career in the rugby media and business world, where his parallel career with Fran Cotton as a player, teacher and account manager finally converged when the pair became directors of the well-known leisurewear company, Cotton Traders.

CARSTON CATCHESIDE
Catchy and the King

Rugby's great entertainers have invariably been nippy little wingers whose love of the unorthodox or ability to beat a man with a jink or a sidestep take them to the try-line for match-winning scores. Think Shane Williams among the current crop of international players, Gerald Davies in the Welsh sides of the 1970s, or Prince Alex Obolensky for England against the 1936 All Blacks. They weren't big bruisers. They were noted for their small stature, tremendous pace and individual touches of genius.

The player who fitted this description in the 1920s was a Geordie who flashed like a meteor across the Five Nations firmament in 1924 to become the first player in the history of the tournament to score tries in every match of his country's campaign. By so doing he helped England to the Grand Slam and left supporters, among them King George V, with a host of memories.

Howard Carston Catcheside – he was always known as 'Catchy' – was born in Sunderland on 18 August 1899 and educated at Oundle School. He started out as a scrum-half at school, but never played for the senior school rugby team because as a teenager he lied about his age to enlist for service in France with the Royal Field Artillery. During the Great War he reached the rank of Second Lieutenant and was still a teenager when he was demobbed. Young enough to serve again when hostilities resumed in 1939, he was promoted to Lieutenant Colonel, took part in the Normandy landings and was awarded the military OBE.

Rugby would be the torch that guided him through his peace-time life. He joined Percy Park, a club in the Newcastle suburbs, in 1919 and filled his leisure time playing for fun with like-minded lads just back from war. He enjoyed the japes that generations of exuberant rugby players have engaged in. Once, returning late at night from an away match, he and a club-mate found themselves stranded in central Newcastle some hours after the bus depot had closed. His mate's family owned a furniture store on the city's main high street, so the pair decided to bed down there for the night. Imagine the surprise for pedestrians on Sunday morning seeing two slightly hungover rugby players fast asleep in the shop window.

Such cheek was to be a feature of his play on the field and it brought him many tries for Percy Park. He wasn't the fastest of wingers, but he was resourceful; and his pale complexion and swept-back fair hair meant that he stood out in any company. His club talents were noted by the county selectors and it was his performances scoring tries and dropping goals for Northumberland in the Northern Division of the County Championship in the autumn of 1923 that earned him a place in the England trials in December. He made an instant impression on the selectors. He scored for the winning North team against the South in the first trial, for the winning Probables against the Possibles a fortnight later and for 'England' in their overwhelming 28–8 win against The

Rest in the final trial at Twickenham on the first Saturday of 1924.

It was after that Twickenham trial that he returned home full of confidence to submit his claim for travelling expenses to the RFU – 'To third-class railway fare from Newcastle to King's Cross, return . . . £4.' Back came a terse reply from the then secretary, reprimanding him for trying to eke an extra penny out of the parsimonious Union and enclosing a cheque for only £3-19s-11d in old money (£3.99½). But he went straight in to England's team for the Five Nations as a winger and scored tries in each of the four matches of a Grand Slam season – the first player in the history of the tournament to achieve what remains a rare feat. Moreover, he had disguised the fact that he was suffering from mumps when he won his first cap at Swansea where he scored two tries against Wales. In the win against France at Twickenham he made a lasting impression on the King, who was a regular visitor to the ground that had opened in the first year of his reign. England were struggling to maintain a lead against the visitors when, just before the interval, the English backs engineered an opening for Catcheside to have a run on the right wing. The French fullback was perfectly positioned to cut him off with a front-on tackle but, just as the move seemed doomed, Catchy high-jumped over the stooping would-be tackler and dropped over the line for a try. The rugby correspondent of *The Times* called it an 'unexpected revelation', but it set England on course for their third win of the season, with only Scotland standing between them and the Grand Slam.

The King was back at Twickenham the month after for the Scotland match and when introduced to the England side stopped to have a long conversation with the jumping try-scorer. The exact exchange was never set down but Catchy's team-mates later stated that His Majesty warned him to be careful if attempting that move again. 'Isn't it rather dangerous?' the King was heard to say. England went on to win 19–0, Catchy scoring a try that brought his tally in England trial and international matches that season to 43 points – a staggering 13 tries and a drop-goal. He was soon busily filling in his expenses sheet again, this time successfully claiming £4: 'To third-class railway fare from Newcastle to King's Cross, return . . . £3-19s-11d; the use of toilet at King's Cross 1d.'

His lack of pace told against him in the trials next season and he was dropped, but in 1926 he was back in the England team as a fullback, having occupied the position for the first time in his career in that season's final trial. He went on to collect eight England caps before a serious injury brought a premature end to a playing career that also included more than 50 appearances for his county. Between the wars business took him to London, where he worked as a ship broker and coal exporter, while his popularity, playing experience and exceptional personality made him the ideal choice when he was invited to join England's rugby selection committee in 1937. It was a job he loved. He served for 25 years, the last 11 as chairman, during which time England won a Grand Slam, three Triple Crowns, three outright Five Nations titles, two shared titles and were twice runners-up. In his last season as convenor of the selectors the other five members of his committee were all former England internationals that he had helped to cap as players.

He had the ability to get on with young and old and during his days as chairman of selectors no international match banquet was complete without a witty top-table speech delivered by Catchy, who invariably signed himself off with his catch-phrase: 'Here's to the whitest man I know – Carston Catcheside.' His mock strip-teases in Paris at post-match banquets were hilarious and invariably led to a blushing violinist or two dashing out in case a revealing garment was removed. The enthusiasm he shared for the game knew no bounds. In 1958, on their way to Paris for a key Five Nations match with France, the England team shared the flight with a young Julie Andrews, who made a big impression on the side. Just before the English XV left their dressing-room at Colombes the next day Catchy announced that he had just been handed a note to read out. 'Well, isn't that nice,' he said. 'Julie Andrews says "Good luck, boys, and for heaven's sake get the ball out to the wings!"' They did. The wingers, Peter Jackson and Peter Thompson, scored three tries and England won 14–0. After the match one of the players found the note lying in the dressing rooms and discovered, to everyone's amusement, that it had been written in Catchy's handwriting.

He retired as chairman of selectors in 1962 and calculated that

he had travelled more than 150,000 miles as part of his duties watching club players, organising trials and attending international matches. In retirement he continued to watch rugby for pleasure in the London area and when he died, aged 87, in Wandsworth on 10 May 1987, the rugby writer Vivian Jenkins wrote: 'Catchy created fun and laughter wherever he went. I defy any of the moderns to enjoy their rugby as much as Catchy did.'

MICKEY SKINNER
The Munch

Many England players are remembered for their stirring try-winning performances, men like Obolensky, Peter Jackson, Richard Sharp and Andy Hancock. Then there are the outstanding England captains whose periods at the helm are instantly recognised by tags such as Wakefield's England, Beaumont's England or even Carling's England. Finally, there are the individuals who stand out for a heroic try-saving tackle.

Mickey Skinner's match will mean only one thing to those who followed England's fortunes in the early 1990s: the brutal World Cup quarter-final between France and England in Paris in October 1991. Le Crunch. The scores were all-square at 10-all when England, under the cosh as France threatened to cut loose, were grateful to concede a five-metre scrum as the game entered its last quarter. The body language of French blind-side Eric Champ and his Number 8 Marc Cécillon made it clear to the English that they would pick up and drive the ball over for a try. France duly won the strike and Cécillon, a bull of a man, went on the charge. The partisan French crowd roared and then Skinner fronted up to the danger. He put in a tackle that was off the Richter scale, picking up the French Number 8 and dumping him three metres behind the scrum. It was the defining moment of the match. The French crowd fell silent, Cécillon was stunned and as Skinner stared out Champ, his opposite number and with whom he had had a running battle all afternoon, England cleared the danger.

Near the end Jon Webb landed a penalty and Richard Hill chipped towards the French line, where Skinner and his captain, Will Carling, jumped for the ball and landed together to add a late try. Skinner's body language was the loudest on the field, giving the impression that he had scored, but later he had to concede seniority to his captain and the try went to Carling. Nevertheless, everyone was aware of Skinner's magnificent contribution to an outstanding England back-row effort that guaranteed the men in white a World Cup semi-final at Murrayfield against Scotland a week later. After the match, it was the *Sun* that christened Skinner 'The Munch' for that all-consuming tackle, catapulting him to banner-headline stardom. He enjoyed every minute of it.

Mind, he very nearly went from saint to sinner the next week when, in a moment of stupidity, he lost his temper and gave away a penalty in front of his posts at a critical time in the World Cup semi-final. Gavin Hastings stepped up to take the kick that would put Scotland ahead. The England players, who could hardly bear to watch, were distracted by Rory Underwood. 'F*** me, he's missed,' shouted England's teetotal, clean-living winger. Jason Leonard gave the definitive version of the team's reaction: 'The boys and I were so shocked at the fact that Rory was swearing that we hardly noticed that Gav had missed his kick,' he wrote later. In the closing stages England's back row, with Skinner colossal again, blotted a much-vaunted Scottish loose trio out of the game and Rob Andrew's late drop-goal kicked England into the final against Australia at Twickenham a week later, where they were beaten 12–6.

Mickey Skinner was born on 26 November 1958 in Newcastle and played his early rugby with the Tynedale and Blaydon clubs. After taking his degree at Leeds Polytechnic, he became a computer consultant and moved south to Bromley in Kent, where he joined Blackheath. In 1985 he began a long association with Harlequins, where his mullet-hairstyle caused a few eyebrows to be raised among the club's more staid members. But there was never any question about his commitment to the club and his barnstorming performances in the back row of a pack that included several England internationals soon brought him to the notice of the London Division selectors. He was far from being an angel of the north, though his on-field toughness was often masked in a lurking grin. And his cheeky-boy antics at 'Quins made him one of the most popular personalities at the club, but not always with the committee. A garrulous individual, he liked a drink and could have won *Mastermind* hands down had he ever chosen to test his specialist subject, the pubs of southwest London. He loved to party and dressed in waistcoats and bow-ties that matched his exuberant personality, but he was far more than just a social rugby player. In 1987, when through injuries England were short of back-row players during their inaugural World Cup campaign in Australia, Skinner answered the call to duty. The RFU were unable to track him down so it was left to Desmond Lynam to issue a nationwide appeal as to his whereabouts on the BBC's Saturday afternoon sports programme, *Grandstand*.

He was eventually located and flown out, but didn't manage to win his cap. Then, the following January, with Geoff Cooke installed as England's new head coach, the Geordie-turned-Londoner was given his Test debut at the age of 29 alongside fellow new caps Will Carling and Jeff Probyn in a side that was unlucky to lose 10–9 to France in Paris. He became a regular choice in the early Cooke years and impressed the England management with the focus he showed when the side was preparing for matches. In the days before kick-off, the pranks and jokes gave way to concentration and serious training. Well, almost always.

There was one notable exception, when the side went on tour to Australia in the summer of 1988. He persuaded a handful of his England team-mates – 'fat-boys' (his name for his fellow forwards) and 'girls' (the backs) that it would be a good idea to go bungee-jumping. He helpfully made suitable arrangements, even organising for the players' cash and valuables to be handed over ready for collection later. As the enthusiasts queued up for their jump, Skinner managed to edge his way to the back of the line. One by one the England players went over the top before Skinner, the last man, turned away, declined to jump and instead scarpered with all the cash. He wasn't every player's favourite tourist on that visit.

In 1991, he lost his place to Mike Teague on the blind-side for the first England win at Cardiff for 28 years and missed out on the Grand Slam, though he did his bit in support of the team as a bench replacement. When the World Cup began later that year, Skinner was again in reserve as Geoff Cooke opened the tournament with Teague, Dean Richards and Peter Winterbottom as his first-choice back row against the All Blacks. As the campaign progressed, Cooke rested Teague and reinstated Skinner at blind-side, and he scored a try in the pool match playing alongside Richards against the US Eagles. He played such a committed and skilful game that Cooke was left with a back-row selection dilemma for the quarter-final against France. He solved it by taking the bold step of dropping Richards, playing Teague at Number 8 and keeping the Harlequin flankers, Winterbottom and Skinner – a decision, it transpired, that enabled The Munch to tackle France out of the competition.

In 1992 he was on the blind-side when England completed their first back-to-back Grand Slams since 1923–24 and he bowed out on a high note by scoring a try in their 24–0 win against Wales in the final match. After that he was an amusing rugby columnist for both *Rugby World* magazine and the *Sun*, and showed the generous side of his character by devoting much of his time to the Wooden Spoon Society, rugby's main charitable cause. He was the obvious choice to narrate a video of rugby's biggest tackles – a rugby video nasty some called it – but whenever The Munch is mentioned in rugby conversations he is associated with his own big hit that silenced the French in Paris and put them out of the 1991 World Cup.

GARETH CHILCOTT
Coochie

The old adage that the best props, like the best ports, mature with age was never better illustrated in English rugby circles than in the shining example of Gareth Chilcott – 'Coochie' to all his friends and admirers. More cider than port perhaps, he was the larger-than-life West Country stalwart whose on-field escapades admittedly resulted in several high-profile sendings-off and a year-long ban for trampling over Bristol's Bob Hesford during his colourful career. Even he conceded, after his fourth or fifth set of marching orders, that his defence of mistaken identity was wearing thin. In his day-to-day life, after leaving school with no quali-fications, he mastered a variety of jobs from French polishing and debt collecting to TV punditry, popular after-dinner speaker and Christmas pantomime villain. He became a much-loved character who, for his deeds on as well as off the field, was seen as a popular jack-of-all-trades who pretty much mastered them all.

Football was his first sporting interest. He was born on 20 November 1956 in Bristol, where he grew up loving Bristol City and hating Bristol Rovers, but his tree-trunk legs and 17-stone roly-poly Friar Tuck shape dictated that he should be a rugby player, and a prop forward at that. It was a chance meeting with a former teacher that persuaded him to abandon the terraces at Ashton Gate and try his hand at rugby with the Old Redcliffians club. Coochie had the ideal build to make his presence felt in the dark world of the scrum and ruck, and he loved playing up to the part of front-row hard man, sending himself up in hilarious fashion by coming out with such gems as the only three calls he ever understood were 'shove, hit him and duck'.

It was all part of his act as a lovable rogue, of course, for when he joined Bath in 1976 he quickly became the backbone of a pack coached by Jack Rowell which was to dominate English club rugby for much of his long career. He was rarely prominent in the loose, and even his best friends held the view that he would not know what to do if given a pass in the open. Even so, with his uncompromising approach in the tight he was the cornerstone of the club's dominant pack. He formed a formidable front row with Graham Dawe and Richard Lee that called themselves the 'Beached Whales RFC' and he remained loyal to Bath for 17 years, playing nearly 400 first-class matches for them before finally retiring at Christmas in 1993. Along the way he picked up 14 England caps, specialising initially on the loose-head, though he could also play effectively on the other side of the front row.

Coochie courted controversy on his England debut against Australia at Twickenham in November 1984. England fielded five new caps in a side that had a strong West Country presence, but they were left behind in the final quarter of the game by a team that went on to make a Grand Slam tour of the Home Unions. During the match he felled the Wallabies' scrum-half, Nick Farr-Jones, with a punch that would normally have warranted a sending-off. He was lucky to escape with a penalty and a stiff warning, but the selectors wielded the axe and he was in the international wilderness for 15 months before answering a recall for the final two matches of the 1986 Five Nations. It was typical of the man that he took the trouble to book in for some French lessons that year in order to understand what their pack were planning to get up to in the scrums. But in 1987 he was in trouble again when four members of the England side, Coochie included, were reprimanded and dropped on disciplinary grounds for their part in a sour, ugly match against Wales in Cardiff.

His final and most valued run in the England side came at the end of 1989 with a string of appearances as tight-head. English rugby, with Geoff Cooke in charge of team preparations and Will Carling as captain, was gearing up for a golden era. Coochie, now 32, had mellowed into a reformed character and played his part in laying its foundation. He fronted up alongside Brian Moore and Paul Rendall to take apart a much-vaunted French front row in an 11–0 victory at Twickenham. Replacements were permitted only for serious injuries in those days but it was clear after five minutes that the French props were in all sorts of difficulty that afternoon. Claude Portolan, who came off in the first half looking like a man about to undergo prolonged root canal treatment, had clearly been scrummaged out of the game. The English front row, it was suggested, had seriously damaged the Frenchman's pride and injury was merely a cover to enable a more experienced replacement to take his place.

One journalist raved about Coochie's performance. 'Chilcott, restored to the front row, had a magnificent match, clearing up the line-out and burrowing around with the urgency of a strapping gnome,' he wrote. For the first time in 25 years France failed to score in a Five Nations match, losing 11–0 to a rejuvenated England side that was later unlucky to miss out on the championship title against Wales in Cardiff before overwhelming Romania in a friendly in Bucharest. Although he damaged a calf muscle in that final game, he was selected to tour Australia with the Lions in the summer, though a recurrence of the injury restricted his appearances. At 33, the prop previously labelled a villain had become a constructive and effective force. Yet his Test career ended there. Advancing years, the return of Jeff Probyn and the emergence of Jason Leonard deprived him of future Test honours.

Fame, or notoriety depending on the point of view, eased his path from rugby player to rugby personality. His wisecracks endeared him to a wide audience. 'After a match I like to go down the local for a quiet pint . . . followed by 15 noisy ones,' was his catchphrase. His standing as a down-to-earth prop who held the game's values and traditions close to his heart was the passport that enabled him to forge a new and rewarding career heading up the corporate business with Gullivers, the Gloucestershire company that is a market leader in the rugby travel business. His ability to be himself – what you see is what you get – has been the key to his success in the corporate world, but throughout he has been ready to acknowledge the good friendships and breaks that rugby afforded him. He is one of the sport's best ambassadors and funniest storytellers as well as being a staunch supporter of the game's charity, the Wooden Spoon Society.

For several Christmas seasons in the 1990s he broke new ground for a rugby player, bringing his booming West Country accent to pantomime. He always seemed to be bursting out of his rugby kit as a player and, as the unlikeliest of luvvies, he similarly seemed to burst out of his tights and doublet on stage. His first appearance was in a supporting role to Rolf Harris, Lesley Joseph and Sylvester McCoy in *Cinderella* at Bath's Theatre Royal where, inevitably, he was the butt of a variety of jokes. 'Didn't you used to be a rugby player? Whatever happened to your career?'. . . to which his Bath clubmates among the first-night audience shouted back: 'It's behind you.' He played the Broker's man in that production – too ugly, his mates insisted, to be an ugly sister.

Gareth Chilcott stories and escapades have spread across the world. In 1993 he and Mick Quinn, the former Ireland fly-half, were among the leaders of a Gullivers supporters' trip to New Zealand for the Lions' tour. The pair were relaxing playing golf one afternoon when Quinn hit his ball into a pond. It landed just beyond the Irishman's reach but close enough to retrieve with a helping hand. Coochie obliged but, after lending Quinn his strong arm to extend the reach, let go just as the Irishman grabbed the ball. On the same trip, the other side of his character was shown when he saved a Spaniard from drowning after a scary white water rafting accident.

It is doubtful that his like will be seen again. The white sweatband around the cauliflowered ears and shaved pate, the unmistakeable moustache and the mischievous grin were the hallmarks of one of the game's best-loved characters, a throwback to the straightforward times when prop forwards rarely had to pass, tackle or sidestep. It's true that rugby as a spectacle has moved on for the better since his playing days, but there was never a dull moment when Coochie was in the front row for club or country.

AUSTIN HEALEY
The Leicester Lip

Austin Healey was the man that crowds watching their sides play against Leicester Tigers, England or the British/Irish Lions loved to hate. Spiky, provocative and a maverick – on as well as off the pitch – he even found himself at loggerheads with his own team-mates and coaches during his eventful career.

The most publicised off-the-field incident of his playing days came on the eve of the third Test of the Lions' tour of Australia in 2001. The sides went into the final Test with the series balanced at a win apiece when a diary under Healey's by-line appeared in the *Guardian* newspaper. In it, the new Australian lock Justin Harrison was described as a 'plank' and a 'plod'. Australia went on to win the decisive Test, Harrison made an outstanding contribution to the win and the Lions' manager, Graham Henry, publicly rebuked Healey, who was injured and unable to play in the match.

Yet Healey had not written the article. When the Lions' disciplinary committee met to pass judgement, the journalist and former Wales captain Eddie Butler held his hand up to authorship of the newspaper article. Although it was acknowledged by the committee that Healey had not written the article, had not had an opportunity to edit its ghosted contents and did not agree with the views expressed, 'Oz', as he was known, was still fined for 'bringing the Lions into disrepute'.

Four years later, however, when Andy Robinson was on Sir Clive Woodward's management team for the disastrous 2005 Lions' tour of New Zealand, Oz did joke in a newspaper column that Robinson was going to a fancy-dress party as a pumpkin. 'They're hoping when it gets to midnight he'll turn into a real coach!' he wrote. Few were amused. Nor were Lions' management's the only ones to run into conflict with Healey. At Leicester, both Bob Dwyer and Pat Howard, Australians with exemplary coaching pedigrees, had spats with him, as did many among the Tigers' playing squad. For part of one season he was not on speaking terms with outside-half Andy Goode, and his banter left many players unsure about his digs. Was Oz teasing them or were there real barbs in many of his comments?

Even Sir Clive Woodward was not immune to the sarcasm of 'the Leicester Lip' in the early years of his reign as England's head coach. According to Oz, Woodward told his players that he had decided to sell his business after England's demise in the 1999 Rugby World Cup in order to put himself in the same boat as them by investing his professional life in rugby. It left a positive impression on many of the players until Oz queried how much the sale had realised. Healey, on hearing that it was several million, replied: 'So that puts us all in the same boat, then?'

Woodward, though, tells an amusing story that illustrates the comic side of Healey's quick wit. When the England captaincy was up for grabs before Woodward announced his first England squad in the autumn of 1997, the bookmakers quoted Healey's chances of taking over from Phil de Glanville as 350:1. When Woodward arrived to make his announcement to the press he was approached by Healey and informed of the odds. 'I can scrape together £20k,' Healey told the new coach. 'If you can match it, that's £7 million each! Name me captain, and we're out of here!'

Austin Healey was born on 26 October 1973 at Wallasey. His small stature led to his being bullied at primary school and he has admitted that beatings from bigger lads frightened him. On his last day before leaving for secondary school he summoned up the courage to fight back and shocked one of his tormentors by getting his retaliation in first and making the bigger lad cry. It was, Healey said, a liberating experience; he never again took a backward step – physically or verbally.

Those attributes of courage and quick wit transferred successfully to the rugby pitch and during his later schooldays at St Anselm's College he developed into a talented scrum-half. He played briefly for Birkenhead Park before moving to Waterloo, where he first fell under the national spotlight for his part in outstanding wins against the holders Bath and then Orrell in the 1992–93 Pilkington Cup. Appearances for the England Under-21 side and the England Sevens team at the prestigious Hong Kong event followed and, after joining Orrell as a winger, he switched to his natural position at scrum-half in 1995 when Dewi Morris retired. For his gutsy early displays he reminded many observers of the young Gareth Edwards. Healey was a natural games-player, with pace and a confidence bordering on arrogance that enabled him to make unexpected breaks that invariably led to match-breaking scores. His talents were soon spotted by Leicester, and a move to the Tigers was the prelude to his first full England cap in 1997. He went on to win 51 caps for his country and was a British/Irish Lion in 1997 (two Tests) and again in 2001.

The wickedly playful side of his personality came out when he was chosen for the 1997 Lions. Compared with today, those were relatively relaxed times and the lucky individuals received notification of their selection for the tour via snail-mail on the morning the team was officially announced. At the time, Austin was living near the Leicester ground and sharing a house with long-term mucker, club-mate and Lions' hopeful, Will Greenwood, who had enjoyed a good run in the centre for a Tigers' side that had reached the Heineken Cup Final. Greenwood was tipped as a bolter to win a place on the tour and thus join the small band of players called up for the Lions before winning an international cap.

On the morning of the team announcement Austin was up early to intercept the post. He duly collected his invitation to join the Lions but when Greenwood, not the earliest of risers by his own admission, eventually stirred, he was disappointed but not entirely surprised to find no such invitation was awaiting him. He congratulated Austin and kindly offered to drive his housemate to a press conference at their club – several Leicester players had been chosen to make the visit, including the Lions' captain, Martin Johnson. As Greenwood pulled in for the reception at Welford Road and parked his battered old Metro, a TV reporter made a point of shouting his congratulations across the car park to *both* driver and passenger. Greenwood was slightly flummoxed, thinking the reporter was winding him up, whereupon Oz produced a letter for Greenwood that he had held back but which had been delivered with his own invitation five hours before. As Greenwood said, 'With friends like that, who needs enemies?'

For all Austin's achievements though, the lasting disappointment of his playing career was failure to make the 2003 England World Cup squad. His versatility – the description of his skills that he hated so much – became his passport to the England squad for much of Clive Woodward's stewardship, and Healey started for England in the Number 9, Number 10, Number 11 and Number 14 shirts as well as once filling in for Jason Robinson against Wales in 2002 in the Number 15 jersey. He had more positions than the *Kama Sutra*. The label 'super-sub' inevitably stuck to his CV but, when the group that went on to win the 2003 World Cup was announced, there was no room in the extended squad for one who was seen as the undisputed jack-of-all-trades. Spectators on the world stage were denied the delight of seeing his impish genius performing in the cup-winning side – something that Leicester supporters had cherished on several big occasions, most notably in 2001 and 2002 when he ripped apart first Stade Français and then Munster in successive finals of the Heineken Cup. He was named 'man of the match' for his visionary play in both those cup final wins.

But the omission from the World Cup squad was hard to swallow. Healey always wanted the last word in his verbal jousts with players. After 2003, all that anyone from the World Cup side needed to say to silence him was, 'Have you got one of these Oz?' pointing to a World Cup medal. He finished playing in 2006, took a job with a Swiss bank and began building a wide portfolio of media commitments. His insight and wit quickly became a staple of the BBC's rugby coverage, where he joined up with Eddie Butler again to form part of the team that brings live coverage of the Six Nations, while he has impressed a broader audience putting his best foot forward on the *Strictly Come Dancing* programme. Who knows? Ten years from now he could well be regarded as a national treasure.

COMMITMENT
PERSONIFIED

RAY GRAVELL
A Most Passionate Welshman

It was Carwyn James, Lions and Llanelli coach of the 1970s, who perfectly summed up Ray Gravell in a memoir in the *Guardian*. He told readers that Gravell belonged spiritually to the army of the last real Prince of Wales, Llewellyn the Last, who was killed by the English at Builth Wells in 1282. It was the perfect description of a man whose bravery on the field and love of Wales – its culture, people and language – marked him out as the archetypal passionate Welshman of his generation. He brought *calon* – heart – to everything he tackled. His dark facial features and full auburn-tinged beard lent a hint of menace to the character he portrayed on the rugby field, while a warm, generous personality complemented his Welshness away from the battle ground. His politics, musical tastes and recreations were deeply rooted in Welsh life and his nation championed him, just as they had their natural Princes of Wales seven centuries earlier. Typically, his autobiography, which came out in 2008 shortly after his sudden death, was published in English and Welsh.

Yet he was totally devoid of the insularity that sometimes attends fervent nationalism. Grav had the ability to get on with everyone and was popular in Lions' teams representing the four Home Unions as well as with Barbarian sides that united the nations of the rugby playing world. He was never heard to utter a bad word about a team-mate, nor was one ever directed at him. Humour was his first language outside Wales. When he went on the Lions' tour to South

Africa in 1980 he sent up his nationalism by reassuring the *Guardian*'s Frank Keating: 'There will be a sharp fall in the number of English-owned second homes burned down in the Welsh Borders while I'm away.' Then there was the time he made his debut for the Barbarians, against Leicester at Christmas in 1975. He was due to play centre and was introduced to his winger, Pio Tikoisuva, in the changing rooms. 'Where're you from,' asked Ray. 'Fiji,' said the strapping Pacific Islander. 'Fiji,' said Ray with great enthusiasm. 'At 20p a mile travelling expenses, you'll make a fortune.'

'West is best' was his slogan, a reference to the square mile of God's country in Welsh-speaking Carmarthenshire where Ray lived his life. He was born in the hamlet of Mynydd y Garreg near the ancient castle town of Kidwelly on 12 September 1951. Educated at Queen Elizabeth's Grammar School in Carmarthen, he left school early (with one O level, in Welsh, he once proudly revealed) to join the South Wales Electricity Board. There, he worked as a linesman under the careful watch of his Llanelli and Wales rugby hero, Delme Thomas. He won a Welsh Youth cap before joining Delme at weekends as a regular in the Llanelli sides of the early 1970s. The stamp of distinction on his rugby was his boisterous, forthright running. Ray had tremendous physical presence to harness to his natural flair and could trouble the tightest of defences.

In 1975 his strong performances with Llanelli were finally recognised by the Welsh selectors and, among six new caps against France that year, he made a memorable debut in a 25–10 victory at the Parc des Princes. Before the match he was a bag of nerves and even thought that he should withdraw and pack his bags for home, so intense were his feelings at representing his country. But a late telegram from west Wales, with best wishes from Mammy and Twdls (the cat), helped dissipate the nerves and launched him on a career that brought 23 caps in the centre during Wales's domination of the Five Nations in the late 1970s. Mind, he had worked himself up to such a fever pitch that, as the two teams queued in the tunnel waiting to take the pitch, Grav gave an excited thump to the Frenchman beside him. Only he could choose to stand next to Alain Estève, one of the biggest, meanest locks ever to play for

France. Fortunately the Welshman could only reach up to strike his opponent's shoulder. Estève looked down at him with disdain and wound a finger to his temple, making the gesture that translates as 'nutcase' in any language.

Grav's pre-match antics passed into rugby legend, particularly his renditions of Welsh songs that were loud enough to be heard in opponents' dressing-rooms. On one occasion an Irish substitute became so annoyed at the deafening noise emanating from the toilets that just before kick-off he went in, threw a bucket of cold water into the cubicle where Ray was singing and scarpered before the great man emerged. Minutes later, when Wales took the field, the rest of the Irish side imagined he must have put himself through an extremely vigorous work-out as he appeared to be sweating profusely.

Carwyn James said that nobody had worn the scarlet national jersey with a deeper sense of what it means to be Welsh than Grav. He was a reliable stopper in defence and an effective attacking play-maker with his aggressive running, proving a good link with his wingers. He was troubled by a shoulder injury in 1977 but returned fully restored to play a key part as the crash-ball catalyst who sucked in defenders in the 1978 Welsh Grand Slam. Many felt that this role was overplayed, for he also possessed an authentic outside burst which was seldom seen when playing for Wales. When he lost his place in the Welsh side the pain of being dropped was intense. He felt so ashamed, he said, that he wore dark glasses to disguise himself back in his home village. The Welsh selectors, of course, came to their senses and restored him after his barnstorming play for the 1980 Lions. But when, later, he was dropped again he wrote to the Big Five imploring them *never* to select him again: 'I couldn't risk the agony of rejection for a third time.'

He retired from playing in 1985, having appeared nearly 500 times for his beloved Llanelli. The highlights of his club career were playing in the 1972 victory over the Sixth All Blacks and later captaining the Scarlets. On the field he was a constant chatterer. Early in his career insecurity plagued him, for he constantly sought approval of his play from team-mates. When he became a senior player he was a source of inspiration to younger members of the side, and as captain his garrulous nature occasionally swayed things the

Scarlets' way. Once, leading his side against Cardiff at Stradey Park, he managed to talk them to victory. Llanelli held a narrow lead but Cardiff were attacking with the match in its dying moments. A well-known Welsh referee was officiating and Grav had been in his ear constantly during a succession of scrums near the Llanelli line. Gareth Davies, Cardiff's fly-half, was in the pocket ready to drop the winning goal, but Grav kept on so much at the official that the poor ref blew up in frustration, leaving Cardiff annoyed losers.

Early in his playing career he had made cameo television appearances (playing himself) in the Welsh language soap opera, *Pobol y Cwm*, and it was to broadcasting and acting that he turned to forge a new and equally successful career after rugby. He engaged a wider audience of young and old with his regular radio programmes in English and Welsh for BBC Wales and S4C, and his film roles included a part in Louis Malle's *Damage* in 1992. For his contribution to Welsh life he was invited to become a member of the National Eisteddfod's Gorsedd of Bards. Rugby remained his consuming passion and his professional duties included commentating on Welsh international and club games, while in his recreation he was in his element as president of Llanelli and later the Scarlets when Welsh rugby went regional. Down at Stradey all visitors were greeted with Grav's firm shake of the arm and big hug.

In his late 40s he was diagnosed with severe diabetes and later had to have his right leg amputated below the knee. The setback was one that he overcame bravely, as he had years before as a teenager when coming to terms with the suicide of his father. He taught himself to walk and the artificial limb was emblazoned in Llanelli's colours. But on 31 October 2007 – 35 years to the day of his proudest club triumph over the All Blacks – Ray Gravell died suddenly from a heart attack while enjoying a family holiday in Spain. The great and good of Welsh public life, together with his huge extended family of friends and colleagues from the worlds of rugby and broadcasting, attended his funeral at his beloved Stradey Park. There were 10,000 at the ground to hear his former rugby colleague Gerald Davies pay sincere tribute to a man whose infectious enthusiasm for life, particularly of the Welsh variety, will never be forgotten.

KEVIN FLYNN
The Quiet Man

Kevin Flynn had one of the most remarkable international careers in Irish rugby. Only Mike Gibson and Tony O'Reilly had longer spans in the Irish team and but for a run of injuries that would have completely demoralised less committed individuals, he would have challenged Gibson's one-time record for Irish Test appearances. Quiet and retiring off the field, he shunned the limelight, preferring to toil away for club and country as a maker of tries. He always enjoyed the buzz of top-class rugby and accepted the knocks that came his way – often the result of the heavy marking he suffered because of the reputation he had as an electric runner and dangerous creator of openings for his wingers.

Kevin Flynn was born in Dublin on 20 March 1939 and gained a glowing reputation as a schoolboy three-quarter who ran with the grace of a gazelle. He entered the Irish side at the end of his first season in first-class rugby as a 20-year-old in April 1959. It was a happy time to join the national side, for a mood of hopelessness was about to give way to a spirit of optimism. Ireland were contenders for the wooden spoon while France, their opponents, were already champions when the boy wonder from Dublin Wanderers, not long out of Terenure College, won his first cap in the last international match of that season's Five Nations Championship. Against the odds, Ireland fashioned a famous 9–5 victory over the French, with the newcomer paving the way with a searing break for Ireland's only try. Sean Diffley, the noted Irish rugby press critic, wrote 'Flynn made a resounding debut. His confidence was amazing. His passing and straight running were right out of the classical mould.' Another critic, Vivian Jenkins of the *Sunday Times*, asked, 'Where have the Irish selectors been hiding him? He looked like the most promising centre one has seen this season.'

According to a story that did the rounds after that match, Flynn was unhappy with his outside-half, Mick English, in that debut match. The youngster had expected to receive more passes, but English kept the ball tight in the second half and either kicked for position or took the game back to his forwards as Ireland nursed a 9–0 lead. At length, the exasperated Flynn shouted to his Number 10 for more possession. He was told in no uncertain terms where to go, not for personal reasons but because English did not want to give the French an opportunity of getting the ball. The unassuming youngster also found himself on the receiving end of a piece of Tony O'Reilly's wisdom later in the match when Jean Dupuy scored a try to take France back into the game. Dupuy was O'Reilly's opposite winger, but sensing an opportunity left his post, moved infield and cut between Flynn and David Hewitt in the centre to score. 'He was your man,' O'Reilly told Kevin in no uncertain terms as the Irish side lined up under their goalposts to await the conversion.

Even so, a glittering and long career beckoned, it seemed. But Flynn was beset by hamstring problems in the years that followed, and his career, though spanning 15 international seasons, was restricted to only 22 Test appearances. He would have won three times that number but for injuries. On his second appearance for Ireland, against France in Paris in 1960, he was floored early on by a dangerous head-high tackle by Jacky Bouquet, his opposite number from the year before. The Frenchman remembered what a danger Flynn had been and was determined to snuff out the flying Flynn's fire. Such incidents were common in the Irishman's career, and though they shook his confidence they never quelled his enthusiasm for Test rugby.

The light shone on him for several seasons in the early 1960s as Irish rugby steadily improved. His clever support play and uncanny positional sense were the hallmarks of his contribution to Ireland's Triple Crown challenge in 1965, when the Welsh narrowly robbed them of glory in Cardiff. He had the enthusiasm for the game that comes naturally to the Irish and brought pace to the three-quarter line, demonstrating his potential as an attacking centre of silky skills. His running had a beautiful balance yet he also showed that he had the vision to create tries for his wingers, as he had for Niall Brophy in that debut game against the French. But after playing against the Scots in 1966, 25 matches passed before he was fit enough to regain his Ireland place.

Of the five tries he scored for Ireland, the three in the 1964 and 1972 Twickenham wins against England stood out in the memory. His two in 1964 were scored while he was at the height of his powers, but it was the winning try in 1972, after he had been out of the national side for six years, that brought the most satisfaction to Irish supporters.

The Irish Troubles were at their height in 1972. Rugby, however, has always united the Irish and it proved a welcome diversion to the seriousness of everyday life. An Irish win at Twickenham was also important for the Irish community exiled on the mainland. In a nerve-racking game, Flynn and the rest of the Irish back division kept their cool to make the match-winning strike in the last minutes of the game. England led 12–10, but the gods had one last smile for Ireland that day. In a desperate last attack, Johnny Moloney fed Barry McGann from a scrum on the English 25. The outside-half handed on to Flynn, who popped through a chink in the English defence and, with the biggest of smiles on his face, went over for the clinching score. His final fling came a year later when, aged 33, he was a member of the side that has gone down in Irish history as their only one to date to hold the All Blacks in a Test.

His unassuming yet valued involvement in Irish rugby continued in the late 1970s when he was appointed a national selector. His three years of service culminated in 1981–82 when, as chairman of the committee, he helped select Ireland's first Triple Crown team since 1949. Ever true to his understated image, Irish rugby's quiet man waited for the changing rooms to empty after the Lansdowne Road win over Scotland, drove home and went for a reflective walk.

CLIFF DAVIES
The Iron Man of Kenfig

Cliff Morgan perfectly summed up the character of Cliff Davies, his contemporary in the Cardiff and Wales teams of the early 1950s: 'To play an international with [him] was something else,' Morgan wrote. Davies, the 5ft 9in nugget of a coalminer, part-time undertaker and all-round good egg was a prop forward who gave his best, on and off the pitch. Fire and iron strength were the hallmarks of his play, but it was the sense of fun that exuded from his powerful frame, whether philosophising about Wales and rugby or leading team-mates with his rich baritone voice in impromptu choral sessions, that marked him out as one of the rugby characters of his generation.

Clifton Davies was born in Kenfig Hill on 12 December 1919 and became a collier working at the coalface before the age of modern mining machinery. It was said that on Saturdays he hewed the coal from the face during the morning shift, clocked off and departed to play rugby in the afternoon before returning in the evening, ready to work the next shift. Early in his career he played for the local Kenfig village club, the team he fondly christened 'The Mules', and in 1939 turned out occasionally for Bridgend. Mining was a reserved wartime occupation, keeping Cliff in south Wales where he joined Cardiff, which organised an interesting fixture list of high-profile charity matches between 1940 and 1945.

He had not received any formal further education, but his love of reading, his interest in people and his easy-going extrovert personality made him a popular graduate of the university of life. To Kenfig and Cardiff rugby friends he was known as 'Tubby'. By the French he was nicknamed the '*Bon Ami*' of British rugby. His first rugby visit there was with Cardiff on their New Year tour to Nantes in 1945–46. The only French phrase he knew was *bonne année* yet he became the natural leader and life and soul of the party off the field. He always travelled light, with a toothbrush in his outside pocket and spare collar in his kit for the après-rugby.

Later the same season he was selected to play for Wales against France in Paris in one of the unofficial Victory internationals, but a mining injury prevented his travelling. No matter. Cliff arranged for his Kenfig Hill and Cardiff soulmate, Billy Jones, to take his place. The Welsh selectors – the 'Onions' Cliff called them – drafted Jones into the team before realising that he had no valid passport. No problem to Cliff. He simply lent Jones his. They were cousins and there was a strong family resemblance. And so W.G. Jones went out to Paris and played for his country as 'C. Davies', with only the Welsh Rugby Union and a couple of Welsh pressmen wise to the wheeze. For many years after, the record books showed Cliff Davies as having played in this match.

In 1947, when official internationals resumed, Davies was called up to play prop and this time was able to make the trip to Paris for the crucial championship game against France in March. It was a very rough match and at half-time Cliff showed his index finger to his Cardiff team-mate, Bleddyn Williams. It had been gnawed to the bone by his opponent in the dark underworld of the front row. Cliff pointed to the opponent responsible, whereupon Williams noticed that half the French prop's ear had been chewed off. Nip for nip, one might say. Typically, Davies and his opponent were the best of pals over the fine cognacs at the after-match banquet and, according to legend, for years afterwards the Welshman sent his French adversary a Christmas card wishing him a 'Happy New 'Ear'. Years later, in the mid-1960s, biting became quite widespread and attracted adverse publicity when an Australian hooker was sent home for biting the ear off an Oxford University prop during a Wallabies tour. Cliff was reported as saying at the time: 'What's the prop worried about? He got his ear back, didn't he?'

All told, he won 16 caps for Wales between 1947 and 1951. He was a consummate scrummager and mauler in the tight and showed remarkable pace in the loose. In the autumn of 1948 he underwent a cartilage operation that many feared would end his first-class career. But he recovered his form and fitness rapidly, forced his way back into the Welsh side for a trip to Paris in 1949 and, aged 30, enjoyed his finest season in the Welsh side of 1950. The campaign opened at Twickenham, where Wales had not won since 1933, but with Cliff lifting the side's morale with a rousing version of the famous chapel hymn *Calon Lan* in the changing room just before kick-off, Wales achieved an 11–5 victory that set them on the path to a Grand Slam.

The *Western Mail*'s pen-picture of Davies on the morning of the Twickenham match informed its readers that 'he can be relied upon for a special effort' and Welsh supporters did not have to wait long to witness it. Five minutes before half-time, fullback Lewis Jones launched a zig-zagging run that finished with Cliff, red shirt hanging loose outside his white shorts, popping up out on the right wing to crash over in the corner for their first try. The Welsh captain, John Gwilliam, paid handsome tribute to Davies's motivational powers at the end of that unbeaten season. 'No team is complete without a born humorist,' he wrote. 'We had Cliff as a guarantee against despondency, and besides his exceptional gifts as a player he always contrived to keep up morale by infectious good humour and his powerful tenor voice.'

He was in his element socially on the Lions' tour of New Zealand and Australia later that summer. The side travelled to the Antipodes by sea via Panama and were accompanied on their journey by Mr W.J. (William) Jordan, the High Commissioner for New Zealand. The long hours on board provided invaluable bonding opportunities for the tour party and Cliff struck up a good friendship playing crib with the commissioner – it was 'Bill' and 'Cliff' between them during their card play. Later, when the side was in New Zealand, they were introduced to the then Prime Minister, Mr S.G. Holland. The PM, familiar with Welsh rugby stars and especially the current tourists, was introduced to Davies and said with unexpected familiarity, 'Pleased to meet you, Cliff.' The miner from Kenfig replied: 'Pleased to meet you, Sid.'

It was during the stopover at Panama City that he endeared himself to the touring party. After exploring the nightlife everyone was broke, except Cliff, who still had a quarter left. He gambled it on a pinball machine, hit the jackpot and shared his winnings with the team, who thus enjoyed another few riotous hours. It was typical of his generosity and had his team-mates eating out of his hand for the rest of the visit in his capacity as their honorary choirmaster. Who else could have possibly taught Scottish stockbrokers or Irish doctors to sing hymns in Welsh? Colleagues recall his commanding presence. Cliff could silence the hubbub of a crowded club lounge simply by standing on a chair to conduct an impromptu choral session. 'He was like a candle in a dark room,' another famous Welsh international said. He went on to form a strong friendship with the Scotsman Graham Budge, a fellow prop, on the tour. Budge emigrated to Canada afterwards but flew back to south Wales later in the year to act as best man when Cliff got married.

Away from the daily physical grind of mining, however, Cliff's weight ballooned in New Zealand and the quality of his forward play declined. For those monitoring the tour back in Wales, his omission from the Test side was a mystery, but he had lost mobility and never quite recovered the outstanding form he had shown in the Grand Slam season. He won his last cap against Ireland at Cardiff in 1951 and retired from the first-class game a year later, having made nearly 200 first-team peacetime appearances for Cardiff.

Clifton Davies once said of his rugby career, 'I used to enjoy every minute of every match.' His contemporaries from that golden age of rugby after the last war and before the era of televised rugby fully endorsed his infectious enthusiasm for the social and playing aspects of the game. No one, moreover, ever had a bad word for Cliff and he spoke ill of no man. His premature death on 28 January 1967, aged 47, left the world of rugby the poorer for his passing.

JASON LEONARD
The Barking Fun Bus

R ugby teams are sometimes divided into the piano players (the backs) and piano shifters (the forwards). The piano players make eye-catching breaks and score thrilling tries that stay in the memory while the shifters graft away as tight forwards in the nether regions of the game, grappling unseen to win or retain possession that can be recycled for the use of the backs. For a tight forward from that dark, dark world to continually impress his country's selectors over a period of 14 years, winning more than 100 caps, is exceptional, a real testimony to the player's fitness, strength and technical excellence. The first to achieve such a remarkable feat – and still the only one do to so for England – was the self-employed carpenter from Essex, Jason Leonard, or 'Jase' to everyone in rugby.

He brought a tremendous sense of fun to the squad with his ready wit. His mentors were the England props Jeff Probyn and Paul Rendall, the famed 'Judge' who ruled over the England players' mock court rituals where players were censured for such off-the-field misdemeanours as not drinking enough beer. The position involved fining players by making them consume vast volumes of alcohol. When Jason first entered the England squad he was amused by the players' nicknames and turned to Rendall to ask: 'Why haven't you got a nickname, Judge?' That no doubt earned him a hefty fine, but it was all good preparation for the days later in his England career when he occupied the high court position himself. His own 'Fun Bus' nickname was coined by Martin Bayfield. The England players were supplied with red, white and blue shirts for training before internationals and on one occasion Jason was sporting a red one. He looked like a London red bus said Bayfield.

Then there was the time shortly after his Test debut when he was asked by a journalist what the (England) shirt meant to him. Irritated by the hack's inane probes for a printable quote, Jase replied with an inane joke. His offhand remark that he had spent an afternoon at home watching in awe as the red rose on his jersey spun through its cycle in his mum's washing machine predictably appeared in print. Fortunately, Messrs Probyn and Rendall were always there in his formative years to pull him up for any unwise remarks or antics that gave England's dreaded backs cannon fodder in their off-the-field banter with the forwards.

Probyn reputedly came to Jason's rescue during England's World Cup quarter-final weekend in Paris in 1991. After knocking the French out, the boys were out on the town watching a cabaret act involving a trickster in a water-tank full of crocodiles. The animals were so obviously sedated and the performer so irritating that Jase decided to take action. He stripped off, intending to dive into the tank and, pretending to be a croc, give the showman a real shock by nipping him on the bum. Probyn and other kindly minders cut him off before he reached the tank.

Jason Leonard was born in Barking on 14 August 1968 and schooled at the university of hard knocks before joining his local club. His easy manner quickly endeared him to team-mates, while his strength as a scrummager attracted the notice of the top-flight London clubs. He was still in his teens when he made his first-class debut for Saracens and within two years was in the England squad for the tour to Argentina.

Brian Moore was England's hooker at the time and, after he had stood shoulder to shoulder with the youngster for 80 minutes in Buenos Aires in the first Test, he vouched for Leonard's solid and reliable qualities as a loose-head. Jason was, at 21, the youngest prop to play for England in 27 years. Having survived a harsh apprenticeship in Argentina, he switched club allegiance to Harlequins when he returned to England and joined seasoned internationals such as Moore, Paul Ackford, Peter Winterbottom and Mickey Skinner in the 'Quins' pack. Even in those relatively carefree days, when players enjoyed a few beers after a match and went back to their jobs on Monday mornings, it was clear that England had found a genuine grafter who would take some moving in the front row.

His dedication to training and fitness, and the discipline he showed in adhering to the strict dietary regimen that became part and parcel of the professional era, enabled Leonard to stay at the top of his game during a decade that saw the demands on leading players change beyond all recognition. The arrival of the open game in 1995, he once observed, was the background to his longevity. He doubted whether he could have maintained the long hours devoted to training and travelling round the M25 for club and national preparations without the advantages professionalism brought. It's true that in his early playing days he was not averse to a pint or several. Once the professional game kicked in, he understood and accepted the new demands and readily swapped the pint for a mineral water . . . well, some of the time. He used to send himself up saying he thought his World Cup MBE stood for 'More Beer 'Ere'.

Beneath the fun-loving surface there was also a mental toughness to his preparation for matches. His approach to Tests was well documented. Two to three days before a big game he focused sharply on the upcoming challenge, adopting a mindset that by match day was finely tuned to minimising error. He absorbed the detail of line-out calls and scrum feeds and was rarely caught out in the fray of match play. His tackle count was high for a prop and he wasn't prone to giving away penalties for technical offences or foul play. His standards were consistently high.

He underwent a delicate neck operation to correct a career-threatening injury in 1992. The injury had occurred in the Calcutta Cup match earlier in the year, but he soldiered on through a busy season for club and country before seeking expert advice. Serious nerve damage was diagnosed. A slipped disc in his neck was threatening the spinal cord and an operation involving transplanting bone from his pelvis was required. The procedure was successful and, with typical grit, he steadily worked his way back to fitness and rebuilt his scrummaging strength. As a result he was able to continue a wonderful run in the England side, setting up a record of 40 straight Test appearances between 1990 and 1995.

Throughout it all he was the one constant in England's scrum equation. Four times he featured in Grand Slam sides (1991, 1992, 1995 and 2003), he was a member of England's 1991 team that lost to Australia in the World Cup Final and he enjoyed revenge in 2003 when England won the trophy. He even captained England once. In 1996, after Will Carling had relinquished the leadership. Phil de Glanville was Jack Rowell's choice as the new captain and the Bath centre led the side in the first of the autumn internationals, against Italy. But he picked up an injury that ruled him out of the subsequent game against Argentina. Jase got the nod and actually scored the only try of the match as England scraped a narrow 20–18 win. His score was the result of a line-out take by Martin Johnson from which the entire pack drove their captain over the line. He thus became the first prop to lead a winning England Test team for nearly 30 years.

When he finally announced his retirement in 2004, four months after taking part in England's winning World Cup Final, Fran Cotton, esteemed England prop of a previous generation, paid the former Barking chippie the highest compliment. Referring to Leonard's magnificent international record, Cotton called him 'rugby's Don Bradman'. There can be no higher accolade than that.

ERIC EVANS
Mr Motivator

Wander around the Twickenham Stadium concourse before a match and there in the south-west corner of the ground will be found an unprepossessing room with the letters ERIC on its entrance. Outside this holiest of holies is the autograph-hunter's dream lair, for the initials stand for the England Rugby Internationals Club, the meeting place on big match days for former Test players. The club's name was deliberately chosen by its members so that the acronym read as a tribute to Eric Evans, the England captain of the late 1950s who created from scratch one of England's most successful sides of the past 50 years.

He was born on 1 February 1921 in Droylesden near Manchester, and grew up supporting Manchester United while learning to become a rugby player as a pupil at Audenshaw Grammar School. He went on to Loughborough College and qualified as a PE teacher, turned out in holidays for his local rugby club, Sale, and won his first cap as a prop against Australia at Twickenham in January 1948. But it was as an expert, burrowing hooker and motivational captain with an infectious enthusiasm to succeed that Eric Evans is chiefly remembered.

His England appearances were few and far between in the three years that followed his debut, but a stern lecture from his father, one of his fiercest critics, after one of his early Twickenham appearances changed his outlook on the game. His father chided him for his lack of fitness and Evans junior immediately resolved to address the criticism, taking himself off to Old Trafford and persuading the management to allow him to train with the famous Manchester United Busby Babes. There, training meant going flat out beyond the limits of pain and he raised his stamina to levels that would not look out of place in today's demanding professional era. Moreover, he impressed his footballing contemporaries to such an extent that he was later invited to direct the soccer players through some of their stamina exercises. Eric was no strapping physical specimen, but his mantra that a fit player moves and thinks more quickly under pressure than an unfit one, no matter what his size, was the secret of his personal success. He believed that, even against technically better players, the advantage of superior fitness helped wear down opponents.

At the same time he honed his rugby skills to become an exceptionally fast striker for the ball in the scrum and an untiring forager in the loose. After featuring in the championship-winning England team of 1953 and the Triple Crown successes of 1954, he was out of favour until recalled in December 1955 to captain the junior side in the first England trial. He led his trial team to a 26–17 win against a bigger and more experienced pack and, when selected to lead the The Rest for January's upcoming final trial against England, he took the original step of writing to every member of his side before Christmas imploring them to go to bed early over the holiday and to eat and drink in moderation. It was contrary to the beer-swilling, hard-partying rugby conventions of the day, but his appeals struck a chord. Aged nearly 34 – though he declared that he was four years younger for the official programmes of the day – he relished the challenge of leading a young XV that rose to the occasion and went on to overwhelm the senior side 20–3 at Twickenham. Not surprisingly, he was named captain of the England XV to face Wales in the opening Five Nations match of 1956 and carried nine of his trial team into the international line-up. All told, he had 10 new caps in his side and, although seeing the team narrowly beaten by Wales, the selectors wisely resisted the temptation to make wholesale changes.

Eric's enthusiasm, voluble leadership and energetic approach rubbed off on a young side, which developed the greatest admiration for their captain. He set them high standards with his own personal fitness and mental toughness, forging the entire team into such a formidable unit that over the three seasons he was in charge England lost only once more. There were several Oxbridge undergraduates forming the backbone of his pack, including John Currie and Peter Robbins (Oxford) and David Marques and John Herbert (Cambridge). Eric had the people-skills to bring out the best in them as players, treating them as valued lieutenants, forwards whom he could trust to make shrewd tactical judgements when his head was buried in the scrum.

England achieved the Grand Slam for the first time for 29 years in 1957, when Eric was at his indomitable best. Because he was so much older than most of his side they looked up to him as a father figure. That team, he used to say, had come together as an unfancied trial outfit under its own flag and wanted to play for that flag. For the Welsh match at Cardiff he engaged his young back row of Robbins, Neddy Ashcroft and Reg Higgins in an intricate tactical plan that set an effective snare for the Welsh fly-half, Cliff Morgan. England thus blotted out Wales's main strike runner to win by a single penalty to nil. It was only their third win in the principality since the war, but it gave the side tremendous confidence for the battles that lay ahead.

When England prepared for the Calcutta Cup game in March, the sides were introduced to the Duke of Edinburgh at Twickenham. Scotland's only new cap that afternoon, fly-half Gordon Waddell, was so thrilled by the prospect of making his Test debut that, as the teams lined up to be introduced to the Duke, he could barely suppress his excitement. Eric singled Waddell out and told his back row to wipe the smile off his face. They did and England secured their first Grand Slam for nearly 30 years, playing brilliant rugby in the second half to wear the Scots down and win 16–3. It was the zenith of Eric's career. The team that he had brought together and nurtured to play in his own image had won through superior fitness and the mental discipline that attends it. 'Real training is speeding up the co-ordination between the body and the mind,' he later reflected.

He succeeded in winning the fervent loyalty of the teams he led. In those days the captain took the lead role in dictating how the team played and, with a little-changed side, England were unbeaten again in 1958 to retain the championship title. That season he had been dropped by Lancashire: too old, they said, after he had made more than 100 appearances for the county. Then Eric twice overcame difficulties to lead his country to victories on successive Saturdays in early February. First, on his 37th birthday, he maintained England's morale in a bruising encounter with Australia when the side was reduced to 13 men through injuries. There were no replacements permitted in those days, but Eric's drive and cajoling inspired the team to raise its game and pull off a last-minute 9–6 victory against the odds through a corner try by Peter Jackson. Then, back at Twickenham the week after, he had to lift himself and the national side in the sad aftermath of the Munich air crash in which several of the Busby Babes with whom he had once trained lost their lives. England beat Ireland 6–0, went on to win in Paris and draw at Murrayfield before Eric retired to rank among the top England captains of all time.

After his playing days he was an industrial relations executive for Shell and BP, drawing on his strong personal qualities to see his company through the rigours of the tanker-drivers' strikes in the late 1970s. His association with English rugby continued as a selector, in which role the directness of his northern humour endeared him to another generation of international players. He died on 12 January 1991, aged 69. His playing contemporaries say with affection that Eric Evans was one of those people who stay with you for ever. Happily, the ERIC room at Twickenham ensures that his name lives on.

BOBBY WINDSOR
The Duke

There is a story set on the eve of the 1974 Lions' tour to South Africa that typifies the commitment that Bobby Windsor showed to rugby union. The captain for that visit was Willie John McBride, who had been a Lion four times previously and was about to make his third tour to South Africa. He gathered his players in a London hotel that was under siege from anti-apartheid demonstrators and began telling his charges of the enormity of the task that lay ahead. He told them of his tough experiences of physical intimidation and cheating by Springbok forwards in the 1962 and 1968 series that the Lions had lost, and invited anyone who was not up for the fight to leave the tour before it started. 'If there's anyone here with any doubts, go home now,' McBride said. 'Nothing will be said. But if you don't leave then you're in for four hard months.' A pregnant pause followed before Bobby Windsor, the Pontypool and Wales hooker, stepped forward to break the ice saying: 'I'm going to bloody well love this, boyo!' And so he did, just as he loved everything about the game of rugby union, from the fighting and open play on the field to the camaraderie and banter off it.

He was born on 31 January 1946 at Newport, but like many who become good rugby players, his early sporting skills were shown as a hard-shooting soccer centre-forward at primary school. His sportsmaster at Brynglas Secondary Modern School was the former Newport three-quarter Hedley Rowland, who converted the young Windsor to rugby as a fullback and fly-half of outstanding talent. Bobby was a dazzling runner and prodigious kicker, but when he left school and became a steelworker he bulked up and quickly slipped into the hooking role. The physical demands of the day job developed a muscular hardness in his sturdy frame which, allied to his natural sporting skills, enabled him to make the transition to the front row with ease. He joined Pontypool in 1973 for the simple reason that their fixture list was less extensive than Cardiff or Newport's, entailing less time off for travel and therefore better suited to his work patterns. His outstanding performances in the Pooler pack earned him Test recognition the same autumn, and he made his Welsh debut in a handsome win over the Wallabies, scoring a rousing try at Cardiff – 'If you want your name in the paper, you have to score a try,' he informed team-mates.

Former Lion and Wales prop Ray Prosser was his mentor at Pontypool. Prosser instilled a discipline and spirit in the club that transformed Windsor and the Valley pack into one of the most respected in the principality. Windsor had become the founder member of the Pontypool front row that played for Wales, props Graham Price and Charlie Faulkner joining him in an all-club Test front row that became known as the 'Viet Gwent' in 1975. Before that, Bobby demonstrated his dynamic loose play and toughness in the tight for Wales and capped a highly productive first season in the Five Nations by gaining selection for the 1974 Lions' tour. There, his sound striking, effective contribution to the eight-man shove perfected by coach Syd Millar and all-round hooking master-classes in the provincial games ensured that he was the first choice for the winning Test series.

Off the field he captivated the tour party and travelling press with his wit – he was a genuinely funny man whom many felt could have made a career as a comedian. Gordon Brown of Scotland was on that Lions' tour and he and Windsor became bosom pals. One of Brown's legendary stories related to a hefty hotel telephone bill that was run up by one of the players sneaking in to the manager Alun Thomas's room. When Thomas was presented with the itemised bill he called the tour party together and demanded that the culprit own up. Reading out the number, he began with the code for Pontypool, at which point Bobby, with mock anger, butted in shouting: 'Right! Which one of you bastards has been calling my missus?' For his sense of fun and brilliance on the field the South African critics nicknamed him 'The Duke' and he returned to a hero's welcome.

But the success had attracted the attentions of rugby league scouts, and Windsor was regularly pestered to turn professional. Wigan offered him £7,000 to sign, with £35 a match and a job promised. Bobby, however, was committed to rugby union and knew that the rules relating to amateurism were strict. Concerned that the WRU would learn of his overtures from Wigan, he went public, telling the *Daily Telegraph*'s John Mason, 'I'm concerned that rumours will reach the WRU and that they may think I've spoken to Wigan. Well, so I have – but only to tell them to go away, or words to that effect.'

The offers persisted, but even during the recession that hit the heavy industries of south Wales in the mid-1970s, when The Duke was among many steelworkers who had their earnings curtailed, he could never be persuaded to abandon his beloved sport. 'To be without a game [of rugby union] on a Saturday would be like cutting off my right arm,' he once said. There is a related story, partly apocryphal but typical of Valley humour, that an investigative journalist struck up a friendship with one of Bobby's near-neighbours in the close of houses where he lived in Bettws near Newport. Anxious to know if there had been any unusual activity at the Windsor household, the journalist telephoned his contact to see if Bobby had gone north. 'Ooh, I don't know,' said the neighbour, 'but if it's any help he turned right when he came out of the door this morning.'

To the relief of Pontypool and all Wales, Bobby remained true to his union roots and went on to win 28 consecutive caps, featuring prominently in the four successive Triple Crown wins of 1976–79 that included two Grand Slams. He toured New Zealand with the 1977 Lions but, on a tour that had more of its share of setbacks, he never quite reached the standards he had set in South Africa. His confidence was badly shaken during this visit by the zany antics of a mad pilot on one of the many internal flights that the Lions took between games. It was not the happiest of tours for the Lions, and it certainly wasn't for Bobby after that incident, which seemed to unsettle one who was normally so unflappable as a player. When he returned home he swore that he would never fly again, but he couldn't avoid it when Wales played in Scotland,

Ireland and France. His wicked team-mates used to tease him unmercifully by singing the Rolling Stones refrain 'This could be the last time' whenever Bobby boarded a plane.

His Welsh career ended in 1979 when he had to withdraw from the Welsh side that ended its season with a thumping win against England. The council workman is a much-maligned breed in south Wales, but on this occasion Windsor and the Welsh rugby-loving public had just cause to vent their wrath. The offenders were allegedly Torfaen Borough Council, owners of the Pontypool Park where the town's club played its rugby. The council were responsible for marking the pitch and on the Saturday before the international, while Bobby was playing against Cardiff, he slid along the touchline with his jersey outside his shorts after tackling Roger Lane. As the game progressed, Windsor felt his back inflamed and the next morning had to be admitted to hospital suffering first-degree burns. The lime used by the councilmen in the pitch markings had lethally reacted with the rain, leaving Windsor in intensive care for a week and ruling him out of the Welsh team.

The incident understandably annoyed him, but it was the beginning of an unhappy time for him. His young wife died from cancer four months later, but barely hours before passing away made Bobby swear that he would go on playing and regain his place in the Welsh team, to show their three children that life goes on. The Duke was back for Wales's non-cap game against Romania in October but recurrent back injuries interrupted his career thereafter and he never again forced his way into the Welsh team. In October 1980 he was again challenging for Welsh honours when the All Blacks came over to help Wales celebrate their centenary season. 'I want a crack at them, and I don't mind if the selectors pick me as a goalpost,' the irrepressible hooker told the *Western Mail*'s Chris Jones shortly after receiving a back injury playing against Bedford. At length, he reluctantly gave up playing after helping Pontypool win the WRU Cup in 1983 but continued his lifelong love affair with Welsh rugby as coach to Pontypool, where he became respected as one of the club's elders.

Now the head of a family that runs to numerous grandchildren and even a few great-grandchildren, he is still the inspiration of his local community in east Wales for the brave way he has overcome prostate cancer in recent years. Rugby's Duke of Windsor will always be up for a fight.

OLLIE CAMPBELL
Dedication Personified

When Ireland came close to dominating the Five Nations in the early 1980s their selectors were faced with the difficult decision of choosing between the merits of two different but exciting out-halves: Tony Ward from Munster in the west and Ollie Campbell from Dublin in the east. East or west? Each was an expert kicker; each could hoodwink defences with a shuffle of the feet or a convincing dummy; each had his champions.

But it was Ollie Campbell who occupied the pivot position in 1982, which was Ireland's first Triple Crown season since 1949. Tony Ward, it was argued, was too individualistic to bring out the best of a talented Irish back division. Campbell, by contrast, was more than just a kicking machine: he was an instinctive genius who loved to run, and he took as much pleasure from freeing a three-quarter with a delicately weighted pass as he did from firing over a 50-metre penalty with a casual sweep of his right instep. He was also an enthusiastic tackler – a rare trait in outside-halves of the 1980s.

Ollie was fond of a story he told against himself that illustrated how far-reaching the Ward/Campbell argument extended in Ireland at the time. He was on business near Castlebar in County Mayo for his family's textile firm and gave an elderly woman a lift in his car. During the journey the passenger struck up a conversation and asked him if he played sport. Ollie replied that rugby was his game, to which the woman replied: 'The one thing I can't understand about rugby is why that Tony Ward isn't on the Irish team.'

Campbell was calm where Ward was erratic, and Campbell was a tactical thinker where Ward was an impulsive opportunist. They contrasted in personality and appearance, too. Campbell was the shy, red-haired perfectionist who had immersed himself in rugby since his schooldays at Belvedere College, the Jesuit academy that gave the world Tony O'Reilly and Ireland's first great captain, Karl Mullen, as well as one Terry Wogan. Ward was dark, played off-the-cuff and was more broadminded in his interests.

Seamus Oliver Campbell was born in Dublin on 3 March 1954 and from an early age he played in the pivot position, but it was not until he began playing senior rugby for Old Belvedere that he became a recognised place-kicker. He used to say that he was thrown the ball to convert a try in his first first-class match . . . simply because his captain assumed that the Number 10 would take the kicks. Everything snowballed from there.

The feature of Campbell's approach to rugby that eclipsed all others was his dedication. Long before Jonny Wilkinson became obsessed by practising, Ollie perfected his place-kicking technique until all hours, in all conditions and all year round. And at a time when the game was amateur. Selected for his first cap as an eleventh-hour stand-in for Barry McGann against Australia in 1976, he missed four goal kicks and was immediately discarded. It looked for a while as if the hours of devotion he had given to the game would be the wasted time of just another of rugby's legion of one-cap wonders. But Campbell's resilience and steadiness were rewarded in the summer of 1979, when he leapfrogged Ward to kick Ireland to a 2–0 series win in Australia. Another strong performance, this time in the Irish trial in early 1980, took him into his first Five Nations Championship. For the next four years Campbell never looked back.

After losing 19–13 to France in the opening match of their 1981 championship campaign, the Irish selectors decided to accommodate both Tony Ward and Ollie, moving Campbell to the inside centre position. In terms of results, the switch was ineffective, for Ireland lost every match, though the margin of defeat was never more than six points. 'It was Ireland's best ever whitewash,' Ollie used to say. John O'Driscoll, his blind-side flanker, was, however, absolutely delighted by the positional move and told him (ambiguously) of his pleasure. Ollie took the comment positively and, encouraged by the big forward's apparent vote of confidence, ventured to ask him why. 'Because now I know that we'll have someone who can make a tackle at outside-half,' was the deflating reply.

It was all part of the legend that goal-kicking Number 10s can't tackle to save their lives. But the remarks of Barry John and the late Clem Thomas exploded that particular myth. John wrote, 'Ollie fills all the requirements of an international fly-half nearly to perfection,' while Thomas, a destructive flanker and wrecker of international fly-halves' reputations in his playing days, added: 'He is simply one of the greatest rugby footballers in the world. He is close to being what Pelé was to soccer.'

Ollie became a prolific collector of points and, having set a new championship scoring record in 1980 gathering 46 points, he equalled that mark in 1982 when his kicking at Twickenham was crucial to Ireland's stirring victory there. He set a new individual match record with six penalties and a drop-goal when Ireland – or Campbell to be more accurate – beat Scotland 21–12 for the Triple Crown. Before that match he had missed a penalty against England, so set himself the task of practising to make perfect for the Triple Crown decider. He spent hours at his club ground kicking goals from the equivalent position to the one from which he had fired astray at Twickenham, succeeding 90 per cent of the time. Three minutes into the Scottish match Ireland were awarded a penalty from a similar position and the metronomic Campbell landed the points, a just reward for his extraordinary application. He could have kicked goals in his sleep that day.

The final statistical milestone he notched was in 1983 when he pulled clear of Tom Kiernan's record for most individual Test points, going on to finish with 217 points for Ireland in 22 matches. He was also the Lions' outside-half against South Africa in 1980 and in the 1983 series in New Zealand, where the hamstring injuries that were to end his career first blighted his wonderful run of success. Later, illness and a much-needed rest forced him to withdraw from the Irish side halfway through the 1984 Five Nations and, to the regret of his country's supporters, he never returned. Although shy and unassuming, Ollie had a sharp sense of humour. When he heard a rumour that he was giving up to join the priesthood, he played along with the story a couple of weeks later by attending the 1984 Ireland–Scotland post-match dinner dressed as a priest . . . and with a girlfriend dressed as a nun. His career was relatively short, even for the amateur era, but it was certainly rich in quality.

BORN TO MANAGE

MICK DOYLE
Give it a Lash

Mick Doyle swept through Irish rugby circles like a breath of fresh air in the 1980s. Ireland has always enjoyed the services of technically brilliant coaches, men such as Ronnie Dawson, Syd Millar and Ray McLoughlin, who could dissect the finer arts of forward play with the skill and precision of a surgeon. Yet for many seasons after the coaching revolution changed rugby in the Home Unions during the late 1960s, Ireland rarely enjoyed success in the Five Nations. Perhaps the coaching approach was too clinical for players who were invariably the backbones of famous Lions' sides yet somehow never managed to deliver when playing for Ireland. Then, after a disastrous whitewash in the 1984 Five Nations, Doyle, a maverick who proved that there was method in his madness, was appointed coach and one of the most colourful periods in Ireland's rugby history began.

Doyle coached his Irish squad to the Triple Crown and Five Nations Championship title in his first season at the helm in 1985. Only a draw with the French in Dublin prevented Ireland from winning their first Grand Slam since 1948. Many have subsequently argued that Doyle's adventurous side of that year was the best that has ever represented the 'Men in Green'. Trevor Ringland, a member of that talented XV, said the coach was a motivator who 'freed players up. He motivated young players to go out and do their best. He was a great character.'

The Doyle mantra was 'give it a lash' – a refreshing daredevil gospel for 15-man rugby. Before Ireland's first Five Nations match under his guidance he told his team: 'I want you to run the ball, and if it doesn't work, I want you to still run it.' He wasn't interested in building a team around a goal-kicker. The Irish players embraced his philosophy wholeheartedly and it worked. The match was at Murrayfield, where Scotland, the reigning Grand Slam champions, led 15–12 with time running out. With virtually the last play of the afternoon the Irish backs created the space to run the ball and, from a perfectly executed scissors move, winger Trevor Ringland crossed for his second try of the match. Ireland were on their way.

Ironically, the team did have to rely on the boot of Michael Kiernan to scrape a draw with France, but behind the larger-than-life front that Doyle presented to the press was a sharp analytical mind. He might well have engendered an off-the-cuff playing attitude in his players, but he impressed on them the need to take responsibility for their own actions on the field. His background preparation was all-embracing in its attention to detail: use of diet, behind-the-scenes organisation and video analysis put him 10 years ahead of his time. The dossiers he compiled on his own players as well as opponents were the basis of team preparations that were conducted with forthright honesty. The result was that Ireland went on to break Wales down in Cardiff before taking the title, back home in Dublin, with a 13–10 win against England.

Doyle was the man of the moment and some said that too much of the Triple Crown limelight shone in his direction. He wasn't to achieve such heights again. The side never quite managed to live up to its reputation after the Triple Crown triumphs, and the pressures of the job took their toll. He reckoned that his rugby commitments cost his veterinary business in the region of £750k, and by the time he took Ireland to the inaugural World Cup in New Zealand in 1987 he was feeling the strain. So much so that within 48 hours of arriving for the tournament he was struck down by a heart attack that effectively ended his coaching career.

Michael Doyle was born in the Gaelic sports stronghold of Kerry on 13 October 1940 and educated as a boarder at Newbridge College, where he fell in love with rugby. He studied veterinary science at University College Dublin before completing his professional qualifications at Cambridge and Edinburgh universities. He won his first cap for Ireland in 1965 under the captaincy of Ray McLoughlin and scored a try on his debut in a 3-all draw against France. McLoughlin, Noel Murphy, Ken Kennedy, Willie John McBride, Bill Mulcahy and Phil O'Callaghan were the personalities he said had the biggest influences on him as a player in a career that saw him win 20 successive caps at a time when the Irish were beginning to take a more serious attitude in their approach to Test rugby. The highlight of his career, he always said, was playing in the back row with his brother Tom in the 1968 Five Nations, while prominent among his achievements were three wins against Australia and selection for the 1968 British/Irish Lions' tour of South Africa, where he appeared in the first Test at Pretoria. Those Lions split neatly into two groups off the field: the 'Wreckers', who partied hard, and the 'Kippers', who were the quieter, reserved members of the party. Doyle was never a 'Kipper'.

He retired from playing in 1968 to concentrate on establishing his veterinary practice. He'd been a perpetual student until then, but found the lure of the game too great and returned to play minor rugby at Naas, where the coaching bug bit. The rest, as they say, was history. He went on to coach a successful Leinster provincial side between 1979 and 1984 and, when Willie John McBride's spell as coach of the Ireland side ended in 1984, Doyle was persuaded to run for office. His first Test was against the 1984 Grand Slam Wallabies, who rated Ireland the best international team they met on that tour, and within months Ireland's rugby renaissance was under way. The press loved him, for he always supplied them with good copy. On the eve of the 1985 game with France he put his approach into perspective in an interview with the *Daily Mail*'s Terry O'Connor. 'When spectators pay £12 for a ticket, they are entitled to get value for money – not technical forward mumbo-jumbo. They want to see the game's skills, and this also appeals to the players.'

After the setback that ended his coaching career and very nearly his life in 1987, it was with typical grittiness that he set about extending his business interests to the agricultural world. Rugby still kept a hold on him and his often trenchant views on the game found expression in a number of Irish newspapers as well as in the broadcast media. There was also an unexpurgated autobiography in which the 'give-it-a-lash' hell-raising path of his private life was charted. 'It's 20 per cent rugby and 80 per cent pornography,' Doyle told Charles Haughey, who helped him launch the book. 'You got the balance just right then,' the former Taoiseach replied.

In 1996 he was given a one-sixth of one per cent chance of surviving after suffering a brain haemorrhage that left him having to learn to walk and talk. Again, he fought the statistically impossible odds and his second book, *Zero Point One Six: Living in Extra Time*, was a graphic account of his recovery. Afterwards he threw himself into work on the board of Headway Ireland, a charity supporting those afflicted by brain damage but, having twice side-stepped the grim reaper, he died tragically on 11 May 2005 in County Tyrone in a car accident. He was 63. All Ireland, and rugby followers in particular, mourned a man who as player and coach broke the mould of conventional, stifled theories about the game and gave his teams freedom to think.

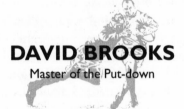

DAVID BROOKS
Master of the Put-down

Arguably the first British/Irish Lions' tour to embrace a modern approach was the 1968 visit to South Africa. The management for that tour was announced a year before the visitors flew out and the man selected for the position from the five men shortlisted was David Brooks, a former Harlequins forward who went on to serve the London club and English rugby in a number of roles during a long and distinguished association with the game.

The Lions of 1968 were a young and skilful group of players who knew how to enjoy themselves and Brooks was the perfect man to take charge of them. The tourists had their ups and downs and lost the Test series, but no one ever got the better of the manager. David

Brooks was a seasoned rugby nut whose years as a press officer at
'Quins had given him a sharp wit with an expert line in put-downs.
The Lions were accused of 'unmitigated drunken revelry' after one
of their Test setbacks. The side allegedly went on the rampage one
evening and caused extensive damage to their hotel. Next morning
the angry hotel manager confronted Brooks with a bill for the
repairs. 'Nine hundred pounds?' queried Brooks as he calmly wrote
the cheque, 'Couldn't have been much of a party.'

His experiences of touring stretched back to the mid-1950s
when he visited Romania with Harlequins. The Romanians, who
were to become strong contenders for invitation to the Six Nations
tournament a few years later, were keen to impress their visitors.
Before one match the 'Quins were shown round a new 100,000-
seater sports stadium. The guide waxed lyrical about the excellence
of the construction and was keen to emphasise that its Romanian
builders were hard-working citizens who had completed the
construction in four months. Brooks piped up: 'What took them so
long?', completely deflating the guide's pride.

His charm offensives made him a legend in his own club. He
could talk his way out of anything, it was said in Harlequins' circles
– policemen, hotel managers and even communist officials came off
second best in verbal brushes with Mr Brooks. There was one
occasion, however, when his charm cut no ice with a well-known
referee on the London circuit. Early in the autumn of 1958 new
laws regarding the tackle came into operation and Harlequins were
puzzled by the decisions made during a match against one of their
local rivals. After the match 'Brooky', as he was known to his clubmates, felt he should approach the referee and opened discussions
politely by noting that the 'Quins were slightly puzzled by his
reading of the new laws. 'What new laws?' barked the referee in
reply. It was the only time that Brooks was left lost for words.

David Brooks was born at Merton Park in London on 12 March
1924 and educated at Rutlish School before serving with the Fleet
Air Arm during the Second World War. He flew Swordfish,
describing the aircraft as 'ponderous in design and purpose', adding
self-deprecatingly 'Quite suitable, I thought.' As a player he joined
the Harlequins as a back-row forward in 1945 and went on to make

more than 150 first-team appearances for the club in a 16-year career that included a season as captain in 1952–53. He played the game for pure enjoyment and retirement from playing did not come easily to him. In November 1962 he threatened a comeback to play for Harlequins against Newport, but twisted a knee taking an inside pass from fly-half Ricky Bartlett in training. 'Quins' skipper Colin Payne was relieved, but not at all happy with Brooky – 'Now no genuinely injured player can get near the doctor's table in the dressing room!' the captain told readers of *Harlequinade*, the club's monthly newsletter. Another contemporary, Mickey Grant, a Scottish international and Harlequin good egg, wrote in the magazine: 'Few Harlequins become legends in our own lifetime, but already an aura of myth is growing around this remarkable character.'

Mobility, Brooks was quick to point out, was not his strength, 'but if I waited long enough play would invariably come back to me,' he once told an interviewer. Even so, he was good enough to play for Surrey and London Counties, though it was for his work in the administrative field that he really made his mark on the game. In 1967 he was on the Surrey committee when they reached the final of the County Championship, then the top competition in England below international level. Worried that the final was getting scant publicity in the daily press, he happened to meet his captain Roger Michaelson (who, like Brooks, enjoyed a successful business career in the wholesale fruit trade) early one morning on the markets. Brooks persuaded Michaelson that he was 'injured' and leaked the news to the press, who took the bait. The upshot was that the final warranted a sidebar of coverage each day leading up to the final, by which time Michaelson of course had made a miraculous recovery. The late John Reason, former *Daily Telegraph* rugby correspondent, described Brooks as 'the cleverest public relations man who had ever appeared in British rugby administration'.

In a more serious vein, his experiences with the 1968 Lions left him in no doubt that British rugby, particularly below international level, needed an organised competition in order to lift its game to the level where the Lions could match or even defeat the Springboks and All Blacks. As president of the RFU in 1981–82 he was not afraid to express his forthright views, and championed moves to introduce leagues and develop relationships with sponsors while recognising in those amateur days that rugby remained primarily a leisure pursuit.

In retirement he was elected president of his beloved Harlequins in 1990 and continued to support the club right down to its grassroots. He was very proud of the advance of the women's section at his club and in his 70s could often be seen on the touchlines giving advice and shouting encouragement. David Brooks died in January 2002, aged 77.

DR DOUG SMITH
Crystal-ball Gazer

British/Irish tourists have been playing Test rugby against the All Blacks since 1904, yet to date only one side from these shores has won a series in New Zealand. That was the 1971 team skippered by Welshman John Dawes, led up front by the Irishman Willie John McBride and spearheaded in the three-quarter line by the try-scoring Englishman David Duckham. The Scots were represented in the ample form of the manager Dr Douglas Smith, a former London Scottish and Scotland winger who had toured New Zealand and Australia as a Lion in 1950.

Doug Smith, an Essex GP, was everything a team manager should be. He possessed a good understanding of his players, placed immense faith in his coach, Carwyn James from Wales, and forged excellent relations with both New Zealand administrators and all parts of the media. Appointed manager with James as coach in 1970, he recognised the technical ability of the Welshman early on. They were complementary characters: Smith the bluff, outward-going Scot; James the scholarly, thoughtful Welshman. From the moment the tour party left Heathrow in May 1971, Smith realised that his contribution would be to deal with administration, PR and discipline, leaving the tactical and playing side of the tour to his coach, captain and a core of knowledgeable senior players.

In his dealings with the players he came over as firm but fair. The journalist John Reason described him as a 'benevolent sergeant-major'. He didn't need to be firm very often, but there was one occasion when one of the Lions' props was torn off a strip for an off-the-field misdemeanour. The high-spirited forward had set the fire-hoses off, causing a tsunami in a hotel where the Lions were staying. Next day, the contrite player was left in no doubt as to what the manager thought of his actions.

Smith had shown his leadership even before the side reached Australia by inviting his team to have a night out on the town during a stopover in Hong Kong. It was the perfect bonding exercise, most of the players taking the advantage of a free evening to let their hair down, together with several members of the British rugby media who were simultaneously outward bound. 'What goes on tour stays on tour' was the motto of the day, and players and pressmen strictly adhered to the timeless maxim. Indeed, many said later that the tourists had so much on the esteemed pressmen as the result of that long night out in Hong Kong that any subsequent criticism of the players would have had to have been very carefully considered before translating to print.

When the side lost its first tour match, to Queensland within three days of arriving long-haul from Hong Kong, Smith was again to the fore, upfront in his defence of an abject performance by the Lions that was not helped by an equally abject refereeing display. The good doctor – arguably the prototype of the spin-doctor some 25 years before the role became popularly defined – was no whingeing Pom and declined to comment on the referee. But he did announce to the press that the team was suffering 'chronic circadian dysrhythmia'! The jetlag diagnosis was delivered in the matter-of-fact manner of an old-school, much-respected GP. It certainly kept the press off the Lions' backs. Who could argue with a medical expert?

But for most, Dr Doug Smith's defining moment in his management of the victorious Lions was the short speech made when the side arrived in Auckland for the long New Zealand leg of the visit.

Gazing into the crystal ball, the spin-doctor turned witchdoctor to put a spell on the All Blacks, predicting outrageously that his side would win the series 2–1 with one Test drawn. Even Colin Meads, who was renowned for keeping his own counsel and who would captain the All Blacks, felt the Lions were being cocky.

The rest is history. The Lions were deprived of their main props Sandy Carmichael and Ray McLoughlin as the result of a brutal battle at Canterbury, but went on to win the opening Test thanks to Barry John's boot. There was a sharp reverse in the second Test when the All Blacks levelled the series, but John and Gareth Edwards gave the Lions a morale-boosting start to the third Test, and with a 13–3 win the tourists knew they could not lose the series. J.P.R. Williams's drop-goal from near halfway in the final Test earned the draw that made Dr Smith the crystal-ball gazer of the century. Jack Sullivan, a former All Black and the chairman of the New Zealand Rugby Council, paid Smith a handsome compliment at the end of the visit when he said, 'This has been the best managed tour that has come to New Zealand in my experience.'

Smith's credentials for the Lions' management role were impeccable. Born on 27 October 1924 in Aberdeen, he grew up there and went from the local grammar school to the town's university, where he was a distinguished all-round sportsman. He played football, cricket and rugby, but after graduating in medicine and becoming an army doctor in London concentrated on the 15-a-side game. He played for London Scottish as a burly but fast winger and his powerful bursts carried him into the Scotland team, where he won eight caps between 1949 and 1953. His persuasive skills assisted his selection for the 1950 Lions' tour of New Zealand and Australia. Playing in an Army Cup semi-final for the Royal Army Medical Corps at Blackheath in March of that year, he had to leave the field with a fractured right forearm. It meant that he would be unable to play in the Calcutta Cup match and he feared that his place in the tour party, due to be announced a fortnight later, might be in jeopardy.

Smith, however, used every inch of medical jargon he could summon to successfully persuade the Lions' selectors that the fracture was minor and would heal in time for the opening of the tour. He also designed a protective strapping to wear in matches. This resembled a mailed fist when he carried the ball while running at opponents Down Under and, by all accounts, he cut a pretty fearsome sight.

His professional qualifications were often put into practice in rugby circles. During a training session at Richmond, the London Scottish centres Iain Laughland and Donald Sloan made a pig's ear of a dummy scissors move. A heavy collision resulted in Sloan breaking his nose. Smith called for a spoon and a bottle of brandy and reset the centre's nose on the spot. He was equally straightforward combining his medical duties as manager on the 1971 Lions' tour, administering sleeping tablets for flights and somehow finding the most threatening hypodermic needles to relieve players' pains. The Scottish hooker Frank Laidlaw was on that tour. One morning he reported for treatment, only to see the manager plunge a needle the size of a screwdriver into a team-mate's groin. Legend has it that Laidlaw's pain was instantly cured.

After the tour he was awarded the OBE. It was, he said, an accolade to a great team. He continued as a doctor in general practice and was London Scottish's fixtures secretary for many years – the unsung hero's job in any club. He served as president of the Scottish Rugby Union in 1986–87. In 1996, suffering from ill-health, he attended a 25th reunion for the Lions he had managed so successfully and was warmly welcomed by all his former players. He died, aged 73, on 22 September 1998 at Midhurst. To a man, the Lions of '71 had great admiration for their charismatic manager. Willie John McBride, a veteran of five Lions' tours as a player, spoke for them all when he described Smith as quite simply the finest of all Lions' managers.

SIR CLIVE WOODWARD
The Winner

It is doubtful whether rugby union has ever experienced anyone like Clive Woodward. His ability to ruffle feathers yet achieve winning results through his lateral thinking and constant challenges to authority and convention made him the sport's most fascinating character for a generation. He is better known today as the manager and head coach who steered England to victory in the 2003 Rugby World Cup in Australia, but long before those heady days he was a noted player who won 21 caps for England, took part in a Grand Slam and twice toured with the British/Irish Lions.

He made his debut as a centre in the 1980 campaign under Bill Beaumont and was a Lion in South Africa under the same captain later that year, playing in two Tests. Early in his international career he endeared himself to England fans with his beautifully balanced running. He relished taking on his opposite centre in attack, and invariably backed himself to create openings by taking bold outside breaks – a skill that was at a premium at Test level during the 1980s. He was at his brilliant best against Scotland in the 1980 Grand Slam decider at Murrayfield. That day his silky running and powerful bursts of acceleration twice left the Scots standing and paved the way for tries by Mike Slemen and John Carleton.

If there was a criticism of him as a player it was that he was mercurial. On tour with the Lions in South Africa, he appeared on the wing in the third Test at Port Elizabeth, a match the Lions had to win to keep alive their hopes of squaring the series. As the match entered its final 10 minutes, and with the Lions leading 10–6, Naas Botha aimed a kick towards Woodward's corner. To the horror of his team, the Englishman gently side-footed the ball into touch. Gerrie Germishuys rushed after the ball, took a quick throw-in to Theuns Stofberg, and gratefully accepted a return pass to score wide out. Naas Botha converted and the Lions, who had enjoyed 70 per cent of the possession, were robbed of both the match and the series.

Clive wasn't Bill Beaumont's favourite player that day, nor six months later when England were leading Wales in the dying moments of a match at Cardiff, where England hadn't won for 18 years. It was 19–18 to Beaumont's side when Brynmor Williams lured Woodward offside at a scrum on the English 22 and Steve Fenwick, from in front of the posts, landed Wales's winning penalty. Perhaps those chastening experiences were the origins of the famous 'TCUP' mantra – 'think correctly under pressure' – that underpinned the Woodward approach as head coach of the national side 20 years later?

Although he was a Lion again in New Zealand in 1983, he never appeared again in a Test for the tourists. He won his last cap for England in 1984 before settling for five years in Australia and turning out for the Manly club in Sydney. Always keen to absorb new ideas, the business principles he learnt working for Xerox, and his fascination with discovering the secrets of Australia's success in a variety of international sports, occupied his inquisitive mind away from the rugby pitch. These would later inform the management strategies he embraced running his England side.

He returned to England and reinvented himself as a successful coach. As a student at Loughborough Colleges in the 1970s he had warmed to the thoughtful approach of the former Scotland Number 8, Jim Greenwood, who guided a host of Loughborough rugby students on their way to international honours. Greenwood had kindled in Woodward interests that went far beyond merely playing his sport. The qualities that had marked him out as a player now set him on his way to achieving fresh goals by becoming one of the top-flight coaches in British sport.

After working with Henley, Oxford University, London Irish and Bath, where he instilled an independence of spirit in his sides, he succeeded Jack Rowell as coach of the England side that played Australia, New Zealand (twice) and South Africa in the 1997 autumn internationals. It was a baptism of fire. England lost two and drew two, but his methodical approach, innovations and readiness to stand up to RFU red-tape carried players with him. True, many of his ideas did not come off, but overall his readiness to back players and take chances, in selection and match planning, was the hallmark of his success.

England's playing approach evolved hugely during his reign as head coach. An important off-the-field rule adopted by his squads was confidentiality – no one was permitted to divulge information that might do a disservice to any other member of the squad or management team. He could be a maverick. It was Clive Woodward who threw Jonny Wilkinson in the deep end of international rugby, making the teenager the youngest England player for 71 years when he made his debut in 1998. England were unsuccessful in the 1999 World Cup, losing to South Africa in an infamous quarter-final. But Woodward's continuing focus on what he believed to be in the best interests of English rugby, and the RFU's patience in sticking with him and often acceding to his requests for additional back-up team members, paid handsome dividends in 2003.

By the time of the next Rugby World Cup, Woodward's players had a string of Triple Crown successes and a Grand Slam to their credit. More importantly, however, they had put together an impressive run of wins, at home and away, against the Tri Nations. Woodward's side were hot favourites for the 2003 tournament and duly collected the sport's ultimate prize. He brought in an extensive advisory team, even appointing a team chef, Dave Campbell, to travel with the team overseas and work with fitness coach Dave Reddin, who devised the players' dietary programmes. His back-room staff for the World Cup also included a kit technician, a vision specialist and even a QC. Each of his support staff made important contributions to the winning of the World Cup. Focus was the byword in all his preparations as head coach, making him British rugby's first modernist manager.

Thereafter, there was a falling out with his RFU employers and Woodward – now Sir Clive after the World Cup campaign – resigned as England manager in 2004 to concentrate on preparing the 2005 Lions for their visit to New Zealand. There, his golden touch deserted him and the Lions were whitewashed by an outstanding All Black side in the Test series.

Sir Clive briefly took up a management position with Southampton FC, football having been a lifelong passion, but in 2006 he moved on to become director of elite performance with the British Olympic Association (BOA). There, he was involved with the panoply of Olympic coverage – 35 sports in all – and was responsible for Britain's preparation camp for the 2008 Games staged in Beijing. More recently, in January 2009, he was promoted to Director of Olympic performance at the BOA, a challenge that he will relish as Team GB prepares for the London Olympics in 2012.

CARWYN JAMES
The Coach of Coaches

Carwyn James was the most influential coach British/Irish rugby ever had. In his finest hour he orchestrated the Lions in their greatest rugby triumph of modern times in New Zealand in 1971, still the only series win the combined strength of the four home unions has achieved against the All Blacks. Then he steered his club, Llanelli, to their historic 9–3 win against the 1972 New Zealanders, and later the same season he gave the pep-talk to the 1973 Barbarians prior to their majestic performance against the All Blacks – the team that won 23–11 was essentially his 1971 Lions reunited. Yet in his native Wales he was to go down as the greatest coach the national side never had, a prophet without honour in his own land.

A quiet, reserved man, he had the gift of bringing out the best in people, an art which came naturally to him and helped him flourish as a master at Llandovery College during the 1960s. He was neither a tub-thumper nor sergeant-major in his approach to management. As a rugby coach, he studied tactics, assessed the strengths and weaknesses of his opponents and sought the advice of friends and experts before adopting a collegiate approach to the task of winning rugby matches. His coaching philosophy was straight-forward: he was the figure who should guide the team, not command it; players themselves should take responsibility for the manner in which the game was played, adapting tactics to match their strengths and instincts.

His early successes came at Llandovery, where he revitalised the teaching of Welsh, became a respected housemaster and in his extracurricula contribution assisted T.P. Williams, the longstanding master in charge, with the running of the College XV. Carwyn always maintained that his simple approach to the sport, which was mastery of the basic skills and treating rugby as a handling game, reflected 'TP's' beliefs. By the late 1960s the College side was the best school side in Britain, its 15-man fluid game setting the template for Carwyn's subsequent successes with Llanelli and the Lions.

He left Llandovery College to take up a lectureship at Trinity College, Carmarthen, in the late 1960s and about the same time took over the coaching duties at Llanelli, the club he had played for as an outside-half. Before this, his initial foray into first-class coaching had been preparing the West Wales combined XV that faced Brian Lochore's All Blacks in 1967. Now, the Scarlets, playing with an originality that warmed the hearts of their loyal supporters, saw their stock rise. They began to challenge London Welsh's supremacy in the unofficial club merit tables and matched the exiles in the number of international players supplied to a successful national side that was embarking on a decade of unparalleled success.

As a committed Welsh Nationalist, Carwyn was true to his principles and fully supported the party's line on South Africa. Yet that did not stop him preparing the Llanelli side that faced the Springboks on the infamous demo tour of 1970. Nevertheless, he sat out the match in the changing rooms, refusing to watch the South Africans and declining an invitation to attend the post-match function. The game itself was a classic: Llanelli narrowly lost a heart-stopping game, 10–9, but scored one of the most famous tries in the club's history. For fully five minutes the ball was kept alive by the Scarlets in a counterattack launched on their own yard line and which culminated, many phases of play later, in a try at the corner by Alun Richards.

That was the brand of open rugby that bore Carwyn's hallmark and which the enlightened Four Home Unions Committee wanted to embrace for the 1971 tour to New Zealand. Carwyn was their chosen coach, and his work with manager Doug Smith and captain John Dawes laid the foundations for a wonderfully successful visit. Although a proud Welshman, Carwyn gained the respect of every member of the squad. He said himself that he learnt more about scrummaging techniques on that tour from Ireland's Ray McLoughlin, the prop whom Carwyn called his 'senior pro', than in the rest of his entire life. When training became tiresome for his talented backs, he had the foresight to leave them to their own devices and allowed them to indulge in impromptu games of soccer. He had the gift of putting his team at ease and was a great listener. He seemed to have great empathy with everyone he met. Even strangers introduced to him were somehow made to feel that he was greeting them as old friends, like a teacher pleased to greet former pupils. 'Where are you now?' he might softly enquire on being introduced.

Above all, he was inspired by an urge to gather knowledge in his academic life as well as in his work as a rugby coach. In New Zealand, Carwyn treasured the players' opinions and even listened with interest to the views of the travelling British press or anyone who could provide an insight into plotting the downfall of the All Blacks. The rest is history. The Lions won the series 2–1 with the last Test drawn, but the team played with such panache that it left a deep and positive impression on New Zealand and world rugby. The legacy was that coaches across the world bought in to Carwyn's thoughts on how rugby could be played. Indeed, when Brian Lochore coached the New Zealand side that lifted the inaugural Rugby World Cup in 1987, he pointed to the 1971 Lions as having a deep influence on the way his teams approached the game.

Carwyn returned from the Lions' tour a hero and was put forward with John Dawes and Dr Doug Smith for an OBE. But his strong nationalist convictions would not be compromised and he politely rejected the honour. He was just as articulate and thoughtful discussing politics as rugby tactics and was a figurehead in Plaid Cymru, the official Welsh Nationalist party. He stood for Parliament as their candidate for Llanelli at the 1970 general election, losing to Labour but polling eight and a half thousand votes: 'The average gate at Stradey,' he used to say. Parliament's loss was rugby's gain. He continued as Llanelli's coach through a golden era for the club in the early 1970s when they recorded their famous win over the All Blacks and dominated the Welsh club scene.

The watershed of his career came in 1974 when the reigning Welsh coach, Clive Rowlands, retired. Carwyn, who had missed out on the job in 1969 when Rowlands was first appointed, was the popular choice to succeed him, and many in the Welsh squad, including former Lions as well as Llanelli players with recent first-hand experience of his theories, expected him to stand for the post. He had earlier been rejected when applying to become a member of the Welsh Rugby Union (WRU), leaving him embittered by the experience, and when the WRU issued a circular letter inviting him to put his name forward to be considered for the coaching vacancy, his reply sealed his fate.

The gist of his response to the WRU was that an effective coach, like a successful teacher, was an extension of the personality. Only the coach could be responsible for pulling together all the strands that go towards placing an international side in the field; it could not be achieved by the selection committee process then favoured by the Union. Basically, Carwyn wanted the job, but on his own terms without the complication of kowtowing to independent selectors. Onllwyn Brace, a noted Welsh international and broadcaster, later said 'He [Carwyn] lived and died by his own ability and would not tout for favours.' Interestingly, Sir Clive Woodward and Ian McGeechan, the most successful British coaches who followed in Carwyn's wake, enjoyed exactly the autonomy he craved, but in 1974 Carwyn was a man 25 years ahead of his time. The WRU were not ready to change their archaic systems. It was rumoured that the WRU were split by the narrow margin of 14–11 against his appointment, but they were not ready for a coach who was prepared to stand or fall by his own judgement. Carwyn was viewed as a potential dictator and, as he predicted, five years later Welsh rugby fell into the most disastrous decline of its 100-year history.

Carwyn Rees James was born on 2 November 1929 in Cefneithen near Carmarthen He was educated at Gwendraeth Grammar School and Aberystwyth University, experiences which shaped his life and actions. He was a passionate lover of intellectual pursuits, in particular the Welsh language, politics and culture, and he was devoted to all aspects of Welsh life, from hymn-singing to rugby football. A brilliant schoolboy fly-half who was capped by the Welsh Secondary Schools, he played first-class rugby for Llanelli, the Royal Navy during national service (as a Russian linguist), London Welsh and twice, in 1958, for his country. It was his misfortune to vie with Cliff Morgan for the Welsh outside-half post in the 1950s, otherwise he would have won many more international caps.

After his rejection by the WRU he coached Rovigo in Italy, inevitably taking them to the Italian Championship title before returning to Wales and turning his academic mind to writing, journalism and broadcasting. His Friday rugby columns in the *Guardian* were eagerly awaited by a loyal readership, and he was in constant demand to broadcast for BBC Wales on rugby and broader Welsh matters. But everyone knew that in his heart he wanted little more than to be out on the training ground doing what he did best: coaching young Welsh rugby players to become world-beaters. The man they called the 'Lion Trainer' and the 'Coach of Coaches' died suddenly on 10 January 1983, aged 53, struck down by a heart attack while taking a winter break in Amsterdam.

THE PRESS GANG

J.B.G. THOMAS
Welsh Rugby's Boswell

J.B.G. Thomas was rugby's man of many words. In a lifetime devoted to chronicling the game he loved, he wrote more words than any other critic, past or present, about rugby football. Books, magazine articles and programme notes flowed effortlessly from the proud Welshman's battered typewriter, but it was as the chief rugby correspondent of the Cardiff *Western Mail* that he achieved lasting fame.

His stint with the national newspaper of Wales established him as a household name in rugby circles, and arguably he did more than any other of his contemporaries to raise the *Mail*'s profile during his long service from January 1946 until May 1982, when he retired as the paper's assistant editor.

Rugby was in the blood. John Brinley George – he was known as Bryn – Thomas was born in Pontypridd on 29 April 1917, but his paternal grandparents were of Carmarthenshire stock and keen Llanelli supporters. The young J.B.G. saw his first match there as a six-year-old, Llanelli v. Pontypridd, and was hooked. He avidly began collecting everything related to the game that he could get his hands on. Cigarette cards, programmes and newspaper cuttings were all assiduously stored for future reference. His father was a butcher in Pontypridd and as a youth J.B.G. was always the first to unwrap the parcel of recycled newspapers that came into the shop to be used as wrapping paper. These were plundered for match reports and pictures and all were kept, meticulously labelled in manilla folders, for the rest of his life. Later, after moving to

Cardiff, where he was a pupil at Cathays High School, he began collecting books and caught the rugby-writing bug.

He captained his school's senior side as a fullback but in his teens he was already finding his name in print. The BBC had pioneered outside broadcasting in 1927 with Captain Teddy Wakelam's live radio commentaries of international rugby matches. J.B.G. followed these intently, charting match facts from the remarkably detailed broadcasts. At length, he was bold enough to write to the *Radio Times*, where its then editor Gordon Stowell was an encouraging influence on the young rugby writer. The *Western Mail* and *News Chronicle* were other outlets for his freelance work as a youth.

But the turning point in his career, he always said, was in 1935 when, at the age of 18, he saw Wales beat the Third All Blacks 13–12 at Cardiff. He was the same age as the Welsh scrum-half, Haydn Tanner. J.B.G. had recently left school to start work at the City Hall in Cardiff, where he met his wife-to-be, Gwen. But, reading 'Old Stager's' match report of that famous Welsh win in the *Mail*'s sister paper the *Football Echo*, he realised that rugby writing was his true calling. 'It was the tender trap. I told myself, that's for me!' he later recalled.

He took himself off to the big matches in the years leading up to the Second World War, seeing firsthand the exploits of 'Tuppy' Owen-Smith and Hal Sever in England's Triple Crown year of 1937 and watching Scotland's Wilson Shaw wrest the Crown from England in the Twickenham sunshine a year later.

War service in the navy followed. He began on destroyer duty and by June 1944, as a lieutenant RNVR in fleet minesweepers, was in the van of the D-Day landings leading the American forces on to Omaha Beach in the critical stages of the great liberation that led to peace. Throughout his war service he carried in the breast pocket of his uniform a copy of the 1939–40 edition of the *Rugby Football Annual* – it was his rugby bible.

The most significant event of his war service, though, had taken place while home on leave in 1943. The then editor of the *Western Mail*, David Prosser, invited J.B.G. for interview. Johnny Hoare, who as 'Old Stager' had led the newspaper's rugby coverage for many years, had died in his 50s and a successor was needed. It was the offer of a lifetime and, having survived the war, J.B.G. Thomas began his professional writing with the newspaper in January 1946. He covered Wales and club rugby in the winter and county cricket in the summer.

His first big story came two years later in 1948, not on the rugby front but with his beloved Glamorgan County Cricket Club. The Welsh county won the championship for the first time and J.B.G. was in the press boxes above the thousands at St Helen's and at Cardiff who watched a side led by Wilf Wooller beat off the challenge of England's best. That success, Glamorgan's victory over the 1964 touring Australians and the county's repeat championship win of 1969, were his favourite cricket memories.

But rugby, of course, was his first love and he didn't have long to wait before covering Wales's first postwar success story. It came in 1950 when John Gwilliam led the principality to its first Triple Crown and Grand Slam for 39 years. The campaign opened at Twickenham, where Wales had succeeded only once before in the previous 40 years. There had been a massive shortage of newsprint in the postwar years but J.B.G. was given more and more space as Welsh rugby started to recover the standing it had enjoyed during its golden era between 1900 and 1911. 'Hats off to Wales! Theirs was a great victory at Twickenham, and restored the waning prestige of Welsh Rugby', he led in the *Western Mail* on the Monday after the match. It was always capital 'R' for Rugby and capital 'G' for the Game when J.B.G. wrote about the sport.

Scotland were beaten at Swansea to set up a battle for the Triple Crown with Ireland in Belfast. The Grand Slam wasn't a term in the rugby lexicon in 1950, for France were still regarded as the also-rans in the International Championship at this time. It was winning the Triple Crown that was seen as the ultimate prize. Ireland had carried off the mythical trophy in 1948 and 1949 and now, with home advantage and the championship title still in their sight, the match with Wales was expected to be a huge showdown.

The game more than lived up to expectation, and it was Wales who took the spoils. In the dying moments and with the scores locked at 3–3, Newport winger Malcolm Thomas dived to score the winning try. 'The Triple Crown is ours! Cymru am Byth! At long last the 39 years' quest has ended and the bogy of continued failure banished', a delighted J.B.G. told his readers. But the story was to be tragically put into perspective by the events of the intervening Sunday. A Tudor IV charter aircraft carrying 82 crew and passengers crashed returning from Belfast to Llandow. Eighty, mostly Welsh rugby supporters, lost their lives in what was then the worst civil air disaster. J.B.G. had enjoyed a night of revels before rushing back by boat, train and car with his colleague Reg Pelling of the *Echo* to start working on a would-be front page Triple Crown story. But he finished that Sunday afternoon helping newsmen report from the scene of the disaster and compiling a completely different front page story. The Triple Crown tale was buried among the sports pages.

There was another Triple Crown to report two years later, by which time Thomas's reputation as rugby critic and historian was secure. To mark the occasion the Welsh Rugby Union commissioned J.B.G. to edit an official souvenir of the Triple Crown, with the proceeds benefiting the Junior Rugby Unions in Wales. The editor set about his task with enthusiasm, engaging the great names from Welsh rugby's past to illuminate an attractive and informative publication. The 35-year-old J.B.G.'s reputation was summed up by Sir David Rocyn Jones, the Union's distinguished president, in the foreword: 'He is a popular and knowledgeable critic who has covered every international match played by Wales since the War. He is respected by official, player and spectator alike, and is a great student of the game.'

He had covered the 1951–52 Springboks tour of Britain and through his connections he was in demand to write for South African journals. The 1953–54 All Blacks tour was to provide a new opportunity. He had for some time toyed with the idea of producing a book on the history of the game, especially the great rugby tours, and his first work, *On Tour*, appeared in the New Year, 1954. When the first draft of the manuscript arrived at the publishers they were staggered by its length. He had to cut it by half, but still managed to add a postscript covering Cardiff's defeat of the All Blacks in 1953 . . . in between the book going to press and its final release.

It is a relatively little-known fact that much of the half omitted appeared six months later as part of another book, *Fifty Years of the All Blacks*. For this publication, Thomas was disguised by the pseudonym David Owen. The book was a record of every New Zealand match played in Britain and Ireland between 1905 and 1954, J.B.G. again teaming up with great players of the past to tell the fascinating story of the first four All Blacks tours to this country.

These were the first of what became a veritable library of works, and by the time J.B.G. published his memoirs in his last book, *Rugger in the Blood*, in 1985, 30 had been penned under his name. Many charted the ups and downs of major touring teams while others adopted a more historical perspective. But all were written with enthusiasm – the reader sensed that the author was dying to tell his tale, to spread the rugby word. And spread it he certainly did, for at the time few books on rugby football were published. He wasn't the most stylish of writers, and would never settle for five words when he could use 50, but he had no superior as a rugby writer when it came to sheer hard graft. The year 1955 was to be a landmark one for J.B.G. and the *Western Mail*. It was a Lions' tour year, to South Africa to take on a side that hadn't lost a home series since the 1890s. Wales was well represented in the tour party and the newspaper sent their man to cover the visit. John Billot, a longstanding colleague on the paper, recalled: 'Expenses were tight. Bryn set off for London in a delivery van sitting on top of newspapers.'

The tour was a rip-roaring success. The Lions shared the series and J.B.G., like his press colleague Viv Jenkins, was so popular with the players that he became an honorary member of the party. Investigative sports journalism was unheard of and J.B.G.'s reports and stories were given plenty of space back home. He was a father figure to many of the tourists, and many of the friendships he forged with players on that tour were to last a lifetime that took in eight more Lions' trips.

Meanwhile in Cardiff the *Western Mail* had appointed a new editor in 1955. David Cole, at 27, was young and go-ahead, with the drive and ambition to broaden the newspaper's appeal. J.B.G.'s rugby coverage would be a key factor in the paper's circulation rising to six figures for the first time in its history.

By the late 1950s J.B.G.'s name and the *Western Mail* were synonymous with rugby. His growing reputation attracted offers to leave Wales and head for a career in Fleet Street. He wrote under the pen-name 'Arthurian' for the *Daily Telegraph* and was in demand to broadcast for both television and radio, skills he had honed as a youngster with his brother, the playwright Gethyn Stoodley Thomas. But he wasn't interested.

Both he and his newspaper went from strength to strength, and the successes of Welsh rugby in the 1960s allowed J.B.G. to ask for and get more rugby coverage in his paper than he could ever have expected working for one of Fleet Street's soccer-dominated sports news desks. Having plenty of space to write about the game he loved was more important to him than big London salaries and generous expenses.

When the Lions and Wales enjoyed a run of success in the 1970s they provided him with the best stories of his reporting career. The 1971 Lions' visit to New Zealand was the highlight of his touring days. Even his newspaper surprised him on that tour, asking for Test reports on the whistle so that the Saturday morning editions – Wales being 12 hours behind New Zealand local time – could carry the first news of the tourists' only winning series against the All Blacks to date.

He was a straightforward writer, never worrying about the angle or the inside story. He told the tale, analysed the game and praised the best players. He never destroyed reputations. A host of Welsh greats, from Bleddyn Williams to J.P.R. Williams, commented later that they knew when they'd had a poor game because J.B.G. simply did not mention them. He had the respect and trust of the players, and even the selectors. He was invariably the first to know the composition of a Welsh XV, but was trusted to keep the news embargoed until a suitable time.

Even when Wales were unexpectedly (or even sometimes expectedly) beaten in the Five Nations, J.B.G.'s pieces would often include a paragraph that started off along the lines 'Wales can still be champions if . . .' He was always optimistic. He was, moreover, always keen to see the interests of the game advanced. When the Welsh Rugby Union announced its intention to commission its

Centenary History for the 1980–81 season, most connected with the game felt J.B.G. should be the automatic choice for the job. He wasn't. Nevertheless, he published his own splendid illustrated history of the Welsh game in a then modern, beautifully designed volume. A wide selection of rare photographs from J.B.G.'s personal archives helped to make the book arguably the most attractive published on rugby up to that time. Viv Jenkins, in his foreword, called him 'indisputably the Recorder of the Century where Welsh rugby is concerned'.

Yet J.B.G. was generous to rival authors. 'The game would welcome them all,' he wrote at the time, 'for there can never be too many.' He was also encouraging to new freelancers trying to make their way, as he himself had done many years earlier. For years he combined his *Western Mail* duties with those of press box organiser for the Welsh Rugby Union. In those blissful days before corporate management of such affairs became the norm, he carried out his duties with the utmost professionalism. 'I'll see what's about,' he would say to hopeful new hacks. He also did much to foster the interests of the Rugby Union Writers' Club. Fittingly, he served as its chairman in the Welsh centenary season, was elected a life member and was the first chairman of the Welsh Rugby Writers' Association.

The only issue that vexed him was neutral officials. He had seen a New Zealander referee the All Blacks to a victory by six penalty goals to four tries against the Lions at Dunedin in the 1959 Test series and campaigned vigorously thereafter for neutrals to be appointed for major internationals overseas. He was equally trenchant in his criticisms of British referees who were lenient to visiting sides to this country. Sometimes he overstated the case and, understandably, his cause did not go down well in New Zealand.

He retired in 1982, not because he wanted to but because he had reached the age of 65. His newspaper gave him a wonderful retirement dinner – 'The Last Supper' he called it. He continued to contribute to the *Western Mail* and was awarded the MBE in recognition of his services to rugby in the 1984 New Year's Honours List.

J.B.G. was plagued by ill-health in his later years. In April 1997, his treasure trove of rugby memorabilia went to auction in Cardiff, a touch-kick from the Arms Park. The remarkable run of cuttings dating back to the 1920s, programmes from an even earlier vintage, and even the whistle from the famous 1905 Wales v. New Zealand encounter were among the Aladdin's cave of items that fell under the hammer. He died a week later, a few days short of his 80th birthday.

JOHN BILLOT
Putting the Record Straight

It was the late Richard Burton speaking in the 1960s who described rugby in Wales as a game of great lies and huge exaggeration. He was referring to the almost universal boasts among Welshmen – young or old, including himself – of having played for or at least featured in a final trial for their country. That many were able to get away with such exaggeration was down to the fact that rugby had never enjoyed the massive statistical back-up of games such as soccer or cricket, and that therefore most rash claims could neither be proved nor disproved.

The writer who did start to put rugby's facts and figures on to a firmer footing was the Cardiff *Western Mail*'s John Billot. In the 1960s, as an integral part of the newspaper team built up under J.B.G. Thomas, he began spending his lunchtimes in the city's main library across the road from the *Mail*'s offices tracking down the ancient deeds of the legendary players of Wales's rugby past. Over a period of two or three years he systematically searched the massive bound volumes of *The Times* and *Western Mail* kept in the library's vaults. The fruits of his labours were realised in the autumn of 1970 with the publication of his magnum opus, *History of Welsh International Rugby*. It was a volume that gave details of every Welsh cap match since the original rout by England at Mr Richardson's field in Blackheath in 1881 supported by lively, concise write-ups.

It was a treasure trove of facts and figures and a fascinating read for those interested in the development of Welsh rugby. So poorly had the game been served statistically up to then that only three years earlier, when Keith Jarrett made his astonishing debut at Cardiff in the famous 34–21 win against England, journalists had had to rely on their memories to state that Jarrett's 19-point haul was a record for an international match.

Billot's researches, however, showed otherwise: the Swansea fullback Jack Bancroft had also scored 19 points for Wales against France back in 1910 in the first ever Five Nations Championship match. They say that imitation is the greatest form of flattery. Within a few years of Billot's pathfinding work rolling off the presses, similar match-by-match histories had appeared for each of the major rugby-playing countries.

Arguably the most impressive 'imitation' was the deluxe leather-bound volume on New Zealand rugby produced by Rod Chester and Nev McMillan in 1977. Their tome, *Men in Black*, was a more expansive (and expensive) creation, but the style adopted was unmistakeably that of Billot's: match number, result and opponents; date and venue; report, teams and scorers. In later years Rod Chester always maintained that the Welshman's volume had been his and his coauthor's inspiration. Indeed, during their research for that book they wrote 'blind' to Billot, addressing their letter 'Mr John Billot, Welsh Rugby Writer, Cardiff, Wales'. The Cardiff sorting depot knew exactly where to redirect the mail.

John Billot's legacy was a heightened awareness among rugby followers of the game's records and players' achievements. The Welsh history was quickly updated in a second edition a year later, after another Welsh Grand Slam. He also produced two interesting volumes on the All Blacks and Springboks tours of Wales, with forewords by two of rugby's greatest names, Cliff Morgan and Dr Danie Craven.

Then, when *Rothmans* added rugby union to their growing list of sports yearbooks in 1972 he was the man entrusted with recording the game in Wales. When that annual's editor, Vivian Jenkins, began to expand statistical coverage in the mid-1970s, Billot provided chapter and verse for the Welsh sections. In fact, he was the yearbook's Welsh correspondent throughout its 28-year existence, a record of service matched only by the Scot, Bill McMurtrie.

Billot was born in October 1929 and had joined the *Western Mail* from school in the summer of 1946, shortly after J.B.G. Thomas had taken up duties as the paper's rugby football correspondent. 'I was the copy boy at the beck and call of the subeditors,' Billot later recalled. Within 18 months he was writing match reports at a time when sport in postwar Britain was attracting huge crowds. It was a happy era and the Cardiff players who emerged to carry Welsh rugby back to its heights – Bleddyn Williams, Jack Matthews and, a little later, Cliff Morgan – are still among his all-time favourite players. Williams contributed the thought-provoking foreword, naming his favourite postwar XV to Billot's updated version of the Welsh history, published in 1999.

By the mid-1950s John Billot had become J.B.G. Thomas's right-hand man, often taking the chief rugby writer's copy from the end of a telephone line. He also typed the manuscript for J.B.G.'s first rugby book, the groundbreaking *On Tour*, and remembered vividly the telegram received from the publishers after delivery. 'There were just four words: 'Staggered by the length'. They cut it by half, but it was still a great read,' Billot added.

Then there was the time he was awoken in the early morning by one of Thomas's transfer-charge calls from Perth, Western Australia. 'It was very early one Sunday. I was shivering in my pyjamas taking a 1,200-word note at extra special shorthand speed about the Lions because J.B.G. was in a hurry to catch another flight. Then back to bed. He wasn't my favourite sports editor that weekend.'

The *Western Mail* had grown to a daily circulation of 100,000-plus in Wales by this time, and the office team that Billot headed behind the scenes and J.B.G. led in the field was tight-knit, hard-working and successful. Welsh rugby was always big news and played an important part in the newspaper's growing popularity, even when the French emerged as a force in the late 1950s and early 1960s.

'They used to let me out on Saturdays to report club matches,' Billot used to say. While J.B.G. understandably led the *Mail*'s main match coverage, it was often from the lesser games that the up-and-coming players emerged. Billot covered some of the earliest first-class matches played by two of Wales's finest fly-halves, David Watkins and Barry John, and urged his writing colleagues to go judge their skills for themselves. He was also a keen follower of Glamorgan's fortunes in the County Championship and spent many summers reporting their progress for the *Western Mail.*

He wasn't averse to a bit of fun. He once invented a hoax story purporting to come from J.B.G., who was holidaying in Spain. J.B.G., so the spoof ran, had interviewed a bullfighter named Dom Stefano Gonzalez Jones of Welsh heritage. Billot ghosted the story that went on to tell how the sand used in the Pamplona rings was of the finest-grained Mumbles variety. The *Mail*'s editor saw the story and wanted to run it immediately. The paper didn't, of course, and Billot was hauled over the coals. 'It was the best story J.B.G. never wrote,' he said.

He succeeded Thomas as chief rugby correspondent and became Sports Editor of the *Western Mail* when J.B.G. finally retired in 1982. 'It was a close run thing between me and the office girl,' he said in his unassuming way. He served several years before retiring himself. During his time at the helm of the sports pages several of today's leading rugby correspondents cut their journalistic teeth on the *Mail.* Among these were Steve Bale (first with the *Independent* and now with the *Sunday Express*) and Chris Jones (with the London *Evening Standard*). Each retains the happiest memories and highest respect for the professional standards John Billot set.

In 1968 one of his ideas turned into one of rugby's longest-running serials, the *Rugby Annual for Wales*. He wanted to produce a rugby yearbook chronicling the deeds not only of the Welsh senior international side but also of what was happening at every level at which the game was followed in Wales – county, club, youth and schools. Later, the Welsh women's game, too, received prominent coverage. His own newspaper, though interested in the project, was unable to give substantial support, but at length he engaged the interest of Arwyn Owen, then sales promotion manager with Welsh Brewers Limited, and between them they produced 37 successive editions of Welsh rugby's bible. Richard

Burton's assertion could no longer hold with Billot and Owen's massive record of Welsh rugby a part of the game's literature. Indeed, only the *Rugby Almanack* of New Zealand (launched in 1935) has enjoyed a longer continuous run.

Billot's approach was straightforward. He charted the progress of Welsh rugby day by day, updating scores and results while continuously preparing copy for the next instalment of the annual. There wasn't a single concession to the electronic age, for he was perfectly happy to work from a trusty old portable typewriter. The production was professional and attractive, his way with photographs reflecting the layout skills he learnt as a newspaperman. It was an affordable and handy reference that was a splendid mix of comment and record valued by everyone from the schoolboy fan to the professional journalist. Welsh rugby certainly lost part of its heritage the day John had to give up compiling the annual owing to ill-health.

JOHN REASON
The Voice of Reason

It was a distinguished recent Welsh captain-turned-pundit who coined the golden rule for the modern rugby journalist. 'Either be loved or hated, but never be ignored,' he once said. John Reason, a predecessor in the press boxes of British rugby, didn't need anyone to tell him that. A generation earlier he was writing controversial columns – first for the *News of the World* and later for the *Daily Telegraph* and *Sunday Telegraph* – that challenged the accepted conventions of how the game was run and how it was played. And he never pulled his punches about the way the players performed on the field. In short, he was the confident voice of reason – admittedly a somewhat strident one at times – that anyone with an interest in the game either loved or loved to hate. Never could it be said that he sat on the fence. Some called him the rottweiler of the press box and said that he was to rugby journalism what Norman Tebbitt was to British politics.

Born on 6 March 1929 and raised in the east Midlands, he began his career as a local journalist in Bedfordshire, working on general news and sport for the *Dunstable Borough Gazette* before moving quickly on via the *West Herts Post* to Fleet Street, where he became the rugby correspondent of the *News of the World*. Rugby's traditions of camaraderie and old-school-tie were anathema to him. No fawning praise for officialdom or effusive hero worship for players ever adorned his columns. Indeed, he was particularly direct in his lambasting of the International Board, the game's controlling body, for its failure to keep pace with the sport's development as it accelerated towards professionalism in the 1980s and early 1990s.

Before that, he was equally trenchant in his criticisms of Unions and the Board for their failure to tackle sham amateurism, while dirty play, especially by the All Blacks, was another subject that exercised his lively mind. He became the *Daily Telegraph*'s rugby correspondent in 1967, and the space the newspaper gave to the game allowed him full scope to air his views. To sit beside him at an international match was an education. He had been technically skilful at a number of sports in his youth and retained a rare judgement for recognising an outstanding games-player. As a journalist, he had the ability to sound off and find out – he conducted his own research, never relying on the say-so of others in collating facts and figures to support a theory. His match reports were classics – concise yet stylish and full of insight.

In 1971 he covered the Lions' only Test series win in New Zealand. The high standards set by the tourists, coached brilliantly by Carwyn James and studded with star backs such as Barry John, Gerald Davies and Mike Gibson – four of rugby's most distinguished names in his view – inspired some of his best writing. A couple of weeks before the first Test he met Keith Murdoch, an accomplished prop who had won rave reviews for his strength in the face of adversity while playing for New Zealand in South Africa the season before. Anxious to meet the man behind the legend, Reason was introduced to the All Black as a travelling journalist by the president of the Otago Rugby Union. 'I don't talk to pressmen,' said Murdoch. 'F*** ya.' John responded by saying, 'Good morning to you too,' and with that exchange the pair went their separate ways. He later mused that, as a first greeting, 'this deserves an honoured place in a book of famous first words'.

A week later he was witness to one of rugby's most shameful games when Canterbury, New Zealand's leading provincial side, turned their match against the Lions into a brutal slug-fest. The province's forwards tried to punch the living daylights out of Lions' prop Sandy Carmichael, inflicting multiple fractures to the Scotsman's left cheekbone. Gareth Edwards, Fergus Slattery, David Duckham and Ray McLoughlin were also the victims of unprovoked attacks. John was direct and accurate in his reporting. 'The refereeing was so bad that it was embarrassing,' he told *Telegraph* readers, adding, 'Canterbury's crude attempts at physical intimidation failed. The [Lions'] triumph of virtue may have been disfigured but it was a triumph nonetheless.' Disfigured indeed. John's photograph of the battered and bruised Carmichael was one of the tour's most sought-after shots and appeared in his book, *The Victorious Lions*, which he published himself. It became a best-selling rugby classic, as did a companion volume, *The Lions Speak*, which was a distillation of tape-recorded insights from Carwyn James and many of the class of '71 that became an inspiration to a generation of coaches.

Then there were his regular mid-week newspaper columns – *The Voice of Reason* and *Talking Rugby* – where he analysed tactics, passed his judgements on who should be in or out of international teams and exposed inadequate officialdom when he saw fit. It was Steve Smith, an England scrum-half and captain, who best summed up how the words of Reason loomed over players. Talking to an Englishman about to win his first cap in Paris, Smith allegedly told the debutant: 'Keep your eye on that clock: it'll go round so fast that you won't remember a thing. Then, when there's 10 minutes to go, just pick up that ball and charge like hell. Anyway, you won't know how you've played till you read John Reason next day – and then it's bound to have been badly.'

Arguably the event of John's career that demonstrated above all the courage of his convictions was the court case that arose from two articles he wrote during the 1979 Five Nations season. Rugby Union players could not accept payment for writing books and articles relating to the game under its then strict amateur code. A number of distinguished players of the 1970s had published autobiographies after announcing their retirement from the game and by so doing had become professionalised, closing the door to any future involvement in the administration of the game.

John was aware that a Welsh player had committed to writing an autobiography and told readers of his mid-week column that the WRU was investigating reports that a £10,000 advance on royalties had already been negotiated. He made it clear in his carefully worded article that if '[the player] has not received the money or plans to give it away, his amateur status is in no way infringed.' The Welsh Rugby Union cleared the player, but John still felt their interpretation of the International Board's by-laws was wrong and called for swift action to halt creeping shamateurism. He published his views in a forthright second article and added to the controversy by writing, 'I have not met anyone in the game who does not believe that the case has infringed at least three of the intentions of the International Board's amateur principles.'

The player later sued the *Daily Telegraph*, John Reason and the newspaper's editor, Bill Deedes, over claims that the book infringed his amateur status, stating that he had planned to put the proceeds into a charitable trust. The newspaper denied libel and, in pleading justification, said that the two articles were true at the time of publication and that the intention to give proceeds to charity should have been made clear from the outset. They said the player had only announced his decision after the appearance of John's first article and contended the articles were in the public interest when they appeared.

But the player was cleared of being a shamateur in the High Court and awarded £20,000 libel damages and costs. The *Telegraph* appealed and the Court of Appeal quashed the decision and ordered a retrial, but the libel suit was pursued no further. The Welsh player was never declared professional and John Reason emerged to serve the *Telegraph* group for another 10 years, fighting without fear or favour against the game's sometimes cosy amateur ways before retiring as their Sunday newspaper's correspondent in 1993. During his journalistic career he had formed trusted contacts among players, coaches, selectors and leading administrators, and in retirement he continued to contribute news-breaking stories to the sports pages.

Outside rugby, he was a master of all he surveyed, turning his mind to property, building, car maintenance and publishing with the same self-reliance as he did to his journalism. It would be hard to imagine the word 'outsourcing' entering his vocabulary. When he died on 9 February 2007, aged 77, the order of funeral service drawn up by his family – his son Mark was a chip off the old block, writing on rugby and golf for the *Sunday Times* and *Sunday Telegraph* sports columns – carried a portrait of John with the epitaph: 'Insufferable All-Rounder.' It said it all.

BIBLIOGRAPHY

Beaumont, Bill. *Thanks to Rugby – An Autobiography* (Stanley Paul, 1982)

Billot, John. *All Blacks in Wales* (Ron Jones Publications, 1972)

Billot, John. *History of Welsh International Rugby* (Ron Jones Publications, 1970; second edion 1971)

Billot, John. *History of Welsh International Rugby* (Roman Way Books, 1999)

Blair, Michael. *Life at One Hundred Miles an Hour* (G & A Publishing, 1987)

Brown, Gordon. *Broon from Troon: an Autobiography* (Stanley Paul, 1983)

Campese, David. *On a Wing and a Prayer: The Autobiography of David Campese* (Queen Anne Press, 1991)

Chester, R H & McMillan, N.A.C. *Men in Black* (Pelham Books, 1978)

Cockerill, Richard (with Tanner, Michael). *In Your Face: A Rugby Odyssey* (Mainstream, 1999)

Collins, W.J.T. *Rugby Recollections* (R.H. Johns Publishers, 1948)

Cotton, F.E. *Fran: an autobiography* (Queen Anne Press, 1981)

Dixon, George H. *The Triumphant Tour of the New Zealand Footballers 1905* (Geddis & Blomfield, 1906)

Doyle, Mick. *Doyle* (Gill & Macmillan, 1991)

Frost, David. *No Prisoners. A Background to Rugby Touring* (Pelham, 1978)

Gallaher, D. & Stead, W.J. *The Complete Rugby Footballer* (Methuen, 1906)

Gravell, Ray. *Grav* (Gomer, 1986)

Greenwood, Will. *Will: The Autobiography of Will Greenwood* (Century, 2004)

Higgins, Aidan. *Scenes from a Receding Past* (Calder, 1977)

Hignell, Andrew. *The Skipper: a Biography of Wilf Wooller* (Limlow, 1995)

Jenkins, Vivian. *Lions Rampant* (Cassell, 1956)

Jenkins, Vivian. *Lions Down Under* (Cassell, 1960)

John, Barry. *The Barry John Story: An Autobiography* (Collins, 1974)

Leonard, Jason. *Jason Leonard. The Autobiography* (Collins Willow, 2001)

Massie, Allan. *A Portrait of Scottish Rugby* (Polygon Books, 1984)

McBride, Willie John. *Willie John: The Autobiography of Willie John McBride as Told to Edmund Van Esbeck* (Gill & Macmillan, 1976)

Moore, Brian. *Brian Moore: The Autobiography* (Partridge, 1995)

Morgan, Cliff. *Beyond the Fields of Play* (Hodder & Stoughton, 1996)

Reason, John. *The Victorious Lions* (Rugby Books, 1971)

Reason, John & James, Carwyn. *The Lions Speak* (Rugby Books, 1972)

Richards, Alun. *Carwyn: A Personal Memoir* (Michael Joseph, 1984)

Ripley, Andy. *Ripley's Rugby Rubbish* (Allen & Unwin, 1985)

Roach, David. *In Strength and Shadow: The Mervyn Davies Story* (Mainstream Sport, 2005)

Scally, John. *The Giants of Irish Rugby* (Mainstream Publishing, 1996)

Sewell, E.H.D. *The Rugby Football Roll of Honour* (T.C. & E.C. Jack Ltd, 1919)

Smith, Steve. *The Scrum Half of my Life: An Autobiography* (Stanley Paul, 1984)

Taylor, John. *Decade of the Dragon: A Celebration of Welsh Rugby 1969–1979* (Hodder & Stoughton, 1980)

Thomas, J.B.G. *Great Rugger Players* (Stanley Paul, 1955)

Thomas, J.B.G. *Great Contemporary Players* (Stanley Paul, 1963)

Thomas, J.B.G. *Rugby: Men, Matches & Moments* (Pelham Books, 1970)

Thomas, J.B.G. *The Greatest Lions* (Pelham, 1974)

Thomas, J.B.G. *On Tour* (Stanley Paul, 1954)

Thomas, J.B.G. *Rugger in the Blood: Fifty Years of Rugby Memoirs* (Pelham, 1985)

Thomson, A.A. *Rugger My Pleasure* (Museum Press, 1955)

Verdon, Paul. *Tribute: Ranking the Greatest All Blacks of All Time* (Cumulus, 2001)

Veysey, Alex. *Colin Meads, All Black* (Collins, 1974)

Wakefield, W.W. & Marshall, H.P. *Rugger* (Longmans, 1927)

Woodward, Clive. *Winning!* (Hodder & Stoughton, 2004)

Wooller, Wilfred & Owen, David. *Fifty Years of the All Blacks* (Phoenix House, 1954)